FROM PRISON CELLS TO PhD

It is Never Too Late to Do Good

STANLEY ANDRISSE,
MBA, PhD

Post Hill
PRESS

A POST HILL PRESS BOOK
ISBN: 978-1-64293-940-8
ISBN (eBook): 978-1-64293-941-5

From Prison Cells to PhD:
It is Never Too Late to Do Good

Cover art by Cody Corcoran

Post Hill Press
New York • Nashville
posthillpress.com

Published in the United States of America
3 4 5 6 7 8 9 10

This book is dedicated to:

William Pierre Frederick Andrisse. My father. My first mentor. My inspiration, then, now, and always. May his soul and spirit rest in paradise. His legacy, love for others, and his strong ethics and morals live on through his five children and ten-plus grandchildren.

Yorvoll Joseph Andrisse. My mother. My best friend. The rock of our family.

My Haitian heritage and culture. My Haitian homeland and my subsequent Haitian cultural upbringings have made me who I am.

Special thanks to:

Stephanie Jo Andrisse. My loving wife. Thank you for your patience, guidance, and love in this process and all that makes up our crazy, busy, joyful life.

My family and close friends. I would not be here without your support.

Barrie Bode and Jonathan Fisher. My mentors. The ones who believed in me and my potential when it felt like no one else did.

In memory of:

Sean L., Dion Stovall, Howard Kennedy, Charles Billups, Jason Pruitt, Kenny Mo, and Anthony Costello.

Proceeds to:

From Prison Cells to PhD, Inc. (aka Prison-to-Professionals or P2P). This book shares it's title with the nonprofit organization co-founded by Stanley Andrisse and Jerry Moore III. The two conceived the idea of P2P while incarcerated together in a Missouri prison in 2009. P2P was established as a 501(c)(3) in 2017. A portion of the proceeds of this book will be donated to P2P.

Visit FromPrisonCellsToPhd.org to learn more about the nonprofit.

"It's never too late to reach your full potential" is a loose translation of the French-Creole phrase that my dad used to tell me often and is included as a recurring theme in the book. That French-Creole phrase is "*Il n'est jamais trop tard pour faire le bien*" (in French) and "*li pa janm twò ta pou fè bien*" (in Haitian Creole). Haitian Creole was the primary language in my household growing up, but we also spoke French interchangeably.

The true translation of this phrase is "it's never too late to do good." My dad's meaning of it was a combo of "it's never too late to reach your full potential" and the American/English phrase "it's never too late to do the right thing." He would tell me this in our several conversations focused on getting me to stop selling drugs and to get me to see that God had a higher purpose for me. I was too young and underdeveloped to get that message and he left me before I had the chance to show him that I finally understood it.

This is a special phrase to me. I leaned on this phrase and his words through many of my tough times and the book is dedicated to my dad for that reason.

CONTENTS

Part 3: Post-Prison

FOREWORD

Names and attributes of some people have been changed to maintain anonymity. It is not my place to pass judgement. We are all at the mercy of a judge much greater than you or I.

I requested written permission for inclusion of certain people's real names. I have those written documentations. Some have requested to remain private and as such I have changed their names. In some cases, I have created composite characters to increase the flow and for privacy purposes.

A timeline was included at the beginning of a chapter if it moved forward or backward a significant amount of time. If a timeline is not included at the beginning, the chapter moves forward sequentially, one hour, one day, one week, or a few months in time.

PART ONE

PRE–PRISON

———

"Father forgive me, give me strength, I was a lost soul."

"My Little Angels"

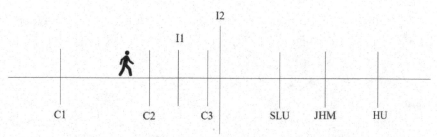

C = arrest that led to conviction; I = sentenced to incarceration; Numbers = number of that event
SLU = Saint Louis University; JHM = Johns Hopkins Medicine; HU = Howard University

Contrary to popular belief, most drug dealers are everyday, regular people.

"Happy birthday!" yelled a coalition of voices. Confetti popped, party blowers blew, and voices were cheering loudly and excitedly as my twin nieces, Tierra and Alanna, walked through the door, both wearing adorable, puffy princess dresses. My precious little angels were turning four (February 2004). Tierra stylishly rocked a cream, laced dress with a pink cardigan, and Alanna was in a similar stylish, cream, laced dress with a purple cardigan. The twins always wore pink and purple, and they always were dressed in the latest fashion. They were beautiful. From the time the twins were just little infants, my brother and his wife Angie were constantly being asked to put them in print ads and commercials. With their cute smiles, and pretty brown eyes, it was no wonder why everyone was immediately drawn to their cuteness.

I was enchanted from the very first time I laid eyes on my precious little angels. I remember the day they were born as if it were yesterday. I was only sixteen. Will was away playing in a college basketball tournament. Angie had the twins nearly three months early. When the doctor came out of the operating room, he congratulated me, mistakenly thinking I was the father. I was too dumbfounded to respond and simply followed him into the NICU where the 1.7-pound tiny little angels were in a tiny little fully encased incubator. I had to stick my hands through a special gloved opening to hold them. They each fit perfectly into the palms of my hand. I was instantly and forever enchanted.

Two little girls jumping into my arms broke me out of my memory daze. "Uncle Stan! Uncle Stan! We missed you. I love you so much. Thank you for coming to our birthday!"

"Not make it to my precious little angels' birthday party?" I exclaimed in an inquisitive voice, my sideways face looking directly into their bright brown eyes and big smiles. "What? I wouldn't miss your birthday party for the world, baby. Not for the world. Even if I were stuck in a million miles of traffic—one million miles! I'd hop in my new flying car and fly right over all of that traffic." I carried them both and circled the room as they made airplane arms. They began giggling and were smiling from ear to ear. "Even if I were locked away somewhere far, far away, and a lion came by and swallowed the key, I'd Harry Houdini my way out of that cage. Get my running shoes on and run over here so fast—in superfast speed!"

Their giggles became contagious and my other eight nieces and nephews surrounded me with laughs, giggles, and smiles. I am the youngest of five. By that time, all of my four siblings had at least two kids. My nieces and nephews ranged in age from newborn to ten years old. So, birthday parties were always fun filled, with lots of little ones running around. When my first nephew was born, I was only eleven, and every year for the next ten years, a newborn was brought into the family. With me being the youngest uncle, I was instantly the favorite.

Alanna asked me, "How fast, Uncle Stan? How fast?" So, I set the twins down and began running in place really fast. All of the kids started running in place with me. I then started slowly moving around the room, still running my legs as if I were in a track meet. I ended up with a train of little kids behind me pumping their legs as fast as they could and all of them yelling, "Superfast speed!" It was the most adorable thing. Ten little ones trailing behind me, ranging from four feet tall to crawling, trying to keep up with the pack. Half of them weren't even able to say, "Superfast speed." So, it came out sounding like "Tupertast peed, Tupertast peed, Tupertast peed, Tupertast peed."

My brother Will came over, laughing at me, and bumped me out of the train to dap me up and give me a hug. Will was six feet-plus. He always had a fresh pair of Timbos on. He had them in lots of different colors. Today he wore the dark tan ones, with baggy cargo khakis and a long-sleeve army fatigue on.

He greeted me with a big smile. "Thanks for making it out, fam. I can't believe the girls are four already! My entire college life has been a blur. Playing basketball and raising infants at the same time? Man, it's crazy." He stopped, looked over at the girls playing with their cousins, and shook his head in enchantment at their beauty and the great job he'd done raising them. But also, at the same time, in frustration. "Now I'm back in the STL. I gotta get paid, my dude. These little girls eat like mini monsters, man. I gotta get some bread in my pockets. It's been nearly eight months since college graduation, and I can't find shit! I just moved into this new apartment in the hood. The bills ain't gonna pay themselves. It's stressful, bro." He looked over at me, shaking his head again. "Let me shut up. How you been, man? You still doing your thang? I see you out here taking trips to Jamaica and MIA and shit. I see you, fam! I'm tempted to jump in the game with you!"

I looked at him and then looked away as we walked outside the door to the backyard. It was sunny and 65oF—a beautiful February afternoon. I flipped my $500 yellow-gold Versace aviator shades out and slid them over my eyes—mostly because it was sunny out, but partly because my high off of the California blueberry Kush blunt that I smoked before coming to the birthday party was starting to wear off. At that particular time in my life, I stayed high 24-7. I would wake up and the first thing

I thought about after making money was rolling up a blunt and getting high. By that time, I was nineteen years old. I had been smoking weed since I was fourteen years old. But for the past year and a half since I'd met my big out-of-state connects, I smoked nothing but California Kush—$750 an ounce. Ten times the price of regular weed—more along the price of cocaine. With the California Kush, I would roll two Kush blunts in the morning, store them in my little stash spot in my car, and be good for the day. I would only smoke half a blunt in the morning, half a blunt in the afternoon, half a blunt in the evening, and then half a blunt a night. I didn't have to smoke twenty to thirty blunts a day like I'd been doing at one point in high school when I was smoking "Reggie"—another name for regular-grade weed.

I did not see myself as a drug addict. It was just weed. I knew the effects were not that bad in the long run. I smoked it because I could. I had a limitless supply. It made me feel good. It made me more creative and imaginative. It helped me devise my plots to make more money and elude the police. Since I smoked all day, I had a "smoker's kit." My kit included spray cologne, cocoa butter lotion, hand sanitizer, ChapStick, eye drops, an assortment of different breath mints, and nail clippers with a file. I would normally smoke in my car with the windows cracked and my beats bumping. This was when I got my best thinking in. I did not want people to know I was a smoker. So, with the windows down, my clothes and body would not smell like Kush. My hands and fingers, how-ever, would still smell like Kush. It was like a ritual. Just before getting out of my car from smoking, I would sanitize my hands, put lotion on my hands, arms, and face, put ChapStick on, put eye drops in to keep my eyes from being red and drooping, put a mint in my mouth, and then spray just a little bit of Axe. Occasionally, I would clip and file my nails to be sure there was no weed or blunt leaves or grim in them. Staying fresh was big for me.

As my brother and I walked out of the house, my Versace shades now covering my drooping eyes, I looked back over at him and chuckled. In a calm, cool, and collected tone, I told him, "Yeah, you know. I'm still doing me." I shot Will a smirk as I gave a head nod to my other brother

Vladimir, sitting with his new girlfriend. I turned back to Will and pulled my shades down to reveal my droopy but very serious eyes, saying, "This ain't no game for a family man, bro. I couldn't do that to you. I couldn't do that to the fam."

I walked over to the outdoor sitting area where my other siblings and parents were. I gave my two sisters Sherer and Yorvoll a hug and a kiss on the cheek. As Haitians, we were brought up to always greet everyone when entering a room—women with a hug and a kiss on one or each cheek and men with a handshake and a hug. I dapped my brother Vlad and gave his girlfriend a hug and a kiss. I walked over to my mom and gave her an extra big hug and squeezed her extra tight. She excitedly smiled and said, "Best, *ki sans ou ye?*" Meaning, "Best, how are you doing?" My mom and I called each other "Best" because when I was very little, I told her that she would be my best friend forever. Even when I went off and got married, she would still be my best friend.

I smiled at her and said, "*Tout bagay tres bien. Nap boule,*" meaning, "Everything is all good. Just doing me." Just doing me, of course, meant something very different when I told it to my mom as opposed to what I had just told my brother a few moments ago. I had my run-ins with trouble and the law as an early teen and in high school. My parents knew I had dabbled with selling drugs and smoking weed. But for all they knew, I was past that stage. My first year of being gone for college had passed without a blip. My grades were good. I was playing football. My girlfriend and I were doing well. To them, I was back on the right path.

My "smoker's preparation kit" worked well. My sister Sherer laughed and proclaimed, "Stan, you always come through smelling and looking fresh! Glad to see you home, bro!"

I walked over to my dad to give him a hug. By this time, he had been waiting in anticipation as I made my greetings with everyone else. My mom was all forgiving and forgetting of my past mistakes and run-ins with the law in high school. My dad, however, the wise man that he was, was not at all buying it. He was very skeptical of my newfound straight-arrow path.

"*Bon swa, Papou,*" meaning, "Good evening, Dad." *Papou* was what everyone called my dad. It is a Haitian term of endearment meaning father. We went through the "how are you doing?" and small talk part of the conversation.

Not long into the conversation, he paused and said, "*Il n' janm twa ta pofe sa ki bien,*" meaning, "*It's never too late to do good.*"

I looked at him, a little thrown off and surprised (but not so surprised) at where that was coming from. I nodded my head as I was getting up and said, "I know, Pops. I know. I remember that every day. You've told me that so many times." I laughed and smiled at him as I walked over to the birthday table. Angie was gathering everyone as it was almost time to sing "Happy Birthday" and then open presents.

I walked over to Will, whispered to him that I couldn't stay too long, and asked him if we could open my gift first after we sang. He replied, "No doubt, fam. No doubt. Thanks for coming."

After we sang "Happy Birthday," I walked over and handed the girls my gift—a new pair of baby Versace shades. "Now you can be supercool just like Uncle Stan!" They smiled in excitement as they put the shades on, and the three of us took a pic with our arms crossed, looking supercool.

My Razr cell phone buzzed right as we were done taking the picture. It was a text message from Jerome: "You still coming to the game today?"

I replied back, "Front row seats. I wouldn't miss it for the world."

He replied, "Hahaaa. That's my man. See you soon."

I quickly went around and gave my departing hugs and kisses because that was also a Haitian tradition. I gave the twins an extra big hug. I picked them both up and gave them big kisses as I told them, "Uncle loves you so much! You will always be my precious little angels." I kissed them one last time and ran off to my car, unknowingly on my way to one of my most life-changing events.

I'm Seeing Dollar Signs

With an extra pep in my step, I excitedly hopped in my pimped-out Grand Prix GTP. Fresh from a hand-personalized, detailed car wash, the buttons on my twenty-two-inch custom-design DUBs shone like diamonds in the sun. I had just recently given her an all pearl-white wet paint job that left her glistening from every angle. The wet white paint job was in perfect contrast to the jet-black limo tint on all the windows. I had "STL" decals with the arch on my back side windows and a decal of the record label I had just started on my rear windshield. My car looked like a drug dealer's car. But I rarely ever transported drugs in this car. I had other cars and means for doing that.

As I got in the car, I immediately tapped a few buttons on my Sony touchscreen-display CD player and a secret compartment opened to reveal several bundles of twenty-dollar bills, two pre-rolled Kush blunts, and a mini scale. I had graduated from counting money by hand a long time ago. With the deals I now found myself in, money was either weighed, eyeballed, or counted in a money-counting machine. I preferred to purchase my drugs in twenty-dollar bills. I saved my hundred-dollar bills; that way, I could stash hundreds of thousands of dollars in a small space like a safe or shoe box. Fifty twenty-dollar bills ($1,000 or, in common street terms, a stack or rack) weighed fifty grams and were about a quarter of an inch in depth. A bundle, a common street term for twenty racks ($20,000) bundled together with three to four heavy-duty rubber bands, was about four to five inches in thickness. I had four bundles on me ($80,000), neatly packed in my secret stash box. Drug money—especially in bulk—smells just as strong as the drugs themselves, mostly because dealers stash the money in the same safe or place as the drugs. I grabbed one of the Kush blunts out and closed the stash box. I was ready to make the trip to KC.

The three-hour drive was nothing to me. I smoked half of the Kush blunt on the way there and before I knew it, I had touched down. Most of the trip was spent thinking of how much money I was about to make. I did a lot of my strategic thinking and planning during these trips. I would set up the appointments for the coming week to two weeks. I would decide on price increases or decreases at this time. I would think up the reasoning behind these fluctuations in pricing, most of which was all bullshit.

Today was a little different. I was meeting Jay's connect today. We had progressed to the point of me meeting his wife, his six kids, and even his mom. I was part of the family. He trusted me more than any of his other lieutenants. He had maybe four to six guys like me—copping one hundred to three hundred bricks every one-to-three months. I was on that higher end and I handled things much more efficiently and effectively. I was running a business. I was a businessman, and he appreciated the effort and thought I put into our business deals.

This deal was bigger than our regular monthly deals. I was copping (slang for purchasing) three hundred bricks of mid-grade weed at roughly $260 a pop ($80,000). This was an insanely low price, half of the $500 per pound that I usually paid and a quarter of the $1,000 that most (early-stage or high school) dealers paid. As an extra bonus, Jay was throwing in a pound of Kush ($6,500 street value) free of charge and a key of coke (kilogram of cocaine) on the front for fifteen stacks ($15,000). Thus, this was a $100,000 deal (in wholesale dollars) with a lot of moving parts. The street value of this deal was about six to eight times $100,000. I would sell the mid-grade bricks for about $250,000 to $350,000 ($800 to $1,200 per pound, more than quadrupling my investment). By the time those three hundred bricks made it to a smoker's bowl or a blunt, the product would have grossed about $600,000 to $700,000 ($1,600 to $2,300 per pound after street dealers nickel and dime it). The fronted key of coke was a very generous payment for the shipment of my product. My drug transporters would pay me twenty-five racks ($25,000) for the key; thus, I would make a measly ten grand ($10,000) off of this transportation deal. The street value for a key of coke ranged from $50,000 to $100,000 depending on how you cut it and in what amount you sold it in. Thus, the final street value of today's deal was roughly $1 million.

I guess in that regard some may consider me to have been a coke dealer. But I vehemently disliked the sale of coke. I tried my best to stay away from it. But at this level of drug dealing, when you have the money to buy anything and make more money off of your money, dealers sell everything. I was not against coke per se at this time. I was not on some high moral pedestal. I just disliked the prison time associated with coke compared to weed. For the same or less amount of risk (prison time and violence), I could make the same or more money with weed. Coke was just not a good business move to me. But, anyway, I was selling keys of coke now. This was my life.

"J-Bizzle! What up, man! Good to see you. What's the movement?"

"StanDrisse! How's it going, bud? You know I'm always excited to see you, bro." We dapped each other up and gave each other the one-arm bro hug. Jay stepped back and instantly broke into one of my record label's songs: "We got pounds for the low man; you can get 'em low, man. Hustle-man, got them thangs going for the low man!" Then he chuckled aloud with a big smile on his face.

"Bricks in the plan, man. Stacks in my hand, man. Hustle, man. Grind, man. Get up on your shine, man!" We then both broke out into laughter. "Hahaaa, StanDrisse in the building!"

After a few more moments of excited small talk, we moved into talk that was more serious. We left my car parked at the Independence Center Mall parking lot and we hopped into his all-black, tinted-out GMC Yukon Denali. There were no rims on this truck, and it looked like it hadn't been washed in weeks. That vehicle did not scream "drug dealer." It more screamed "daddy of six" as it was filled with car seats, muddy cleats, and McDonald's Big Mac wrappers. It was perfect. This was one of our transportation vehicles. It had four rows of seating. That day, the back row was removed. Underneath was a hidden compartment where the gas tank should be—capable of stashing up to roughly a thousand bricks (half a ton of dope).

"Those Versace shades are fresh, bro. I see you. I need me a pair."

"Yeah, you know. I stay with the exclusives. Crushed diamonds with the embezzled Versace image—special-ordered."

"Okay. Okay. Man, I've been telling my guy a lot about you."

"Yeah."

He looked over at me and smirked as he was turning a corner. "Yeah, man. You've been gaining a lot of weight."

I told him, "I'm getting paid!"

"Money over bitches…"

"I'm yelling it to my grave." As I finished his sentence with him, we both shared another moment of laughter. "Man, I'm pretty sure Lil Wayne's 'Money on My Mind' was on auto-repeat for half of the trip down."

"Well, bro, you definitely making big moves. It seems like just yesterday you were getting that first thirty pack."

"Yeah. It wasn't that long ago, huh."

"Now you in the big leagues, man." He turned and smirked at me again. "My man wants to meet the magnificent magician."

"The magnificent magician, huh?" I was thrown off by this comment. His man wanted to meet me? For what? That seemed odd. Drug dealers didn't like to meet new people.

"Yeah. That Harry Houdini shit you pulled off. After paying up front for that two hundred and making 'em disappear in less than a month, he thought it might be good to bring you in deeper to the organization."

"Deeper into the organization?" I shook my head and looked out the window as we pulled up to one of the several familiar houses he had taken me to before for our previous drug deals.

"The numbers'll be better for you, man. Me and you! We'll pick up your three hundred mixtapes and your key. Then, I'm picking up another five hundred from him lata'. He's dropping the ticket since I'm getting it all at once."

I was still a little skeptical but I shook my head in agreement.

He saw the doubt in my face. "I've told you before, bro. I don't have another StanDrisse!" He said my rap name with a prolonged ending as I said it in my songs. "I've got a few guys getting semi-big tickets but none of them are selling mixtapes like StanDrisse."

"But why the fuck does he wanna meet me? Just take my money and make the deal. I don't—I don't like meeting new people, man."

"That's funny, man. Those first few deals you never wanted me to take ya' money. You always wanted it at the same time—same time, man. Now, you just want me to take ya' money?"

"I trust you."

"Then trust me on this, bro. This is the right time."

On the way to the drop-off, we had a little more conversation on the details of the deal. We pulled into an abandoned lot near the heart of a KC neighborhood where, not too far in the distance, kids were out playing.

Almost simultaneously, the other dealer pulled up in an old-school Chevy with the back end visually lower due to all the drugs in the trunk. I walked out of the car, nine tucked in my waist and my hand clutched tightly around the handle of a briefcase with a lot of money in it. After some brief introductions, the deal went sour fairly quickly. It started to become clear that the prolonged small talk was a ploy to allow time for the accomplices to arrive. We were being set up. Another car squealed into the abandoned lot. The second car of assailants never got out. They simply rolled down the windows and four heads popped out and opened fire. Half of the drug exchange was made, and we kept all the money. Shots were being slung around as I scampered back to the truck. Jay's two boys jumped out immediately when they saw the second car creeping up. I heard shots ringing like it was the Fourth of July. I felt the heat of several bullets whip by my body. I immediately dropped to the floor—briefcase of money in hand. I reached for one of the hundred-pound duffle bags of drugs and grasped it in the same hand as the briefcase of money.

As I was crawling backwards on the ground, I reached into my waist for my 9-mm Glock with my right hand. From this point—as I was crawling half-backwards and half-sideways—I was unsure of exactly what else took place and the exact timeframe or length of the event. I had fallen into a hazy dream world. The first thing that popped into my head was a clear visual image of the faces of my little angels. I could hear their cute little giggles and see their heartwarming smiles. I was falling in and out of consciousness.

I was brought back to the real world when I heard a loud scream: "Agghhh, Drisse, get the fuck in the car! Get in, get in!" One of Jerome's friends had just been ripped open by a bullet from an assault rifle. Blood was oozing from his internal organs. Yet he was still firing back at the car that was now driving away.

Jerome shouted, "Stan, Stan, are you in the car? Did you get hit? What the fuck is going on?"

"I'm in. I'm in!" Left hand still clenching the briefcase with eighty racks and the duffle bag with a hundred bricks. I was laid out fully flat in the back row of the truck with the duffle bag and briefcase on top of me to shield me from flying bullets. My heart beat fast—*Is it time to die*? Thoughts raced through my head—*Was I set up*?

"Jerome! Jerome! What the fuck was that?"

"Agghhh, fuck. I'm hit, man. Shit!"

"Jerome! What the fuck is going on? Who was that?"

"I need to go to the hospital. I'm fucking dying, bro. Take me..."

"Jerome, fucking answer my question!" I shouted.

"I don't fucking know, bro. Ask yourself that same fucking question." Jerome's boy, who was now bleeding to death, turned around and pointed his gun directly between my eyes.

"Are you part of this shit? Did you set this shit up?"

"I got bullets flying at me too, bro! How the fuck am I part of this shit?"

"Tavon, put the fucking gun down!" His boy did not respond. He still had the gun pointed dead on my forehead. "Tavon! Tavon! Put the gun down!" He finally lowered the gun. "Drisse, man, I don't know what happened. This is my guy. We've done this a million times."

We ended up splitting the hundred bricks evenly. He promised me that he would get to the bottom of this. I did not want to explain to my transporters the full truth of what just went down, so I gave them some bullshit story on how the deal fell through. I ended up giving them ten bricks for the transportation.

My brain was frazzled. I could not gather myself. There weren't many cars on the road, but with every car that passed, my eyes got big with fear. This was not normal. I didn't even have any drugs on me—my transporters had the drugs about a mile or two ahead of me. I fell into one of my many recurring inner-self battles.

What am I doing? What if one of them got killed back there? What if I had gotten killed? God, I miss my little angels. Uncle Stan loves you. I just want to hold and kiss you and tell you how much I love you. Best, I'm sorry.

Then the devil on my shoulder chimed in.

Shut the fuck up already. This shit is all part of the game. Stop being a little bitch. Everything is all good. Nobody died back there. This is the big leagues. This is what big money looks like. Get your shit together.

My voice of reason chimed back.

This is not what I signed up for. I didn't sign up to be in broad-daylight shoot-outs with little kids running around. What if a stray bullet hit one of the kids? Fuck, I need to text Jay and ask him if he heard any news. What if someone saw us? Fuck, we may be on the news. I need to text Jay.

The devil jumped back in.

Not what you signed up for, huh? Bundles of hundred-dollar bills? Trips to the Caribbean? Not what you signed up for? Chill the fuck out! I didn't hear you complaining about guns when you were taking all those damn pictures with the TEC-9 and the sawed-off. Oh, so you just want to look tough? I chuckled at myself in disgust. *Settle down. We're not texting anybody. That's not part of the script. Let's get home. Get the drugs safely stashed and start counting some money in the next couple of days. Jay will figure this mess out.*

I arrived in St. Louis at about 3:30 in the morning. I did not catch a single wink of sleep. I could not shake what had just happened. I just laid in bed for a few hours and was back up at 7:00 a.m. As I got out of bed, I noticed I still had the same bloody clothes on. Still in a daze, I kept asking myself *Why am I doing this?* I jumped in the shower, got dressed, and headed over to my mom's house. My mom, my sister, and her two sons were heading to Sunday mass like we did every Sunday.

"*Bonjou*, Best. *Ki sans ou ye.*" (Good morning, Best. How are you?) I managed to open my mouth successfully without sounding too shaken and disturbed. I kissed my mom on the cheek and gave her an extra big hug—holding her for a few moments longer than usual.

"*Bonjou*, Best! *Mwen bien. Epi ou mem?*" (Good morning, Best! I'm good. And you?) my mom very excitedly replied with a big smile.

"I'm so happy to see you, Best!" I replied with full sincerity.

"*Em, sac passe?*" she jokingly replied.

"*Onyen, tout bage bien.*" (Nothing, everything is all good.) I somehow was able to muster these lying words out of my mouth.

My mom laughed. "*Ou te wè m 'yè swa.*" (You saw me last night.)

"Tete and Lana's birthday?" I was completely perplexed. "That was yesterday, huh?" I had just gone to my niece's birthday party less than twenty-four hours ago. But it felt like a lifetime.

"*Ou top brway brason?*" (You went out drinking last night?) She giggled—thinking that I went out drinking and partying last night. "Jesus will forgive you for you sins." She giggled again.

My First Encounter

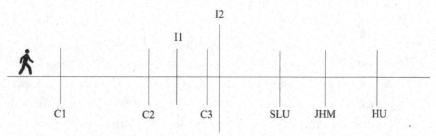

C = arrest that led to conviction; I = sentenced to incarceration; Numbers = number of that event
SLU = Saint Louis University; JHM = Johns Hopkins Medicine; HU = Howard University

M y family lived in the now infamously known area of Ferguson-Florissant. There were several high schools in this area. Despite all of its negative publicity, Ferguson-Florissant was not (neither at the time of my childhood nor at the time of the incidents surrounding the death of Michael Brown) one of worst areas in the greater St. Louis metropolis; it was, however, adjacent to one of the worst areas. St. Louis has been consistently ranked in the top three for murders per capita for almost two decades now—many years sitting atop that murder rate list.[1]

St. Louis City is divided into four areas—North, East, South, and West St. Louis City. East St. Louis (which is actually in Illinois) and North St. Louis are the areas where most of the violent crimes take place. Ferguson-Florissant and its surrounding municipalities (Jennings, Riverview, Dellwood, Kinloch, and a few others) are all adjacent to North St. Louis City. These areas were predominantly Black (roughly 65–80 percent) and low-income when I was growing up and are even more so now (roughly 90–95 percent Black). As was brought to light after the death of Mike Brown, despite these areas being predominantly Black, the police officers, politicians, lawmakers, city councilmen/women, and teachers were predominantly white. That set the stage for a number of inequalities and disparities that are now nationally known—the increased number of Blacks getting pulled over and searched, the insane number of ludicrous tickets and fines, etc.[2] But this was my home. I love St. Louis. I will always love St. Louis. For what it is and for what it hopes to be.

After sending my three older siblings to local public schools (University City and Hazelwood East), my parents were not too pleased with the public school education in the North St. Louis area. Our cousin, who also attended Hazelwood East, was heavily integrated into the streets. While at Hazelwood East Junior High, he joined and was beat into the Bloods. This was the late eighties and early nineties. Bloods and Crips were highly prevalent in the St. Louis area. I recall seeing my cousin beaten, bruised, and bloody many times. I remember him sharing countless stories of his roller-coaster adventures in gang life. I was close friends with many of his gang-member younger siblings. We all aspired to being them. My cousin is ten years older than me, so I was very young at this time (from around four to eight years old) when I was hearing these stories and witnessing his entanglement in gang life.

One of my cousin's Blood brothers was killed in a gang-related fight. This led to a retaliation gang war between the Bloods and Crips in our area. I recall one of the pivotal nights in that gang war when a frenzied gang-member friend of my cousin's informed him that they knew where the person that killed their Blood bother was. I recall my cousin scurrying to get his revolver, hopping in his old-school Chevy, and darting into the night.

I was in an adjacent bedroom pretending to be playing video games but eagerly listening to what was going down. I was somewhat scared but oddly intrigued, not at all understanding the implications of the situation. I never ended up hearing what happened that night. But soon after this incident, my cousin decided to join the army to leave the craziness of gang life and St. Louis.

Because of these tragic experiences, my parents decided and were able to send my brother Will and me to a private high school just down the road from Hazelwood East.

I wanted to go to Hazelwood East, partly because they had a nationally renowned football program and consistently sent players to D1 and the pros; and partly because I wanted to be around more black people (or maybe it was I didn't want to be around so many white people). Whichever combo of these two, it partially led me to accentuate the stereotypical black teenage experience.

Being a September baby, I was denied early entry into Kindergarten and thus was a full year older than most of my peers in all my subsequent grades. This gave me an academic and athletic advantage. As a freshman at Rosary High School, I was the captain of my football team. Although our team was not the greatest, my brother (a senior) and I (a freshman) were a dynamic duo on offense and defense. Will was the best player on the football and basketball teams, and he set the stage for me to follow in his footsteps. I was also captain of my basketball team, which set a school record for most wins by the JV squad.

I was popular with the ladies. I got good grades and was in all the advanced classes, so I was in with smart kids. I excelled in sports, so I was best friends with all the jocks. And I had been smoking weed and drinking for a while, so I was also cool with the "bad kids" as well. Not to mention that my cousin had an image in the streets that I inherited. Life was good from my teenage perspective.

Joyriding

"Brandon! What up! Let's get drunk and smash out," I mischievously said to Brandon over my cordless phone.

"You're crazy, but I'm down. Just give me about an hour so I know for sure my parents are asleep," Brandon said, equally excited.

It was a school night in the last week of freshman year, but we didn't care. We met up with some girls in Riverview to smoke some weed. We pulled up like bosses—or at least that's how we felt. No one else our age was driving, so the girls were super impressed and extra flirtatious. We partied and bullshitted for a little while, then moved on with our night. Stan and Brandon, as they called us, had more exciting things to get into.

We hopped back in the car high as fuck. "So, how was it?" I asked Brandon, giggling like a fourteen-year-old boy.

"She knobbed me up, bro. She knobbed me up," Brandon said childishly, bobbing his hand in an up-and-down motion.

We both burst into laughter. "Yeeaaahh!" we shouted, fist-bumping each other.

"Let's keep the night going," I said roguishly. Brandon looked at me like, *I just got doomed up, I'm down for whatever.*

I had recently learned the hustle of installing and "uninstalling" car stereos. It was a popular thing to get custom stereos at this time, and they sold like hotcakes on the streets. So, I convinced Brandon that we should go on a car stereo-jacking spree. We had never done that before. But, for some reason, it seemed like a good idea.

A little context to this good idea. Along with my freshman year being filled with athletic accolades and good grades, it was also riddled with detentions and suspensions. Rosary High had a demerit card system where getting your "Gold Card" signed five times resulted in a detention and five detentions (twenty-five signatures or five Gold Cards) resulted in out-of-school suspension. A third suspension in one year would be grounds for expulsion. This last week of school, I was on signature seventy-three, two write-ups away from expulsion. Most of these write-ups were for sagging, using slang, being a few seconds late for class, cracking a joke in class, getting my shoulders massaged by a girl in class, etc. I never got warnings like my non-Black friends. In cases where a flirtatious girl would start rubbing my shoulders, I got the write-up, not them. Needlessly, I had inherited and owned the "bad boy" title bestowed on me.

Just as my intel had provided, we found a whole bunch of cars with their doors unlocked. We had gotten into maybe ten to fifteen cars, and we had several stereos, as well as some watches, loose cash, and other stuff.

"Jackpot!" I whispered to Brandon as I uninstalled another stereo. After showing him how easy it was, we split up. He took one side of the street and I took the other. We had been at it for maybe fifteen to twenty-five minutes. We had just about hit the whole block. It was maybe 3:00 a.m., so no cars had gone by yet. Then, we saw headlights. Both of us were in separate cars at the time and I ducked down in the driver seat. The car was moving at a snail's pace. I was thinking, "Hurry the fuck up and pass by." And as it got closer, I realized it was a cop car.

I whispered to myself, "Holy shit!" I looked over to see if Brandon had noticed and he did. The cop pulled up to a house, stopped, got out, and began talking to one of the neighbors. Apparently, we had been seen and someone called the cops. The cops had dogs with them, and apparently the neighbor even saw what car we were in, because the dogs went and sniffed our car. Brandon and I both saw what was quickly transpiring and we slowly crept out our cars and began running in separate directions. The cops hadn't seen us yet but possibly heard us and let the dogs loose.

By this time, I had already been a track star, and I put all my track talents to use that night. I began running as if I were in an Olympic track meet. I was not running in the streets; I was running in between houses and through yards. I began leaping fences in single bounds as if they were hurdles. On one of the fences, I overestimated my talents and got entangled in it. My arms and legs got sliced open; blood began gushing down my arm.

I screamed in silence as I couldn't make a noise in fear of getting found. To my dismay, the giant fence I had just gotten entangled and scarred up by had two giant dogs behind it. They immediately began barking and veraciously coming at me with drool hanging out of their mouths. I quickly climbed back over that fence and fell to the ground, got back up, and headed to the street. I began running again—as fast as I could. It had been a good five to ten minutes now. I was likely about one to two miles away from the original location already. I was exhausted, but my adrenaline was rushing. I hid on the side of a house and began praying.

"Lord Jesus, please don't let the cops find me. I am sorry. I promise I will do good." I began bargaining with my higher power.

Just as I had rested enough to begin running again, I saw headlights turn the corner. It was the cops again. I began running. They saw me and sped their car up. I cut the corner in between two houses. They released the dogs again. I did not have a good enough head start this time and I was running out of gas. The dogs caught up to me.

I screamed as the two dogs began biting at me and ripping and pulling at my clothes. "Awwww! Awwww! Get them off me! Get them off me!" I was absolutely terrified. The cops stood there for a while and let the dogs bite at me before calling them off. I was huddled in the dirt in tears, lying there in the fetal position as several white cops towered over me with their guns drawn and pointed at me. They were yelling things like "Get your hands up!" and "Lie down!" There was a lot of commotion; then they handcuffed me and threw me in the cop car.

❖ ❖ ❖

I had been locked up for about twenty-four hours before they brought me back into the interrogation room. I had denied talking the first two times, so they threw me in a cell. I didn't have an ID yet, so they had no idea how old I was, but clearly, I was a minor. I was fifteen but looked like I was ten. I told them I wanted to talk to my lawyer or my parents before saying anything.

"Tell me who you were with, you fucking little scumbag," the detective yelled at me, punching his fist into the metal table. With tears in my eyes, I told him again that I was not going to say anything until I talked to my parents or lawyer.

"What are you…like, a hundred pounds? You know what they do to little shits like you in juvey? They get fucked in the ass and mouth!" the detective stated to me.

I was scared but I tried my best not to show it. I naively thought to myself, *I didn't even steal anything. They couldn't send me to juvey for this.*

When my mom and dad walked into the room, I wanted to immediately run over and hug my mom, but my hands were handcuffed to the table. Fortunately, she was thinking the same thing. She ran over and gave me a huge, long hug and kiss on the head.

"*Tout bagay bien?*" (meaning, "Are you okay?"), my mom asked.

My dad did not crack a smile. He just looked at me with laser-beam eyes. I could feel them burning into me. My disappointment in myself immediately skyrocketed once I saw his face.

"Mr. and Mrs.…." A pause subsumed the cop's address as he could not pronounce our last name and he clearly saw that we were immigrants. "An-Andrisse-e," he mustered. "Your son is in a lot of trouble. He is looking at several felony charges. He stole over $500 worth of belongings from several different people."

My lawyer had arrived with my mom and dad. The cop explained to them how I had been denying talking.

"Sir, with all due respect, why were you asking a minor to talk without his parents in the room?" my lawyer abruptly interrupted the detective.

"Mr.…?" The cop paused.

"Jangle," my attorney stated.

"With all due respect back at you, this young man does not have an ID. I have no idea how old he is. And he refused to tell me."

After conferring with my lawyer, I finally provided the detective the name of the guy I was with, Brandon, but said that he did not do anything. The cops had picked up Brandon's Gold Card in the car and had already asked me if Brandon was with me but I had not answered anything up until my parents and lawyer arrived.

"So, you say Brandon was not involved. Okay. Just give us an official statement naming him as the person you were with, and we won't charge him; and we will reduce your charges for being honest and cooperative. If we have to use his demerit card, ask the school, and investigate, we will *definitely* charge *both* of you to the highest extent of the law," the detective exclaimed with authority.

After getting the detective to agree on paper that they would not charge Brandon and would reduce my charges, my lawyer advised me to make the official written statement that Brandon was with me but had not done anything. I did as the lawyer advised. They ended up picking Brandon up and bringing him to the station but never charging him. I was, however, charged. I had taken and moved belongings from three different people, so I was charged with felonies for each person I had taken from. After spending some time in juvenile detention, writing personal letters of forgiveness to each person I had taken from, and eventually meeting them in person months later, each of them (all older white people) saw my ten-year-old-looking innocent face and decided to not press charges against me. Especially considering that all their belongings had immediately been returned without damage.

The cops and the system were not satisfied with that. Although the felony theft charges were dropped, the system hit me with a felony tampering for even opening the unlocked cars. This charge did not require the owners of the belongings to press charges. My friend Brandon, who happened to be white, also opened unlocked car doors just as I did. But he never spent a single minute in a cage, nor did he ever even get charged, much less convicted, as I did for opening those unlocked car doors. I chalked it off as, I was the one who thought of the idea, I deserved the conviction. Brandon did not. I did not understand the full racial aspect of the situation. I did not understand the school-to-prison pipeline that was paved for people with skin tones like me. Why did either of us deserve a conviction? Why did I, a Black boy, deserve a conviction more than Brandon, a white boy? Why did I think I deserved one more than Brandon? Why did I feel like a criminal even before I was convicted? Did Brandon feel like a criminal?

I, the ten-year-old-looking Black kid, spent time in juvey, got a felony conviction on my record, and was placed on probation for three years until I turned eighteen. Once I got home from being locked up, my parents grounded me for three months—no phone, no TV, no friends, and even no sports. Fortunately, my football coach begged my parents to let me play, stating that he'd personally take me to and from practices and games. At the ripe age of fifteen years old, I was branded a felon. And more sadly so, I believed I was a criminal.

Immigrant Family

Throughout the entire criminal legal proceedings, my dad stood firm and astute. But, as soon as my parents brought me home from juvenile detention and we stepped foot into the house, my dad immediately broke down into childlike tears. The bawling-type crying you see from an infant when a mother walks away. I had never seen my dad cry before, and this was much more than crying. He was plopped down on the couch, curled up, both hands covering his face in shame, loudly sobbing with tears pouring down his cheeks. My mom, who had already been quietly crying the entire time, was now no longer crying and was huddled next to her husband with her arms wrapped around him, consoling him.

My entire family was there. My parents must have called them over so that they were there when I returned home. We were that type of supportive family. My oldest siblings—my two sisters who were in their mid-twenties—had already moved out of my parents' house. My middle sibling—my brother Vlad—who had just returned from a tour in Iraq and was visiting for my sister Sherry's upcoming wedding, was home too. My closest sibling in age, my brother Will, who had just completed high school and was headed to college on a basketball scholarship, was in the family room as well. Even my oldest nephews were in the house.

I was the baby of the family. Everyone cradled me. I was everyone's son. My oldest sister, who is also my godmother, is thirteen years older than me, and my other sister is twelve years older than me. My brothers are nine and three years older, respectively. They all watched over me, trying to make sure I didn't make the mistakes they had made. And they all seemed to have high hopes for me, even beyond their own hopes. Being a younger sibling, I didn't quite understand that.

Seeing my dad break down into tears, all I wanted to do was console him. So, I walked over to try and comfort him, which none of my siblings had done. My gentle, caring, and protective mother immediately blew up on me.

"*Pa manyen li!*" she screamed angrily at me (which translates to "Do not touch him!"). My mom never screamed at me. I was her best friend. The roles had quickly turned around. In the public face, at the jail, my mom was the caring, consoling parent, and my dad was the stern, hard parent. But, in the private space, my dad was gentle and vulnerable, and my mom was the fierce enforcer.

"*Ale nan chanm ou epi fèmen pòt ou! Ale!*" she screamed again. "Go to your room and close your door! Go now, go now!" I was stunned and hurt. I went to my room and my sister Sherer handed me her son Chris to take with me. Handing me my nephew was this small but impactful gesture of love. Even in my wrongdoing, even as I was seemingly being cast out from the family in this moment, I had a family member to console me. Even if it was only my ten-month-old nephew.

I remember taking lil Chris to my bedroom and setting him on the carpeted floor and hugging him tightly as I broke into deep, sobbing tears. He laughed and cooed to cheer me up. And momentarily he did. My family was always there to support me, even in my low points.

From my room with my ear pressed against my bedroom door, I listened to my family debate as a unit what they were to do with me. My brothers mostly stayed quiet. My sisters chimed in. It was decided that I'd be grounded for three months, where I could not leave my room except to eat breakfast, lunch, and dinner. It was summertime, so I would miss all of the summer fun and summer practices for football. Additionally, I was ordered to read Plato's *The Republic*, a philosophical dialogue on justice. I would eventually read that five-hundred-plus-page book in several weeks in hopes of being let free on good behavior. I was not. Instead, I was given readings on Aristotle and Socrates to round out my learnings of the origins of Western philosophy. I learned concepts like hedonism, the pursuit of pleasure. Hedonism is a school of thought that argues pleasure and suffering are the only components of well-being. Ethical hedonists would defend either increasing pleasure or reducing suffering for all beings. I was absolutely certain I was a hedonist. Not so much seeking pleasure, but I wanted very much to reduce suffering for me and, more importantly, for others.

❖ ❖ ❖

I would inform my dad of my learnings and it was at this time that I started regularly journaling. I still keep an incredibly detailed journal of my emotions, feelings, and activities to this day. Mostly I would tell him about my learnings in hopes of him reducing the punishment. But it also gave us time to spend with each other.

"Kisa ou konnen?" (meaning, "What do you know?"). He would excitedly stop in my room first thing every day after work. I would tell him new things I had learned and occasionally we would sit and play chess. I don't recall ever beating him at this age. As we'd sit and play chess or talk about philosophy, I learned a lot about my dad and our immigrant family.

My family were immigrants, all of us born in the Caribbean island of Haiti—except my closest brother Will and me. Will came over in my mother's belly and I came a few years later as my immigrant family was still trying to get our footing in this odd new world. My mom was from Port-à-Piment, a small village town outside of the capital of Haiti, and my dad was from Port-au-Prince, the capital. Having the framework of US poverty makes it difficult to truly understand what life in a country such as Haiti, the poorest county in the Western hemisphere, was like.[3] My parents came from meager Haitian beginnings, which means by US standards they came from extreme poverty.[4] However, they would never explain it to you as such.

❖ ❖ ❖

My mother and father's coming to the US is deserving of its very own book. As such, devoting a chapter to this story cannot begin to do it justice. My mother and father met in what would be equivalent to high school, as teenagers. My dad was the youngest of ten siblings, all of whom were women. He had one brother who died before he ever had a chance to get to know him. My dad, despite being the youngest, as the only man of the house, was very much looked at as the provider. My mom, on the other hand, had only one biological sibling—a brother who had kyphosis (a hunched back) along with many other illnesses for which he would not receive the proper medical attention he needed. He'd eventually die during my mother's young adulthood. This was not the first family death my mother experienced. My mom's mom, Odette, died when my mother was only two years old. Since pictures were not yet common for certain classes of people in Haiti at that time, my mother sadly only has a few pictures of Odette and none of the two of them together.

By their early twenties, my parents had my two oldest siblings, my sisters. My father went to university in Haiti and worked as a professional for several years there before deciding that he wanted better for his family. Haiti was in the midst of deep political and social turmoil at the time,[5] undergoing several coups from 1934 to '57, then a period of semi-dictatorship in the Duvalier era from 1957 to '86. My dad had moved his family out of the ranks of Haitian poverty and was now living in lower-middle-class Haitian life, which would still be sub-standard by US guidelines.[6] By the time he started having feelings of wanting to leave Haiti, my oldest brother Vladimir had just come along. With three kids—a six-, nine-, and ten-year-old—my parents decided to leave Haiti and come to the US, where I and my closest brother were born.

Our new immigrant family bounced around from Miami to New York to Detroit to eventually landing in St. Louis. All these moves were due to my father not being able to find or maintain employment. For years, we were bouncing around, sleeping on couches and living room floors of Haitian family that we had in each of these US cities. Despite all its claims, the US is not very welcoming to most foreigners—and especially people from Haiti at this particular time in history. Haitian refugees were flooding to the US port of Miami in boatloads. Stories of Haitian gangs and violence flooded the national news daily. So, you can imagine walking into an employer with a thick Haitian-Caribbean accent and then saying you were from Haiti. Most employers, like most people at this time, saw the news and held the same bias towards "those refugees."

My dad and mom first came to the US by themselves. They lived in Miami, then New York. In New York, with the help of family, my dad found a job and rented a small, one-bedroom apartment. After having left and not seen their children—a young boy and two preteen girls—for nearly two years now, my dad thought they were finally stable enough to bring the kids to the US with them. My sister recalls her fears as a preteen without her parents, being told by caregivers that they had been abandoned and that their parents would never return to Haiti. Within a month of my siblings' arrival to the US, my dad was fired from his job. My parents and siblings were homeless for some time as the home of the relatives my mom and dad were staying with before my siblings came along was too small to fit everyone. During this time of homelessness in NYC, my mom was pregnant with my closest brother.

Scrambling to survive, my dad reached out to his cousin Delance, who was living in Detroit. Delance was able to find my dad a job during this time of need. My brother Will was born shortly after my family moved to Detroit. Out of appreciation and thanks for pulling my dad out of the ranks of homelessness with a six-person family, Delance became Will's godfather.

After reaching a point of somewhat stability, with a job and a one-bedroom apartment, again my father was let go from his work for seemingly no reason except for being an immigrant from Haiti. Once again, now in a new major US city, my immigrant family found themselves homeless and lost in a society they could not quite understand.

Delance was out of options in terms of helping my dad with employment. My mom was now pregnant with me. My family now consisted of two teenage girls, a preteen boy, a toddler boy, and me in my mom's belly.

My mom began to doubt my dad's decision to uplift the family and leave Haiti, although the move was largely my mom's wishes from the beginning. Haiti had become an extremely dangerous place in the late seventies, at that time under the political dictatorship of the Duvalier era. Feeling a sense of defeat, my parents were ready to ship back to Haiti and call this entire three-year US excursion to an end.

So there we were—a family of almost seven. In Detroit. No immediate family. No friends. No money. No place to stay. My parents were church-going Christians, and one day at church the pastor asked all people with birthdays to stand up and be celebrated. Even though she was barely able to speak English, my mom was courageous enough to stand up and introduce herself. After church, Marjorie, a young Christian woman, spoke with my family. They explained their strife. And Marjorie took my immigrant family into her one-bedroom apartment—all almost seven of us. She took us in for several months, rent-free, until my father was able to find a job—this time in St. Louis.

Thomas was a childhood friend (and distant cousin) of my dad who had left Haiti many years ago and was now established in St. Louis. With the help of Thomas finding my dad a job, within a month we were able to rent a small, one-bedroom house on Richard Avenue in University City in North St. Louis City. I came into the world shortly after arriving to St. Louis. My parents did not have health insurance at the time, so my mom was unable to go to the hospital to birth me. I was brought into this world on the mattress in my parents' room in our one-bedroom house. I was delivered by Thomas, who was assisted by my oldest sister, Sherer. Thomas and Sherer later became my godparents.

We lived very happily and, unknowingly to me, well below the poverty line for several years at Richard Avenue in U-City before moving on up to a bigger house in the Ferguson-Florissant area.

Life as an immigrant family was different. We ate different. We talked different. We lived, believed, and prayed different. We even looked different than most Black kids—slightly in our physical features being mixed with Taino natives of the Caribbean and Africans; but mostly in our dress as my Haitian parents didn't know, understand, or live by hip-hop or R&B Black culture. Thus, Nikes and Jordans were not a thing in our household. Being different put added pressure to fit into what American "Black" was supposed to be.

This was the beginning of my journey.

❖ ❖ ❖

Papou and Will, c. 1986

First Deal—Intro to Hustling

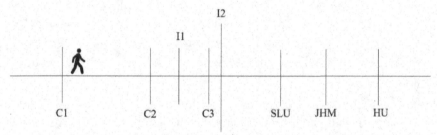

C = arrest that led to conviction; I = sentenced to incarceration; Numbers = number of that event
SLU = Saint Louis University; JHM = Johns Hopkins Medicine; HU = Howard University

"S tan. Stan! Stanley! Earth to Stan! What the fuck dude? C'mon."
My coworker Andrew was laughing at me as he began doing a dance in front of me to get my attention. "C'mon man, let's step out back and hit this joint real quick before the next rush."

"Oh okay. Yeah. Yeah. Cool. Let's get it in real quick." I was off in a daze daydreaming, looking through the order window outside into the world and all the possibilities that awaited this young, entrepreneurial, spirited sixteen-year-old kid. I was a cook at the neighborhood Cecil Whittaker's Pizzeria in Florissant, Missouri. Andrew was in his late twenties, misguided, lost, and had a history of violent criminal activity. He was six feet six and solid, with fists the size of anvils, and scars all over his face and body that marked his many war stories he was always happy to share. I was drawn to those stories. He was funny as hell and even more loyal—the kind of guy you definitely wanted on your team if something popped off.

"Hit this shit, man. This some of that kill that Geno brought in." I took a deep pull and instantly started coughing. Andrew burst into laughter. "Man, Stan, you remind me of my homeboy I used to run with back in the day. A bad muthafucka, man. Little dude, about your size. But had the heart of a fucking giant and a knockout punch harder than Mike Tyson." Andrew took a smooth pull like an OG and continued his story, looking off into the distance. "Yeah, me and that dude got into all shit."

"You still kick it with your boy?" I asked, wanting to meet this seemingly legendary character.

"Naw. He got popped for a body about ten years ago. I ain't seen him since." The end of the conversation dissipated just as quickly as the disappearance of young Black bodies from the community. Andrew and I walked back into the kitchen high as a kite. "Did Geno tell you his man got hit?"

"What?"

"Yeah. This is the last of this good that he will have for some time. That's fucked up. Everyone up here including all the sluts up front loved that shit. He was making a killing," Andrew said as he started the next pizza order. I immediately went back into my daze, mind in the clouds as I unconsciously and artistically covered pizza shells with toppings. I was thinking about our high school drug dealer, Tom Pelantro. He was a senior and I was just a sophomore. The other night he pulled up to a party with a shiny new whip sitting on 22s. It was like something out of a movie. The doors slowly popped open and smoke poured out. Three long-legged girls with skirts barely covering their fallopian tubes stepped out, pulling their skirts down and fixing their hair and lip gloss.

I was drawn to all of the things I shouldn't have been. I spent the rest of the shift making pizzas, daydreaming about possibilities, and intermittently taking smoke breaks that left me in a constant high. After work, I hopped in my hooptie that I had just bought. I spent all summer busting my butt to save up $1,000 to buy a 1980-something Hyundai Excel Hatchback. My mom and dad were still upset with me for getting arrested and put in juvenile a year ago, so they wouldn't allow me to get my driver's license or help me get a car until after I graduated high school.

I had to walk several miles a day to three different jobs until I saved up that $1,000 to get my own car. Determination and resilience have always been a part of my character.

Driving home, I was still fixated on my daydream. The thoughts were racing through my head as if it was a Nascar speedway. *Geno's man got popped. Pelantro riding on DUBs. Girls in short skirts. Everybody including the managers and frontline folks at Cecil Whittaker's Pizzeria* (CWP or C-dub-P) *smoke weed. Me and my boys smoke all the time. I could pop off a few bags while innocently smoking a little bit.* The dollar bills were falling from the sky. I just needed a connect. And the first person that came to mind was my boy Rich.

It wasn't long before this sixteen-year-old kid was running the C-dub-P. Rich was my good friend from Jennings, one of the most notoriously deprived hoods in North STL. As a white boy from the hood, he was always into something. We met at a bonfire party in Riverview, a primarily Black, low-socioeconomic area in North STL near Jennings, where he was about to get jumped. Rich was being Rich. Talking mad shit with no real idea on how he was going to back it up. But he did run with a band of crazy muthafuckaz from Jennings though. One of them being his brother Steve. Not even really knowing Rich, but unwilling to see an unfair fight, I jumped in swinging. Steve ran over and began handling folks like he was a professional MMA fighter. It was nuts.

The fight was over just as fast as it had begun. Girls were yelling. People were running. The cops had apparently been called, unrelated to the fight. I think the neighbors called for underage drinking. So, I dipped off with Rich and his crew. After we were safely off in someone's car, we were still amped up and recollecting the excitement that just took place. Rich sparked up a blunt and so began one of my longest-lasting friendships.

❖ ❖ ❖

Jennings and Riverview were rampant with drugs, violence, and poverty. Rich was well entrenched into that world. He connected me to Tre. Tre was the man in Jennings. Tre was super smart. I think he had completed high school and was maybe eighteen or nineteen years old, but I didn't know, and I didn't ask many questions back then. It was a good quality to have. Questions made folks suspicious as if you were a snitch, looking for dirt. And snitches…well…you know what happens to snitches. That wasn't my reasoning at the time. I just had always been one to be a listener and not a talker. So, I spent many, many hours and days just listening and learning from Tre. I was his apprentice. It wasn't long before I earned my masters in the game.

Tre was an architect with the hustle. He strategically planned his every move in the game. He trusted me. Throughout my life that is a quality that I have maintained. People very easily trust me. I guess it's because I always tell it how it is and am one hundred on everything. Tre introduced me to all the key people in his life, including his mom and his connect.

One school night, we were just riding around, making drops. It was already past midnight. Tre said he had to run to the East Side to pick something up. I shrugged my shoulders and nodded in agreement. I was used to getting to school on only a couple hours of sleep. In my head, I was thinking, *Shit, I've heard all types of crazy stories about the East Side. Muthafuckaz don't play on the East Side. What could we be going there for?* I didn't express any of these thoughts, though. I just remained calm, cool, and collected. As we crossed the bridge over into the East Side, it was as if we entered another dimension. The houses were boarded up and abandoned. Fiends and winos were stumbling around everywhere. Packs of folks were hanging on the corners, looking at us as we drove by with a look of "Why the fuck are you pulling up in our hood? I don't know you."

We pulled up to an old, abandoned building that looked like it used to be some sort of housing unit at one point in time. Now it was just another piece of architecture defining the brokenness of the hood.

Tre looked over to me with the little smirk he often gave me. "This is our stop." His smirk deepened as he continued to look at me for a short while. I imagine he was assessing my level of fear or reaction.

I was, as I often am, reactionless. "Okay. Are we going in? Let's go." We hopped out and walked through the pitch-black darkness around to the back of the building. There were no streetlights on this block. I could barely see my hand in front of me. Someone or something could easily have jumped out at you at any time, unexpectedly. Tre navigated the space with ease and certainty. We finally walked in a dark doorway and immediately down a set of stairs where we encountered another door; however, this door was locked. Tre texted someone and a few seconds later I heard several locks unlatching. The door opened.

"Tre! What's up!" said the guy who greeted Tre with a dap. The guy's voice was so raspy it was as if he had one of those voice boxes, but he clearly did not. I chalked it up to years of weed smoke. He looked over at me, looked me up and down, and then gave me a strong head nod. I nodded back.

Tre jumped in. "This is my guy I had been telling you about."

Tre's boy quickly remembered. "Ohhh. Okay. Okay. Your guy," he said in a slow, methodical way as if the wheels of excitement were turning in his head. "That's what's up. Welcome to my hood, my dude. They call me 'Key.'" Then, he dapped me up with the equal amount of love and respect he had just given Tre.

The abandoned building was being put to use as a pretty high-scale recording studio. Tre's boy was a producer, and he was recording someone that night. The music was bumping, but only in the soundproof booth. Tre's boy was also the man and apparently good at multitasking. In addition to recording and holding a deep conversation with us, he was breaking down and bagging up what looked to be a kilo of coke. I had never seen that much coke in my entire life. But, as I often do, I remained reactionless as if I had been in that situation before.

That was only the beginning of the firsts for that night. The first time I had been on the East Side. The first time I had been in a professional studio. The first time I had seen that much coke. If Tre was the Aristotle of the hood, his boy Key was Plato[1] and tonight we were attending Key's Academy on the East Side. The ceremonial vigil was of course blessed and started by the lighting of a Kush blunt.

Key talked about his hood and the economic problems in the hood. He talked about the rampant poverty and how what he was doing in the rap-and-hustle game was providing economic opportunity to those suffering in his community. He talked about the violence and improper portrayal of violence in his hood. "The D-boys don't want no problems." They were simply protecting their economic interests and investments. He emphasized that people were struggling and that he often found ways to give back. He talked about police and how the streets were a lawless game, but the successful D-boy sees and abides by law. He talked about Black Wall Street.[2] I had never heard this before. I was perplexed and completely driven in on every detail and word spilling out of his brain.

The conversation moved into talking about jack boys. Folks that rob and steal instead of hustling to deal with the rampant poverty. It was at this point that he pulled out an all-black 9-mm Glock from his waist and set it on the table.

"You strapped up? You ready for the jack boys?" Key looked at me. By this point, we had smoked two or three blunts and several hours had slipped by. Tre or I hadn't really been talking much beyond grunts and head nods in between puffing on the blunt.

I didn't know how to respond. "Am I strapped up right now?" I mustered a raspy response. "Naw. I ain't strapped up."

Then, he picked the nine up, pulled the clip out, cocked the bullet out, and handed it all to me. "This is yours, lil homie."

I was dumbfounded. I had never held a gun before. Unlike my normally non-reactional demeanor, it was clear that I had not seen a gun before or knew how to use one. He grabbed it back from me and said, "Here, let me show you how to use it." He reassembled it, showing me the different mechanisms of the gun.

It wasn't until years later that I realized how intentional this entire night was and how instrumental it was in my continuance and deepening into the game. Not too long after this night, Tre ended up getting popped by the drug task force in a raid that seized over fifty hydroponic plants in an apartment he had in Jennings. He was hit with a five-year bid. He had drug money, so he got out on bail. I remember riding with him before his sentencing date.

He told me, "Never forget that this shit here is illegal." I never saw Tre again after that day.

Tre was my first drug dealer. He introduced me to the game. I had only hustled for Tre for maybe nine months. But, by this time, I was a sixteen-year-old high school kid moving about five to ten pounds of mid-grade weed every two to three weeks. The game moves fast.

✦ ✦ ✦

I was making big money for a high school kid. I not only took over C-dub-P, but almost all the restaurants on North Lindbergh. My right-hand man, Jonathan, who never sold a bag of dope—but did every-thing else for our budding organization—worked at another restau-rant on North Lindbergh in Florissant, which is the other side of the now-notorious Ferguson-Florissant District. He found us a few more connects at other local restaurants. Another close friend of mine, Hazel, worked at Applebee's on North Lindbergh. Hazel was a pretty white girl with curly, dark hair, and a developed body way past her age of seventeen. She was perfect for the team. She ran our dope between the different restaurants. We'd move about one to two pounds per week at each of about five or six restaurants in the area.

We also had a strong hold on the local high schools. One of my closest childhood friends, Taron, went to Hazelwood Central. Anthony had connections at Riverview High. Rich and Steve were running packs at Lutheran North in Jennings.

Taron, or T-Dash, grew up in Castle Point, an adjacent municipal-ity to Ferguson. Castle Point was one of the grimiest parts of North St. Louis. Compared to Ferguson, it had smaller houses, lower incomes, more Black people, more racial profiling, and more struggle. Taron was a tall, skinny Black kid. He and I had been playing football and basket-ball in the streets since we were about nine years old. Taron never really knew his dad. And his mom was very often in between jobs. She didn't like that her boys were slanging dope, but Taron was paying most of the bills, helping put food on the table, and keeping eviction notices out of the mailbox.

Jonathan, or J-Dub, grew up in Moline Acres, which was adjacent to Ferguson and Castle Point. It suffered from all the same injustices and difficulties. J-Dub lived with his mom and two sisters in a small two-bedroom, one-bath house. His father was not really in the picture. They were on the far low side of the socioeconomic spectrum. Johnny never really jumped in the game of selling dope. But, as my right-hand man, him and his family received many of the financial perks.

J-Dub and I met freshman year of high school during basketball tryouts. Our friendship started on the court and transitioned to our love of smoking trees and sharing laughs. J-Dub helped me break down and bag up my first brick. One of the initial reasons I started selling weed was to be able to smoke for free with him. That sentiment quickly changed as I learned the economic empowerment side of the game: *Economic empowerment for my people, for my team, for my loved ones and family, had become my primary goal.* I was a hedonist and I wanted to reduce suffering for my people.

Rich and Steve grew up in Jennings. Jennings is adjacent to Ferguson and was a much rougher area than both Castle Point and Ferguson. It was one of the lowest socioeconomic places in North St. Louis. Rich and Steve's mom and dad were potheads and the entire family including their little brother could kill a fifth of liquor and be ready for another on any given day. All three brothers were fighters, scrappy-ass white boys. They were one of three white families on the entire block. Rich had ambitions on eventually moving out of the hood. He wanted a better life for him and his family. He saw hustling as the means to that end.

Hazel grew up in a single-mom household as well. They, too, were struggling financially, and she saw hustling as a way to make ends meet and add to her contributions to the household.

That was the core of my first team, Fab Five 1.0: J-Dub, T-Dash, Rich/Steve, Anthony, and Hazel. J-Dub was my right-hand man. He took trips with me. Stashed money and dope. Sought out and investigated new connections. And was the first person I'd go to about any issue or help I may have needed. T-Dash was my other right-hand man. Rich was my business partner. Rich wanted to make the most out of every brick. I wanted to sell more bricks. Steve and Anthony were our enforcers. Hazel's spot was the stash house for money and drugs, and she was a runner.

My family was better off than everyone on my team. I was the only one with two parents consistently in the household. Despite some issues, I had a much more stable home than they did. Thus, hustling was about economic empowerment for me. It was about seeking financial stability for my team. It was about helping people get to a better place in life. I found myself using words and phrases that Tre and Key used. I would hold mandatory meetings with my team where I gave individual coaching sessions on how to move the product and how to stack your chips to put yourself at a better economic position.

We were teenagers who were moved into dealing with and handling adult problems. I saw a problem: poverty. Financial instability. And I saw selling drugs as a means to solving that problem.

✤ ✤ ✤

Day One Family

Cortney, Jonathan, and I. (c. 2007)

Vlad, Rich, and I. (c. 2006)

The Thundercats

With Tre out of the game, we had to find a new connect. Rich had been telling me about the Riverview Thundercats for a while. The leader of the Riverview Thundercats was Mike. They ran the drug scene in Riverview—weed, coke, heroin, ecstasy, pills, everything. No one fucked with them. They carried guns, started fights, and struck fear into competitors.

Mike was the polar opposite of Tre. Mike was a loose cannon, but he was plugged up with some Mexicans on the weed, coke, and heroin. It wasn't long before I was getting ten bricks weekly from Mike. This was the beginning of me carrying my strap around with me at all times. Mike lived in Riverview, a block away from my girlfriend at the time, whose dad was a Riverview cop. The irony never missed me, driving past their house with ten to twenty pounds of dope in my trunk and a 9-mm Glock tucked under my seat. Dealing with Mike was the beginning of me being paranoid. He was unpredictable; I never knew if today would be the day he decided to pull some crazy shit and jack his own man.

Mike's business quickly grew with this new Mexican connect. He eventually expanded his operations and ended up buying a house in the Dellwood/Ferguson area. Mike was a nineteen-year-old kid, and he had his own house that he bought with cash. I was Mike's favorite drug dealer because I was moving the most weight. This became a common trend amongst me and my connects.

Mike was moving big weight, one hundred pounds per week or two, but was reckless. He broke rule number one of selling dope: "Don't get high off your own supply." He and his right-hand man, Chris, fell victim to the horrors of heroin.

✦ ✦ ✦

It wasn't too long after one of Mike's many party nights that I was back in Ferguson at Mike's house to pick up another fifteen bricks. I was banging on his door for a good five to ten minutes. No response. So, I started walking around the house to look in the windows. I saw that Mike and Chris were awkwardly slumped on the couches. Their faces looked busted up. I pried open one of the windows and slipped inside. As I write this and as I look back on events such as this day, I think very deeply on why I took the actions that I took in these instances. I didn't think twice about sneaking into a dangerous drug dealer's house that clearly showed signs of some wild shit going down. Understanding the adolescent brain is challenging.

As I came in, the house was completely silent. I could hear the floorboards creaking under my feet. I was tiptoeing with my hand on my nine, finger on the trigger, head peeping around corners. I saw Mike and Chris passed out on the couches. I kicked each of them a few times, finger on the trigger, head still on a swivel. No response. They were out. I searched the entire house. Their safe was wide open and empty. No drugs. No money. No AK-47. No sawed-off. Empty. They had just picked up about sixty pounds of weed, a couple keys of coke, and several jars of pills—and it was all gone. Several hundred thousand dollars in street value of drugs, gone. And about $100,000 in cash money, gone.

Mike and Chris were barely breathing. They were nodded off on heroin. I called the cops, wiped my prints off the window, and dipped out. They both survived. I stopped fucking with Mike and Chris for a long time. They were too hot.

✦ ✦ ✦

Now I was in a dilemma. Both of my connects were gone, Tre and Mike. My team had all elevated themselves to a stability level never before seen in their families. Rich and Steve helped catch their mom and dad up on their defaulted house loan. Taron and his mom were comfortable and eventually moved out of Castle Point. Jonathan was helping pay the bills. I helped Hazel buy a condo. I bought or helped everyone buy new cars. We were all rolling around in new whips.

With things getting dire, after not having any supply for some time, I skipped school several days in a row and took a trip back into East St. Louis by myself. I never got Key's number, but after wandering around the streets of East St. Louis for a while I finally found that neighborhood with that abandoned house from probably over a year ago at that point. Nine tucked in my waist. Dressed in all black and gray. I didn't want to wear any colors that might insinuate gang affiliation because I didn't know what gangs ran these streets. Even my STL cap was black and gray and tilted up with no lean to either side. I walked around the block asking folks if they knew who and where Key was. As I looked and sounded super suspicious, naturally no one had any answers for me. From dope boys on the corner to fiends stumbling around the block, I asked everyone. I could have easily gotten myself killed snooping around the most dangerous parts of the St. Louis metro by myself.

On day three of snooping around the abandoned house, an all-black Escalade on 24s pulled up and stopped as I was just chilling in front of the house leaning on my Grand Prix. The wheels kept spinning as the mysterious black car just sat there. I couldn't see anyone inside but didn't want to make a move for my gun because that would look suspicious.

The passenger window finally rolled down after several long moments that felt like a lifetime. A cloud of smoke poured out and a head popped out. I could see two gold teeth shining as I recognized Key's big grin.

"What's up, lil homie! Someone said you were looking for Key," the voice from the car shouted.

I hopped off my Grand Prix and shouted with both my arms in the air gesturing peace, love, and a happiness to finally see the man I'd been looking for. "Key! What's up, big homie! It's Tre's boy, Stan."

"I remember who the fuck you are," he said, laughing in his raspy-ass voice. "You still got my nine?"

I laughed and pointed to my hip. "You told me to always stay strapped and to look out for them jack boys." I smiled. "I still remember everything you taught me."

He told me to jump in and take a ride with him. So, I did. I told him about our situation and he happily helped resolve the problem. The team was back in business.

Missouri Valley

When I went off to college, I told myself I would be done. That would be a new era in my life. I left the streets of STL. I wasn't around those same influences. I was ready to make a change. After some uncertainty as to what would be next after high school, near the end of my senior year, I had gotten a full scholarship to play football at Missouri Valley College. Living in small-town middle Missouri, I thought this was the perfect way to transition out of the game. Little did I know that I was stepping into a gold mine. The temptation was too much to resist. Everybody smoked weed. Within two weeks of football summer practices, I made that trip back to the Lou and comped fifteen bricks just in time for the start of fall classes. The entire trip, Anthony's and my cell phones were ringing off the hook. Before we even touched down, all fifteen bricks were sold. I came back Sunday night before classes on Monday morning. We were up all night dishing out preordered product. We didn't even go to class those first two days. We sold fifteen pounds in two days. All quarter pounds and half pounds, nothing less. At that time, I was getting it for $700 a pound (P) and selling quarter pounds (QPs) for $350 and half pounds (HPs) for $650—so about $1,300–$1,400 per pound. Do the math. In two days, we doubled up—we paid $10,500 for fifteen bricks. And made $21,000 in two days. We had $10,500 in profit in our pockets in just two days. The money was too easy. I immediately was strategizing the plot for the future. My roommate and I were the most popular people on campus. We had at least twenty to thirty people in our room every hour of the day that first week.

We had to change the strategy. Selling QPs and HPs would not work. We had to make about sixty different sales. That was sixty interactions or transactions. That was sixty times that one of those interactions had the chance of being a bad interaction. If we sold Ps only, that would drastically cut down our interactions. But that thought occurred too late. Before the end of the first week, our room got raided. Literally, just minutes after our last sale, we were laughing and joking out in the parking lot and three random old white guys walked up to our group of about fifteen guys (mostly football players).

"Is one of you Stanley Andrisse?"

We were high and clowning at that moment and ecstatic that we were ten racks richer—and I knew that we were clean out of goods, not even a blunt to smoke for the ride back to the Lou, where we were planning to comp more. So, I was a little cocky in my reply, laughing and smirking. "Yeah, that's me. Who wants to know?"

"Detective Smith of Marshall Police Drug Task Force." He said his name assertively and with authority as if to try and scare me. "I am here with campus police." My entourage quickly dissipated.

"We have suspicion that you have been selling narcotics on campus. We will need to search your vehicle." Again, Detective Smith responded in an authoritative voice.

"Well, Mr. Detective, actually, no, you may not search my vehicle. I know my rights; you can't search my shit without any probable cause."

"Well, Mr. Andrisse, we actually do have probable cause. I just told you, we have suspicion of you selling drugs on campus." Again, being very assertive. This time mixed in with a smidgen of dickhead. "Okay, tough guy. Mr. St. Louis drug dealer. I won't search your vehicle. We will just call the K-9 unit to come."

I really just wanted to flex a little bit, unaware of—or at least naïve to—the way Black bodies are taken from this earth in moments such as these. After some jostling, I let them search my car. I didn't have any weed in there. In fact, I had just vacuumed and cleaned the whip, so it was pristine, fresh, and clean. They found nothing but my scale in the trunk. I told them I used to work for a pizza parlor and that's what we weighed our orders, food, etc. on. They didn't buy it, but they couldn't do anything. So, they then proceeded to search our room. They tore our room apart. Flipped everything up. Went through ceiling panels. No drugs. But they did find a shoebox full of money.

"Aha! What's this?"

"Looks like a shoebox full of money, if I were to answer your most direct question, detective." Again, I explained, "I used to work at a pizza place and was the delivery driver. All my money was paid in cash. I don't have a bank account, so my shoebox is my bank!"

They only found some of the money. Most of the money was stashed in my secret stash spot that I had installed in my whip.

The small-town detectives and campus police were still not buying it, but they had no evidence. So, that meant no consequences. The intelligent, reasonable, or scared mind would have probably said, "Damn, they are on to us after just one week. It might be a good idea to not re-up." Nope. Not mine. The reward (tens of thousands of dollars weekly) outweighed the consequences (kicked out of football, losing my scholarship, being suspended from school; prison was not yet a serious consideration). What the fuck was a $20,000 scholarship when I could make that in a matter of weeks? I was not seeing that $20,000 scholarship as an investment in my future career that could bring hundreds of thousands over a lifetime. Nor was I seeing that the $20,000 in drug money was an investment in my self-destruction.

❖ ❖ ❖

Wednesday came around and still I had not been to a single class. Instead, I decided to take the day off, take my money, and head back to the Lou. I comped thirty bricks this time and made the trip by myself. I convinced a single mother to let me use her off-campus house as a stash spot in return for selling her the dream of one day moving out of Marshall with the help of my drug money. Without a single wink of sleep, on Thursday morning, I finally decided to go to my first college class. I walked into class and all eyes were on me. Everyone seemed to already know me. That wasn't what I was shooting for. I knew I had to scale back and change things up a bit. My cell phone had not stopped ringing. "The shop is closed," I told everyone. The market would open back up promptly on Sunday night.

Two elbows (two pounds) were the least anybody could get from me. This cut down on my interactions and left me to about five customers. I rerouted the others to go to these five people. Most of all the sales were now made off campus at one of the groupies' houses (not the stash-spot groupie). And the market was only open on Sunday nights and Thursday nights—just like football. I started devising cell phone codes: "Are you ready for some football?" "Oh okay, a Sunday night party. That's what's up," "Should we invite the groupies?" "Yeah, let's invite those five we invited last time," "Okay cool." I started fronting the bricks. I was making so much money, I was not too concerned with losing money or someone getting over on me. More money, less conflict. I was the preferred campus supplier. I was your favorite drug dealer's drug dealer. Over time, less people knew about me. I was able to die down that initial fame—which was good.

❖ ❖ ❖

Unfortunately, the initial heat did not turn out well for Anthony. After failing a drug test, they suspended Anthony and me from football for a month and made me move to a new dorm. I told Anthony to not smoke in the room anymore and to hit me up for blunt rides. Due to the heat from the local police, they kept a watch on Anthony's room. He ended up getting caught smoking and was kicked out of school. I felt terrible. Anthony was the first in his family to go to college.

People would come up to me and ask if I still had them thangs and I would just say, "Naw, the spot got too hot, so I backed off." At one point, a football friend of mine and I were smoking a blunt before class, and he was telling me about this new fire that was on campus.

He pulled out the bag of weed that he rolled the blunt with. "Smell this. This is some heat! You need to get on this shit, Drisse." This was the creation of StanDrisse. My football helmet had my last name and my teammates just blended it all together.

I looked at it, giving him an "oh shit" face. "Yeah, man, that is some fire. Who did you get it from?" He mentioned some local person. I didn't know the guy, but I definitely knew it was my weed.

Connected like Dots

Business was booming. I had just solidified several new connects. Shit got crazy real fast. Before long, I was selling twenty-five to fifty bricks per week—and only having to interact with five or so people and only on two days of the week. By less than one month in, I had found three new connects—Texas, KC, and Cali. I was making big money. I flipped things up on my STL connect and I became his supplier. I was now selling three different classes of weed. My KC connect was my most stable and consistent connect. It was mid-grade brick and the closest and easiest too. My Cali connect was the fire—Purple Kush. The Purple Kush was going for $500 an ounce or $1,500 a QP (so, $6,000 per P). I'd get about five Ps of it for $1,500 per P, which is a ridiculously good price, so $6,000 for five Ps. It didn't sell as fast, but within a month or two, I'd sell out and have quadrupled my investment, making about $24,000 off of those five Ps. The logistics of the Cali connection were difficult, so I only comped the Kush every four to six months. It was like a commodity. I'd let it go dry for a little while after I sold out so people would be begging for it when it came back. It was mainly for my team of dealers and me. The regular smoker could not afford it. But for us, the Kush was all we smoked.

The KC connect was the mid-grade brick. This was my consistent product. Easy to transport—six by four by one inch—smaller than the book in your hand. Always in double-vacuum-sealed Vaseline packaging, so no smell at all. Sometimes in clear packaging, and sometimes in brown or all-black. You could stick a knife in one and hear the *pssst* sound as the aroma would escape and immediately fill the room. In the height of my hustle, at roughly $400–500 per P and selling them in the range of $800–$1,200, I was doubling or tripling my investment. Let's do the math—50 Ps per week at a cost of $20,000, then selling them for roughly $1,000 a P equals $50,000. So, I was profiting roughly $30,000 per week on the mid-grade alone. At the height of my hustle, I was selling about two hundred-plus Ps and profiting easily over $100K per month or two as a nineteen-year-old college kid. Add in the eighteen racks for the Kush, and I was close to $125K every two months or so. Business was booming! And running like clockwork. Tick-tock, tick-tock. I once broke it down. At one point in time, I was profiting about $10,000 a day and about $500 an hour—every single hour of the day. If I were to calculate this as a nine-to-five, forty-hours-per-week wage, it would be $1,250 per hour or twenty dollars every minute. What the fuck is a nine-to-five? Why work for eight to ten dollars per hour when I was making twenty dollars *per minute*! This was beyond lawyer/doctor money. I was on my way to becoming a millionaire. It was only a matter of time.

When I share my story now, this is always a point that is consistently misunderstood. People hear drug crime, and they think street-level dealer. I was not a dealer. I was a distributor. There is a vastly different level of money and a significantly increased negative impact on the community.

The irony of how I met my KC connect never escapes me. I had just sold out of twenty or thirty bricks. I was drunk and high, partying with the football team on campus, and this big, buffed-up white guy was talking shit. I was in this guy's face on the porch of the dorm, cursing and screaming, getting ready to fight him until it was broken up by security. The next morning, a short, muscular white guy with freckles came knocking on my door. He was laughing hysterically. He invited me to come smoke with him and he was telling me about last night. When asked to describe me, he has stated "fearless" and loves telling folks this story. He recalls it as a scene from the video game *Mike Tyson's Punch-Out!!*, where the main boxer is this small character that faces these giant boxers. I was that small action figure. He said that he heard that I was the man on campus and wanted to introduce me to a better deal. He and I became good friends real quick. It was the beginning of the end.

✦ ✦ ✦

Bricks in the Bedroom: This was roughly my weekly quota.

Let's Take a Cruise

"Yo, yo, yo, yo! StanDrisse! What's up, bud!" my white should-be-fellow juvenile delinquent and long-time best friend Brandon jovially replied to my phone call.

"So, you up to take a lil cruise?"

"Does Brandon want to take a lil cruise?" He laughed again. "What kind of fucking question is that?"

Little did he know what kind of cruise I was talking about. I had just completed my first year of college, but I couldn't tell you what subjects or classes I took except for Moneymaking 101, Advanced Flipping Bricks, Intro to Money Laundering, and collegiate football. I was even more set on making a million, be it hustling or football. By this time, I had received multiple street and hood awards and praise for my accolades in selling dope. Much more praise or accolades than I had gotten in the classroom. Business was good in Marshall, but I had made my mark and I decided I was moving back to the STL: one, to pursue a higher-level collegiate football scholarship opportunity at Lindenwood University, a D-II school in St. Charles, Missouri; two, to move closer to my long-time girlfriend; and three, most importantly, to connect my original team to this new money stream. They had been calling for me to come back.

We were about thirty to forty minutes into our four-hour drive and completely on cloud nine before Brandon started to catch on that this was more than a regular trip.

"So, we are taking a little bit longer of a cruise this time, huh?" he jokingly asked.

I replied, "Yeah. Just a little longer."

The day started off with asking Brandon to cruise with me down the street to pick something up. Two hundred-plus miles and four hours later, that little something happened to be fifteen Ps of compressed Kush street-valued at $75,000. His entire car reeked. He didn't have the Inspector Gadget stash spot as I did, so we put it all in his twelve-inch subwoofer speaker box. This was one of my early trafficking experiences, where I was still doing much of the legwork. I soon acquired much more efficient ways of drug trafficking.

First Hundred Pounds—"Who Knew It Came in Bales?"

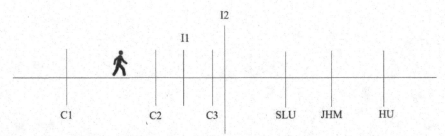

C = arrest that led to conviction; I = sentenced to incarceration; Numbers = number of that event
SLU = Saint Louis University; JHM = Johns Hopkins Medicine; HU = Howard University

The silence was so quiet it was as if my thoughts were amplified on a megaphone or airport intercom system. I enjoyed the quiet. I needed the quiet. So much of my life was noise and chaos. Much of it was self-inflicted chaos. I cherished my alone time when I could think. This was my way of balancing the noise.

Pre-rolls, check. Nine-millimeter, check. Money, check, I was thinking to myself as I was just finishing up counting the $30,000 in all twenty-dollar bills for the third time. I had three $10,000 bundles each wrapped up with two heavy-duty, tan rubber bands. The bundles of twenty-dollar bills, the three pre-rolled blunts, and my gun would all be stored away in my secret stash box in the car.

By this time, I had several stash houses where I would hide money, drugs, and guns. I was at my main stash house. It was a little thousand-square-foot, two-bedroom, one-bath duplex in an incredibly quiet, predominantly older white working-class neighborhood in St. Charles, Missouri. This was far away from the jack boys of North St. Louis; I had just bought this spot all cash. I put it in the name of a white, blonde friend of mine.

Outside the house was just as quiet as inside. The only audible sounds in the 2:00 a.m. air were the thoughts running through my head. The synchronized click of my doors unlocking rang loud in the quiet and calm November night of my sophomore year. Despite concealing a gun and three bundles in my baggy $1,000 Evisu jeans, I inconspicuously hopped in my freshly detailed, limo-tinted, all-white Grand Prix GTP. Normally, she'd be sitting on DUBs, but I had just taken them off for this trip. I was heading to Dallas, Texas, for my first hundred-pack pickup.

The eleven-hour drive offered me more alone time to think and be at peace. It was a pretty easy drive down I-44, which was labeled the drug corridor of the Midwest as it linked the cheaper-priced drugs in the Southwest to the high-priced markets in the North.

❖ ❖ ❖

This was before the days of Google Maps and readily accessible laptops with Wi-Fi everywhere you went. I MapQuested my route to Dallas and had a huge US atlas that I kept in my car. I used my atlas to find the hotel we were meeting at and to get a motel nearby.

I was nineteen years old, by myself, eleven hours away from home, and about to link up for my first hundred-pack pickup. In my head, I had to have been thinking, *How did I get here?* but I don't recall if I was. I walked into this hotel room, nine tucked in my hip, with tens of thousands of dollars bundled up in rubber bands. There were three Mexicans in the room. Two of them spoke no English, and one of them had a sawed-off shotgun sitting on the table, finger on the trigger, and was looking me in the face, quite expressionless. Sitting next to him was a big red Tupperware bin with one huge hundred-pound block of dope. I had never seen so much weed blocked up like that. My first instinct was, *Where is the rest of my dope?* I played it cool, though. That was me, staring down the barrel of a twelve-gauge, potentially walking into a setup or a jack move, yet I was as cool as the other side of the pillow.

Calm, cool, and collected, I dapped up my boy Juan. "What it do, ese! *Qué esta pasando?*"

"What up, my nigga!" Juan replied, both of us using terms of endearment outside of bounds. But this was how we showed our love for each other. *"Escalofriante! Muy bien.* I'm happy to see you, homes!"

"I bet I'm happier." I laughed and threw a huge smile to my boy and the other two guys in the room. They still didn't crack a smile or even change expressions. I remained jovial, despite being ready for something crazy to kick off. I pointed to the huge block of dope and jokingly said, "So, this is what a hunnid pounds of dope look like, huh?"

Juan nodded his head. "One-hunnid pounds, fresh from across the border, homes." He smiled at me. "You got the dough?"

"Like Wonder Bread, of course, I got that dough." I smiled again to try and lighten the mood. Out of my small briefcase, I pulled out a slender lockbox and quickly put in the code to reveal my three bundles. "Thirty stacks!" The two other Mexicans finally cracked what might resemble a smile.

Juan, however, was smiling ear to ear. "My man! Is it all here?"

"Well, actually, I threw in an extra couple thousand dollars for gratuity and taxes." Juan looked at me, perplexed. I started busting out laughing. "I'm joking." They all chuckled at that. "Thirty stacks on the dollar. Nothing more. Nothing less."

Juan and I shook hands and made the exchange. I walked over to the other two guys to shake their hands. The guy sitting down, who was an older Mexican guy, maybe in his forties or fifties, finally took his right hand off the shotgun and shook my hand while fully smiling this time. I assumed this must be Juan's uncle, father, cousin, something. His Mexican connect. He never told me. I never asked.

Juan offered for me to use the room to load up the dope. I agreed to this knowing that, as soon as they left, I would dip to my motel. He handed me the hotel keys and we gave our departing goodbyes, bro hugs all around. *"Gracias, amigo,"* the older Mexican said, while hugging me with his left arm, all the while holding the shotie in his other hand. He tucked the shotgun away in his coat and the three of them disappeared out of the room.

It was a recurring theme in my life to play the Black card. I looked like a gangsta because I was Black. So, when I was put in gangsta situations, like this one, I was indeed believed to be a gangsta, because I was Black. As I walked into the room, dressed the part, $10,000 worth of gear, my Mexican compadres saw my Blackness and thought, "This muthafucka is a gangsta. He *will* pull the trigga if need be." Thus, they had their trigger fingers ready, knowing that because I'm Black I must be gangsta.

❖ ❖ ❖

As soon as they left, I went into a mini panic attack. I had no idea how I was going to weigh this thing. I had no idea how I was going to get this to my car. We were on the third floor of an outdoor hotel. There were no elevators. How the hell did they get it up here? The other motel was about a ten- to fifteen-minute drive from there. It was already getting dark, and I would have to be reading from the atlas or attempting to memorize the route. How was I going to get there without getting pulled over? So many questions, and not many answers. I pulled all the sheets from the bed and started stuffing them into this giant red Tupperware bin. The bin was a big red circle and had rope handles on it. I made it look like it was stuffed with dirty laundry, instead of a hundred pounds of Mexican weed.

I slid the bin over to the door and propped the door open with the bolt. I bent at the knees, counted "one, two, three," and lifted the hundred pounds of dope off the floor. I propped the door open with my foot, slid the bolt away with my shoulder, and let the door close. As I was doing my best to try and look like I was carrying a light load of laundry instead of a hundred pounds of Mexican dope, I stumbled down the stairs and my gun slid down my pants and loudly clanked to the ground. My heart was literally out of my chest at this point. I wobbled down to the bottom of that flight, set the hundred pounds down, and swiftly jumped back up the steps to grab my nine. This time I stuffed it in with the laundry. Now my laundry was even dirtier, a hundred pounds of dope and an illegal 9-mm pistol. I finally got it to my car, but the bin was too big to fit in my trunk, so I had to just sit it in my back seat.

I breathed a short-lived sigh of relief as I made it safely to my limo-tinted car, seemingly undetected. I pulled out my pre-printed MapQuest papers detailing my route back to the motel where I was planning to break down and package up the supply. Taking extra care to drive the exact speed limit, while very alertly weaving through the streets of Dallas/Fort Worth using my pre-printed MapQuest directions, I finally made it to the motel. After fifteen minutes that seemed like a lifetime, a wrong turn down a dead-end street resulting in a suspicious-looking reverse U-turn, and one stare-down with a squad car at the stoplight entering the motel, I breathed another long sigh of relief as I turned the engine off, safely parked in front of my motel room.

As I stepped out of my car, I noticed that I now had neighbors that were not there when I got the room earlier: a white family—dad, mom, and two younger kids. I gave them a friendly smile and head nod. The mom smiled back, but the dad gave me this weird "I know what the fuck you're doing" look. It was as if he had drug dealer Spidey senses. How the hell would he know that I'm a drug dealer? I guess, young Black guy, nicely dressed, fancy car, thirty-dollar motel, by himself. Maybe that was suspicious. In any case, I was paranoid as fuck. I sat in my room for ten to fifteen minutes, hoping they would leave, but when they did not leave, I went to the front desk and asked if I could change rooms to the other end of the motel.

They gave me a room at the back end of the motel with no other guests in sight. I parked my car, double-checked the room for wires or cameras (paranoid drug dealer stuff), then lugged the hundred pounds of dope into the room. I had no idea that when you comped big weight from the Mexicans it just came in one big block.

I was thinking to myself, *Who knew it came in bales? How the fuck do I weigh this shit?* I was used to getting neat, Vaseline vacuum-sealed packs that had no smell. How did I know if this was fifty pounds or a hundred pounds? I needed some supplies to break this down. I wasn't prepared for a big block of dope. I needed a human-size scale. So, I sat my dirty laundry basket at the edge of my bed, left the room, and went back to the front desk to ask where the nearest Walgreens was. I wrote down the directions as the clerk gave them to me and was on my way. It was pitch black outside by this time. After using my giant US atlas book and the scribbled directions, I made it to and from Walgreens and was back in my hotel room with a person-sized scale, a fifty pack of gallon-size Ziploc bags, a bunch of Vaseline, and trash bags. I got a pretty crazy look from the cashier, but I paid cash and kept it rolling. I kept a giant roll of industrial shrink wrap and lots of black duct tape. Duct tape and shrink wrap were a must-have for a drug trafficker. I used them for a variety of reasons.

At about 9:00 p.m., I started breaking down the block. I eye-balled what looked like ten pounds and began hacking away. By this stage in the game, you could lay a half gram or a half ton of dope in front of me and I could pretty accurately tell you the exact weight. On my very first attempt, I hacked out an exact ten-pound block. I weighed it, vacuum-sealed it, shrink-wrapped it, Vaselined it, shrink-wrapped it again, then duct-taped it.

At about 10:00 p.m., I checked in with my girlfriend for about fifteen to twenty minutes to be sure I told her goodnight, sweet dreams, and to see how her day went. She was just starting nursing school by this time. So, we'd small talk about that.

"Hey, baby! What's up!" I happily answered the phone.

"You're alive?" she said in a sarcastic voice. We both chuckled endearingly.

"Alive and well, baby! Alive and well." I laughed again and was now smiling ear to ear.

"It's good to hear your voice," she said, this time in a suddenly much more serious and real voice. We joked with each other occasionally about being alive or not in a ditch or not in jail, but she knew all too well the life that I was living. She hated it. But I would always tell her that everything was all right and not to worry. By this point, we had long been over the "Don't ask, don't tell" discussion multiple times. She understood that I was not trying to hide anything from her. It was to protect her and me. If I got popped and she were to be subpoenaed, she could very honestly say, "I know nothing about his drug dealing."

By 11:30 p.m., I was finally done breaking down the bale of dope. It was actually closer to 102 pounds. I had my two subwoofer boxes in the hotel room. I stuffed fifty pounds of dope in each one. Now, I just needed to put them back in the trunk and connect the wires. By this point, I was very pleased with myself, from my impeccable and swift wrapping skills to all the money I envisioned making with my low-price Mexican dope. This was very short-lived. My car was backed in directly in front of my motel room. I popped my trunk from inside my room and, as I opened the motel door, one fifty-plus-pound subwoofer box in hand, I stared in the eyes of two police officers sitting in their cruiser directly behind my car. My heart instantly dropped, and my eyes shot open as if I was a deer in headlights. This was it. This was the end. I was about to go to prison for a really long time. Unlike my thinking one year prior after the campus police incident, where I saw my consequences as just getting kicked off the team, I was well aware that I had moved into looking at federal prison time.

Images of my soon-to-be fiancé whom I just told everything was fine flashed through my head. My beautiful little angelic nieces and their tiny, sweet voices flashed through my head. My mom, my dad, my family, my life all flashed through like a slow-motion movie, all in the matter of milliseconds. All the while these images were flashing through, I somehow managed to place my subwoofer box very calmly and unsuspiciously in my trunk, close my trunk, and walk back in my motel room.

As soon as I walked back in, I screamed a silent "HOLY SHIT! What the fuck!" at the top of my silent lungs. I kept telling myself, "Breathe, breathe, breathe. Just stay calm. Breathe, breathe, breathe. If they were here for you, they would simply come get you. Breathe, breathe, breathe." What the hell were they here for? Did the white family tell on me? Did the Walgreens cashier report me as suspicious? Did the hotel manager report me? Did my connect snitch on me? What the fuck was going on? "Breathe, breathe, breathe." Five minutes went by. Ten minutes went by.

Fifteen minutes went by. Twenty minutes went by. No knock on the door. I finally calmed myself down from my mini panic attack and convinced myself to fall asleep. "If they were here for me, they'd have come get me already."

When I awoke at 1:00 a.m. from my phone alarm, I immediately peeped out the corner of the curtain. The cop car was gone. I walked outside my door with my ice bucket in hand and surveyed the area. All looked clear. I had fallen asleep fully clothed, shoes on, packed and ready to go. So, I ran back in, grabbed the other fifty-plus-pound subwoofer box, placed it in the trunk, wired it up, jumped in the driver's seat, and got the fuck out of dodge.

❖ ❖ ❖

It was about one hour up 75 to get from Dallas to the Texas border. I breathed another sigh of relief as I crossed the Texas border. I was only a few miles out of Texas when I was flagged by a state trooper.

"Son, do you know why I pulled you over?" the cop stated as he stood at my driver-side window. My heart was pounding to what I felt like was clearly visible to the naked eye.

"No, sir. I do not know," I sputtered out confidently, managing to not show any signs of distress. I knew that I had been on cruise control, exactly four miles over the limit. In my head I was thinking, *Driving while Black in the racist state of Oklahoma.*

"Well, I've been behind you for the past few miles. Did you see me?" the cop asked.

"Sir, I saw headlights. Yes, if that's what you're referring to," I answered.

"Well, you've crossed the white line once or twice. I just wanted to make sure you were okay. Where are you going?" he asked as he flashed his flashlight into my back seat. I very strategically had a laundry basket full of college clothes and my Lindenwood University football sweatshirt very clearly in view.

"Sorry, sir. I didn't realize I crossed the line. I'm headed back to college. I was dropping in to visit my girlfriend for fall break. Trying to make this long-distance thing work. Silly college kid, I know." I laughed and smiled at the cop. He smiled back at me.

He gave one more flashlight glance through the car and genuinely stated, "Okay. Grab some coffee or some pop if you get tired. Safe travels."

"Thank you, sir," I replied and quickly sped off, sighing a hundred-pound sigh of relief. Thank goodness for vacuum seals and Vaseline. After driving for a couple more hours, I took the officer's suggestion, and around 3:00 or 4:00 a.m. I stopped at a hotel in Pine Bluff, Arkansas, to get a few hours of sleep. I was emotionally and physically exhausted. From having a sawed-off pointed at my face, to the heart-dropping surprise visit by the cops at the motel, to getting pulled over on the highway. In the past twelve hours there had been three sure-fire opportunities for my life as I knew it to be taken away from me and I somehow dodged all three bullets.

Branching Out

Although I was back in the Lou, my original team had dissipated. Taron and his mom had moved to Atlanta to be closer to some of her family. A move that was heavily driven by the lack of me being around to help supplement the household income. Anthony and his family moved to Miami-Fort Lauderdale, as he had fallen into deeper and harder drug use since he had gotten kicked out of college. Many, including myself, felt that I was to blame for Anthony getting kicked out and for him moving from recreational drug use into hardcore drug abuse.

These moves opened up new avenues for drug trafficking. Taron decided to go back to school at Tallahassee Community College, which is only a few hours from ATL. There, he met a few guys making big moves from Detroit. It wasn't long before T-Dash's Detroit boys were pulling up to the Lou, picking up ten to twenty bricks from me and trafficking them to ATL and Tallahassee. We called it "T-Dashing." And just like that, Taron and his mom were back in a place of stability.

I was skeptical of Taron's boy at first. He'd pull up in his bright red, candy apple-painted, new-school Monte Carlo, rolling down the streets with suicide doors wide open. I thought, *Man this guy is way too flashy... even for me.* But Taron trusted him. And he was paying cash money. And I didn't have to traffic the weight. And Taron got in on the cut.

❖ ❖ ❖

I made a few trips to Miami. Mostly to see Anthony. Our once extremely close friendship had grown distant beyond our actual physical distance.

It was a point of deep sadness for me. This reflected the increasingly snowballing of terrible things headed my way.

"If anyone can make that shit happen, it would be my boy Stan," Anthony assuredly introduced me to his MIA X-man. It wasn't long before I had my trafficking team in Miami picking up several jars of ecstasy pills. About ten thousand to be more exact, over several trips; at about two dollars a pill. Sold at wholesale for about six dollars a pill ($60K); street-valued at twenty dollars a pill ($250K). It was a crazy time filled with lots of "Xcellent" code language like "Xactly," "Xpedition," and "please Xtrapolate."

Pat was my X-Man and part of my trafficking team. I met him through my C-dub-P girls, who loved them some Stan. They had been begging me to come party with them at a rave. They'd come into work the next day after these raves completely spaced out, eager to tell me all about the party. I had zero interest in doing X, trying X, seeing X, or selling X. But I finally gave in and went to one of the raves. It was nuts. I didn't even comprehend how the shit was legal. *Wait, hold on*, I thought to myself, *I do understand why it is legal*. It was a bunch of white people doing drugs. A whole lot of them! I mean at least one to two thousand people were jammed into this ginormous skating rink. There were strobe lights and black lights all over. People were dressed in bright colors and weird outfits. There were girls in cages dancing half-naked. The music was so loud I could feel the beat in my chest. It was nuts. There were so many drugs all over the place. We were all teenagers. A couple of the girls weren't even eighteen yet. But this is where I met Pat. Surrounded by a group of attractive girls who were blowing Vicks vapor nasal inhalant into his nose, his eyes, his ears. He was in a daze. He had his shirt off. Two of them were rubbing his chest and other parts of his body.

I had no idea what was going on. By this time in my life, I was a regular on the streets of East St. Louis. But this place had me spooked. I didn't fear for my life. I was simply confused and baffled. This was Pat's domain. He was running this and several other huge raves. He was the host of the party, which was backed by drug money. Pat would charge twenty-five dollars to get in. Twenty-five dollars times a thousand people is $25,000. Then, he had a team of folks pushing pills throughout the venue for twenty to twenty-five dollars a pop. He could easily sell a jar (a thousand pills) in one night. Pat was moving all types of dope (weed, X, coke, pills), which is why the C-dub-P girls wanted to introduce us.

❖ ❖ ❖

My team had transformed overnight from close childhood friends trying to have fun and make ends meet (Anthony, Jonathan, Rich, Taron, Hazel) to hardcore dangerous drug traffickers. By the time I was nineteen or twenty, I had a completely new team. The original Fab Five were still benefiting financially from my entrepreneurial endeavors, but they were no longer operational managers. They were more like board members or shareholders who were invested in StanDrisse stock. The dividends paid well, with minimal risk on their part. I kept my original Fab Five away from this new dangerous circle of drug dealers.

My new team, Fab Five 2.0, consisted of (1) Jason and Carlos and their team from Sauget/East St. Louis/Collinsville, Illinois; (2) Bryce, Nicole, and Jeremy and their team from Wentzville, Mexico, and Centralia, Missouri; (3) Dominic, Austin, and their team from St. Charles/St. Peters, Missouri; (4) Charles and his team from Kinloch (adjacent to Ferguson); and (5) Pat and his team, which were our state-to-state drug transporters. My old Fab Five sold pounds of weed to help pay bills and support family. My new Fab Five sold everything under the sun, trafficked drugs all over the country, and every one of them carried guns. The transition happened overnight. The money was coming in truckloads. I was the head of it all. However, everyone on my Fab Five 2.0 team was a boss in their own right. I was just their drug distribution center. We were dumping dope in North St. Louis, East St. Louis, St. Charles, middle Illinois, middle Missouri, and, secondarily, in ATL, Detroit, and Florida.

I met Jason and Carlos (Los) through one of Rich's childhood friends. Jason reminded me of Crunchy Black from Three 6 Mafia. He had suffered from third-degree burns all over his body as a child when someone retaliating from a drug-deal conflict with his father set their house on fire. His dad was serving life without parole for murder. Jason didn't know his dad very well. Did genetics or systemic generational poverty play more into the outcomes of Jason and his father? Back then, I didn't ponder much on that debate. He never told me this story. Jason didn't talk much or smile much. His face was contorted to the point that it looked like it hurt to smile and talk. Los told me the story. Los was the suave guy of the click. He reminded me of Rico from *Paid in Full*. Interestingly, I don't know much about Carlos except that his grandma's house in Jennings was where we made all our drug deals. As with all my drug dealers, he welcomed and invited me to meet his grandma. He was actually proud to introduce me. I brought new life to several generations of impoverished families. Sadly, I was put on a pedestal as some kind of messiah.

Regardless of whether it's a grandma from *The Brady Bunch* or a grandma from a gun-toting, coke-slanging, gangbanger from the East Side, the interaction is all the same. You have to respect Grandma. And you have to listen to at least one "back in my day" story and you have to sit down and eat. Grandma Carlos made some fire collard greens.

Jason and Carlos would pick up about twenty bricks every couple of weeks. I'd park right outside of Grandma Los's house waiting for them. Grandma Los would often peek out the door and wave to me. I'd give a head nod to her. They lived in a war zone. I often had twenty to forty bricks on me. The jack boys were walking up and down the street. Kids were playing on bikes and shooting hoops in the streets. But those same kids often were the jack boys. My eyes were always on a swivel. I'd check all my mirrors at least a hundred times. I was a sweet lick waiting to happen.

I loved Jason and Los drops. Aside from being in a war zone, they were always superefficient and smooth. Never short on money. Never had to front them any bricks. Never much small talk. One of them would hop in my passenger seat. He'd confirm the amount of money. I'd confirm the number of drugs. Then neither of us looked at or counted the money or drugs. He'd hand me several bundles of cash. I'd hand him a duffle bag of drugs.

❖ ❖ ❖

Nicole was one of my best drug dealers. She was a pretty white girl with dark, curly hair, olive skin, and swag beyond belief. When Nicole and I connected, my long-time girlfriend and I were on a break. There was a fling going on between us early on, but for me it was all business and manipulation. Nicole was moving about ten bricks a week and she helped run drugs locally as well. Her Achilles heel was that she was addicted to coke.

Nicole introduced me to Bryce and Jeremy. The three of them were moving about twenty to twenty-five pounds per week all over middle Missouri and Wentzville. Bryce was a younger white guy, maybe seventeen when we met, and was self-reported as coming from white-trash trailer-park life. Bryce looked up to me, a big-city, big-time drug dealer with all the right answers to move out of poverty. I laid the blueprints out of how to be a successful drug trafficker and Bryce followed them to the tee. Jeremy was a Black guy, in his early twenties, originally from the predominantly Black Meacham Park in St. Louis, but moved as a teen to Wentzville, a predominantly white area about an hour and a half on the outskirts of St. Louis. Growing up as one of the only Black kids in this environment, Jeremy was seen as the bad guy and eventually *became* that bad guy.

✦ ✦ ✦

Dominic and Austin were the start of a new brazen culture in our country, Hip Hop America.[1] Rap and hip-hop culture no longer belonged to Black people. By the turn of the new millennia, white rapper Eminem was topping charts and paving his way as arguably the best rap emcee of all time. Lurking in the outskirts were people like Dominic and Austin: deeply suburban white kids, with all the privileges and advantages of upper-middle-class whiteness, who were entrenched in hip-hop and drug culture. Both Dominic and Austin reminded me of G-Eazy, supercool, super hip, artistically super talented white guys. Growing up in North St. Louis, I had never met white guys like them before. The white people I knew were either well off and disliked rap, hip-hop, and more or less

Black people, or they were poor and embodied the same struggle that hip-hop embodied.

I met Dominic in college. We played football together at Missouri Valley. We actually played the exact same position, defensive back. We were both relatively small for football, but ridiculously fast and agile. During team sprints, it would be him and me battling amongst the fastest runners. Dominic eventually switched to wide receiver, which pitted us against each other every single day in practice.

Word eventually got out that I was the man on campus and Dominic invited me over to his dorm to fill me in on his "grass business." Dominic and Austin own a grass-cutting business for which they were legitimately doing business and illegitimately laundering money through. That meeting in his dorm room felt odd from the beginning. Everyone that had been on my team, white or Black, was poor or came from meager beginnings and was looking for financial stability and empowerment. This was not the case for Dominic and Austin. Despite skepticism, I proceeded to build the relationship.

Unlike my other dealers who readily took and sought advice from me, to Dominic, I was just another supplier, replaceable. Upon initially meeting back in MOVAL, he assumed he was a bigger fish, moving more weight. This sentiment held throughout the extent of our business relationship.

Dominic would invite me to his house for most of our drug deals. I would walk into his dad's large St. Peters home with a bookbag or shoebox with ten to twenty bricks every couple weeks, and within ten to twenty minutes I would be gone. Most of Dominic's friends knew me but thought Dominic was selling to me. Dominic and Austin were local celebrities.

❖ ❖ ❖

I played football with Charles and J. P. at Lindenwood. They were both from Kinloch, which is adjacent to Ferguson. Kinloch was one of the roughest areas in North St. Louis.[2] It's primarily Black, heavily impoverished, and excessively policed. And, like Ferguson, it was run by white leadership with little investment in Black lives. Charles and J. P. were at Lindenwood for the same reason I was there. We weren't focused on education. We were chasing our dream of going pro. Be it football or hustling.

J. P. and Charles were moving the least but making the most (per pound) of my Fab Five 2.0, about five pounds or so per week or two. Despite all my coaching on lowering their prices and moving more weight, they decided to stay the "weed man" on campus and continued nickel-and-diming.

That rounds up my Fab Five 2.0. I was a master at building relationships and coaching people. I was managing a business team. I would have regular individual feedback and evaluation sessions with them. I would designate new appointments and hand out promotions for excellent performance, and there would be sanctions or opportunities for improvement for poor performance. "Everybody eats" was the motto. If the team thrives, I thrive. The more money they make, the more money the business makes. The very unfortunate truth that I seemed to deeply suppress was that this was an illegal business, and I was increasingly moving into the territory of it being an *extremely dangerous* illegal business.

❖ ❖ ❖

Outskirt Records. A record label started
by several people from my Fab Five 2.0.

Outskirt Show at The Pageant. (c. April 6, 2006)

Outskirt Records show on Main Street, St. Charles. Charlie Hustle introduced me (white shirt) and my brother, Vlad, who was on the stage as a hype man. (c. January 2006)

Charlie Hustle's 21st Birthday in 2006. RIP Charles Billups (on the left). We miss your energy, good vibes, and loving spirit.

Intro to Jennifer

Jennifer and I met in February 2000, my sophomore year of high school. The buzz around the school was that there was a new girl starting up soon. It was game night, and I was the team captain on the JV basketball squad. At one point in the game, I dove headfirst out of bounds into the crowd to save the ball. I grabbed it in midair and tossed it no-look right back to Jonathan as he soared in the air for a near dunk layup. I fell pretty much right in the lap of the new girl. She was in shock. I smiled and winked at her as I pulled myself up back onto the court. She smiled back and laughed.

After my game, I went directly to sit in the crowd where the new girl was.

"Hey, new girl! I'm Stan," I told her, smiling as I sat next to her.

She gave me an attitude look and said, "My name is Jennifer and I know who you are."

"Oh, so you know who I am? I know who you are too." I smirked at her. "So, what you know about me?"

She laughed. "Don't flatter yourself. Not much. But when you jumped into my lap, I asked who you were."

I laughed. "Um, huh, whatever. Why you stalking me?" She laughed and we continued talking the remainder of the varsity game.

That was the starting conversation of a nine-year roller-coaster-ride relationship. Her parents, Kate and Rick, hated me for the first few years of our relationship. Mostly because her dad was a Riverview cop, and I was a known drug dealer in the area. But, over time, he grew to like me. What her parents cared about most was how well I treated their daughter.

When the money really started coming in, they chose to let my goodness overshadow any doubt. When Jennifer and I bought our first house, we dropped thirty grand cash into renovating it on top of a twenty-grand down payment. Although we never shared with them the exact budget, he knew the price of fixing up houses, and he knew we dropped a considerable amount. He and I together fixed up the house, and through this six-month process became really good friends.

❖ ❖ ❖

Flashing red lights popped up in my rearview. I was being pulled over by Riverview police. Although Riverview was 90–95 percent Black, the cops were 90 percent white. I was minutes away from Jennifer's house, picking her up to go out for dinner.

A voice came over the police car intercom. "Step out of the car with your hands up!"

I was thinking, *What the fuck? Is this really happening? Why aren't they walking up to my car window?* As I looked back in the mirror, both officers were out of the car, hidden behind their car doors, with their guns drawn. *Wow. What the hell is going on?* I thought to myself as I slowly opened the car door with my hands up.

One officer rushed over to me, threw me up against my car, and immediately handcuffed me. By this time, I already had multiple arrests, charges, and a conviction under my belt. The Riverview cops knew very well who I was.

"Sir, why am I being handcuffed? Am I being arrested?" I asked politely.

"Shut the fuck up, son. We know who the fuck you are!" the cop that handcuffed me said. He was a young white guy. Probably about my age or maybe a few years older. He pulled out his gun and put it next to my head. "Where's the fucking dope, Stan?"

"What are you talking about?" I said innocently.

"Don't fucking play games with me, you little piece of shit!" he yelled in my face, spitting on me. "Where's the fucking *dope*?"

It took everything inside of me not to spit back on him. I replied, "I don't know what you're talking about, sir."

He laughed. "You think we don't know your twenty-two-inch DUBs riding through our fucking neighborhood. You think we don't have your fucking face posted up in our goddamn office. I don't even need to run your fucking custom 'DRISSE' plates to see that you're a goddamn, drug dealing scumbag. We know who the fuck you are! Search his car."

"You don't have permission to search my car," I stated.

The cop laughed. "Says who?"

"The law," I stated.

"We are the goddamn law, son," he said, laughing. "Sit your Black ass on the curb. Our canine unit will be here any second."

"You guys wouldn't happen to know Sergeant Barnhart would you?" I asked as I was sitting on the curb.

"You're fucking his daughter, aren't you?" the cop asked. "Is that some type of threat?"

"She's my girlfriend, and no, that's not a threat. But I assume he wouldn't be happy about an illegal search and seizure."

"Don't worry. Our dog will smell something," the cop stated.

"There's nothing to smell officer," I asserted. The dog was simply a safety net. They started tearing my car apart before the dog even arrived. I had just dropped off five bricks, so I was literally drug-free, but they did find over $5,000 in cash in twenties and tens. The car did not smell like any weed or drugs. It was clean as a whistle, but the dog did take a liking to the bag in my trunk that had held the five bricks just less than twenty minutes ago.

Rick showed up to the scene after about an hour of having me in cuffs on the curb. He was pretty upset with the officers. He questioned why they pulled me over and if they found any drugs and why they had me in cuffs. They stated that I had just sold the drugs and that's why I had so much money. Rick explained to them that I was a local promoter and rap artist and that my shows garnered cash income. Unknowingly, he told the same story I had just told them. On Rick's voucher, they let me go freely.

Jennifer was in her dad's car, scared to death. She thought they were going to shoot and kill me. Rick explained to us how they don't like me ever since several years back when I swerved past a Riverview cop that had someone pulled over. That cop hopped in his car and chased me down. Had Jennifer not been in the car with me that day, Rick stated they would have taken me out back and beaten the shit out of me or killed me. Rick saved me then as well.

Rick laughed at the situation. "You better take those rims off your car and change your plates, Stan." Jennifer and I didn't see it quite as funny as he did. "You both still hungry for dinner? I think Kate made spaghetti." And thus, I survived yet another life-threating interaction, not even utterly understanding the implications or weight of what just happened. I could have easily been Mike Brown, laying there dead in the streets, and all that would have been said was, "Oh, another young Black thug, selling drugs, dead in the streets. Who cares? Black lives don't matter." They would have plastered my already plentiful mugshots all over the news and said how terrible of a person I was, and how I would have never amounted to anything in my life.

None of that weighed on me at the time. It was all just part of the game.

Part of the Game

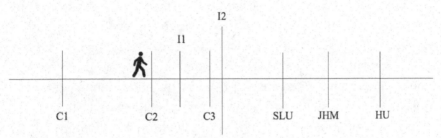

C = arrest that led to conviction; I = sentenced to incarceration; Numbers = number of that event
SLU = Saint Louis University; JHM = Johns Hopkins Medicine; HU = Howard University

Jack Boys

For the entirety of my hustling days, I had heeded Key's words as if they were gospel. "Watch out for them Jack Boys. But if you get jacked don't retaliate unless absolutely necessary. Violence is bad for business."

Jennifer was with me each of the three times I had been jacked. As Key advised, I never retaliated. The first time, I was seventeen at a high school party in Riverview. A well-known local gang banger (and neighbor to the party host) essentially saw me as some young county boy that wasn't 'bout that life. He asked to buy an ounce off me ($100). As I handed him the bag to examine the quality of the weed, he made sure to move in a way that I could see the gun in his sagging pants. He stated he was going to show his friend next door before purchasing. I stated I'd go with him but again, flashing his gun, he insisted I stay there. He never came back. My team was infuriated and wanted to fight this gang banger over $100. I declined. Years later, the neighbor was fatally shot while pulling one of his jack boy stunts. Another black body lost in the game.

The second time, I was eighteen, a freshmen in college back in STL for the weekend visiting Jennifer and dropping off dope. To optimize my time, I had her come along on the runs. I had just met my KC and Texas connects and the money was coming in fast. I was dropping dope to one of my longtime C-Dub-P coworkers. I had zero worries about this deal. I pulled up out front of C-Dub-P. He hopped in the backseat. I tossed him two bricks ($2,000). He said he was going to run and grab the money from his car. I nodded in agreement and continued lacing my new red, white, and blue Air Force's I had just purchased. Seconds later, Jennifer nudged me and informed me that he was driving off. I jumped out and began running after the car. But with my shoes flopping from not fully being laced, they easily got away. I simply cut him off and stopped doing deals under five to ten pounds.

The last time was the most frightening. I was nineteen and making lawyer/doctor money. I frequently stopped over at my cousin's apartment just to chill with family. Leaving his apartment, Jennifer and I were jacked at gunpoint by two men in ski masks. As I was opening the passenger door for Jennifer, they popped out of the bushes. One of them pistol whipped me and the other grabbed Jennifer, pushed her against the car, and pressed his front side against her backside as he put a gun to her head. They demanded our wallets. Jennifer was in deep fearful tears asking me to oblige. I did. I gave them our wallets and they ran off. Jennifer was inconsolably crying and asked me to take her to her dad. I did. He was ready to kill someone. Possibly me. I had half a bundle ($10,000) tucked in my baggy sweatpants that night. I swung it around next to my scrotum as the jack boy was patting me down. For me, the night could have been a much greater loss. I distanced myself from family as I had a strong hunch my cousin set me up.

Jennifer was forever traumatized by these events. I, however, was blind to the trauma. She was never able to shake the fear of being held at gunpoint. She was scared to go anywhere by herself. Constantly looking over her shoulder. Constantly fearing for her life and my life. Constantly fearing being sexually assaulted. That last part deeply saddened and enraged me—but this was all part of the game.

Mom and Pops

It was spring break of my freshman year. Things were booming. I had just met my new connect not too long ago. I had brought some dope back home to distribute to my STL folks. I stashed it in the Christmas tree closet. Why would anyone go there? It was spring.

I left for a few hours and came back home to my mom crying uncontrollably.

My dad brought me into their bedroom and asked me to sit down. For ease, I've recollected this in English instead of Haitian Creole. "Your mom spent the last several hours trying to flush a bunch of drugs down the toilet." He paused, just looking at me. "Son, what are you doing? Why are you doing this?" I didn't have a response. I just sat there. "Will people be coming after you or us? Do you need money to repay them?"

"Pops, pops, no one's coming after us. I don't need any money," I interjected.

My mom was still shivering and shaking. Through tears and snuffles, she explained how it took hours to flush the dope. She began unsuccessfully by trying to flush the entire brick. That didn't work, so she pulled the wet brick out and began trying to break it by hand but couldn't. So, she ended up getting a butcher knife and continuously stabbing the multiple bricks until they were in small enough chunks to be flushed. All the while she was paranoid that the cops or the drug dealers were going to come in and arrest or hurt her.

"Mom, I would never let anyone hurt you. I can promise you that," I told her confidently—and naively.

"You have to stop. Or you will not be allowed back in this house. I will not let you endanger your mother." He paused and looked at my mom. "My wife." He shook his head, holding back tears. "I will not."

I thought about explaining to him how I was not going to stop. I thought about explaining how people needed me. I thought about explaining how I gave people hope, about how I helped people survive. I thought about explaining how I gave people from the hood, people that I cared about, people that were family to me, financial empowerment. I provided them a ticket out of the hood, out of poverty.

But instead I just told him that he'd be seeing less of me and that I loved him. My dad and I didn't talk much after this incident. It remains one of my biggest regrets. Cutting ties with those you loved was part of the game. And at this particular point in time, I had a full house ten hands in a row. I was all in the game.

Visiting Jake

It was fall semester of my sophomore year. This would be my fourth visit to Jake in the past couple of months. He owed me nearly $10,000 and had gone silent on me. I knew he was home. I had just called his home phone from a payphone. He picked up, I hung up, and jetted over to his apartment. My connect got word that Jake owed me ten racks and asked if everything was okay. I assured him that it was not a big deal. I was moving hundreds of pounds; ten bricks were nothing.

I took the Walmart approach: outsell your competitors by having lower prices and making transactions convenient. I was literally throwing bricks to my team. Jake was an up-and-coming hustler from small-town Missouri. He went from selling ounces to moving bricks, and I coached him the entire way. I not only sold bricks. I gave my team the business plan to success. I gave them promotional and marketing techniques. We discussed budgeting and future sales projections based on past performance. I gave them performance evaluations and critiques. Jake would be listening and learning attentively each time I delivered these lessons. He and his wife Chrissy loved me…so I thought. They'd invite me over for movie nights where we'd chill and smoke. I'd play with their toddler daughter.

But now something was wrong. I had moved back to STL after leaving MOVAL. That was one obstacle: he no longer saw me frequently anymore. In order to streamline my process and be more like Walmart, I convinced him to take on fifteen pounds instead of his regular three to five pounds.

I knocked a little more forcefully, but not quite a police knock. I did not want to alert the neighbors. I had fifty bricks stashed away in my car that I had just picked up from KC. No one answered the door.

Jake lived on the fourth floor of an open-air, five-story apartment building. I could not make a scene by knocking loudly and yelling at his door. So, I took an alternative route. I went around the back of the apartment complex where it was damp and muddy from raining in the past days. I looked up four balconies to see that the lights were on in Jake's apartment and that his balcony sliding door, the curtains, and the blinds were open. It was a beautiful, sunny fall afternoon. I thought to myself, *Fuck it, let's get this over and done with.*

I walked over to the first-floor balcony. I peeped in that apartment and saw no one standing in view. I peeped in the other balconies above and surveyed all around to be sure the coast was clear, considering it was about to look very suspicious climbing up four stories of balconies, and considering that I had a whole bunch of dope in my car. But this was part of the game.

Nobody enjoys two-a-days and suicides and 5:00 a.m. practices. But they are part of the game. This was part of the dope game—people management and taking disciplinary action. So, I jumped, and on my very first attempt, my fingertips clasped onto the nine-foot-high balcony baseboard. Luckily, I was in tip-top shape as football season was in and I was in the midst of two-a-days and suicides and 5:00 a.m. practices. I pulled myself up as if doing a pullup and swung my now-muddy, fresh baby-blue-and-navy Nikes to the balcony edge, lifting myself up and hopping over the balcony rail. I pressed my back against the apartment wall and surveyed my surroundings once more. One balcony down.

The blinds were closed on this one but were opened on the next one, meaning I would have to be extra careful to not be spotted as these folks were likely home. I remained close to the building's wall. I stood on the balcony's rail. The next jump was not as high as the first but was more frightening, because if I was not successful on the first attempt, jumping and landing back on the thin balcony rail was highly unlikely. What was more likely was me tumbling down to the muddy ground on the first floor, breaking my neck, and police and paramedics coming to find a bunch of dope in my trunk. That was not an option and actually never crossed my brain in the moment. I simply jumped and clasped on. Now dangling about twenty to twenty-five feet in the air, I swung my muddy Nikes onto the base, hopped over the rail, and backed up against the wall. Two balconies down, one more to go.

As I had suspected, there was someone home at this apartment. There was a woman in the kitchen cooking and dancing. I climbed on the rail and repeated what I had done. Moving a little too quickly, my muddy foot slipped as I jumped, and I didn't get as much elevation as I needed, thus only barely grasping onto the next balcony with the fingertips of one hand. A surge of fight-or-flight flew over my body, but I was never fearful as I was now dangling nearly four stories up in the air with four fingertips of one hand holding my life together. I got myself steady from swinging and commenced to do a one-arm pull-up to the point where I could grab on with my other hand and swing myself up.

I finally made it to the top. By the grace of God or maybe the will of the devil, I was at Jake's apartment. My frustration was moving towards anger as I had seen my life flash before my eyes when I nearly fell off that balcony. That movement towards anger had me ready to pull my 9-mm out and knock on the glass window with the barrel of the gun. I decided to take a deep breath and dial back my emotions. This was simply business. And as an ever-hopeful spirit, I thought Jake would be willing to have an amicable conversation after I barged into his fourth-floor apartment.

I left my gun tucked in my waist and politely knocked on Jake's sliding door window and flashed a smile at him and his wife, then motioned for him to come let me in. This motioning was unnecessary, considering the sliding door was open and the screen door was unlocked. But I waited for him to come over and slide the screen open anyway.

"What the fuck are you doing! Are you fucking crazy? Are you fucking out of your fucking mind?" Jake screamed out frantically as he opened the sliding door, bouncing back and forth as if ready to box me or wrestle me. Jake was not a big guy, but he was an undefeated high school state wrestling champion, touted as being one of the best ever in the state of Missouri. "You are fucking breaking into my house...with my fucking wife and kid here, man. What the fuck, man!" Jake's baby girl, Addy, had started crying by this point.

"What? Breaking in? I didn't fucking break in. You just opened the door for me!" I shouted back at him. "Jake, Jake!" I tried to grab him to settle him down, but he flung my hands away.

"Don't fucking touch me, dude! Do not fucking put your hands on me!" Jake retorted angrily.

"Jake, calm the fuck down. I'm not here to start any bullshit," I said in a quiet voice, using hand gestures in an affirming but calm manner, suggesting for him to get it through his head that I was there in peace and to help. Neither my words nor my gestures were getting through to him. Not only was his baby crying, but his wifey, Chrissy, who was holding Addy, was also crying.

"You think you can fucking bust into my house like this with my wife and kid here! You fucking piece of shit!"

"Jake, CALM...DOWN. I just want to talk," I repeated softly but authoritatively. As I was backing up to slide the door shut, Jake rushed me and wrestled me to the ground. I tussled him off me and pulled out my nine.

"Awwwwwwww!" Chrissy shrilled out, practically loud enough to shatter the windows in the house.

"Chrissy," I said softly. "Chrissy!" I shouted now. "Stop screaming. I am only here to talk. I just want to talk."

Jake jumped up and rushed towards me again. "Stay the fuck away from my wife, you son of a bitch!"

"Jake, you have lost your rabid fucking mind! I have a fucking *gun* in my hand." My head tilted sideways, eyes squinted. "Wrestlers can't body-slam bullets, man."

"So, you're gonna shoot me in front of my wife and kids!" He laughed.

My headed tilted even further to the side like "What the fuck is this crazy white boy thinking?" "I'm from muthafucking North St. Louis, country boy. You think this will be my first time seeing brains splattered against the fucking wall?" I had not seen brains splattered before. I had not shot anyone before. I had never intended on ever shooting anyone. But I played on my Blackness and the criminality associated with it. Jake finally calmed down and sat down on his three-seater couch.

Jake explained how he had gotten jacked in his hometown of Mexico, Missouri. He apologized for dodging me for months. I apologized for pulling a gun on him. I hugged him, his wife, and daughter before I left. I ended up setting up a settlement plan with him. I assured him that things would be okay and that I'd help him and Chrissy get back on their feet, as they had missed a few bills due to getting jacked. I never saw Jake again after that day.

People management often called for climbing four stories and whipping out pistols in front of wives and kids. Sadly, this was part of the game.

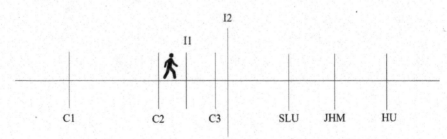

C = arrest that led to conviction; I = sentenced to incarceration; Numbers = number of that event
SLU = Saint Louis University; JHM = Johns Hopkins Medicine; HU = Howard University

Rollin', Okay

Juelz Santana's "Oh Yes" was blasting inside the car as Johnny and I were bobbing our heads.

"Come *fuck* with the boy!" Johnny jokingly said as we parked the car next to a gas pump in the middle of butt-fuck nowhere. Johnny and I were on a trip to go handle business in Texas with folks I was working with in the "music industry." One of my Texas connections and I were putting together a mixtape. I met this guy during one of my stints in jail. I asked Johnny to come along without giving him many details. My friends, including my girlfriend, knew asking Stan too many questions could get you caught up in Fed time.

So, here we were in the middle of nowhere and all it took was a short phone call six hours ago. "Hey, Johnny, wanna go on a blunt ride?"

"Sure! Where are we going?"

"Texas."

"Okay. Let's ride. When do we leave?"

"I'm outside your house."

"Like, right now?"

"Yeah." I started laughing. "But take your time. Pack your bags for, like, one or two days."

That was around midnight. Now it was about 6:00 or 7:00 a.m. and we were somewhere just across the border of Oklahoma from Arkansas. We opened the car doors laughing and smiling, high as a kite with the munchies. I walked over to fill the tank and Johnny headed inside.

"Get me something to eat!" I jokingly blurted out. "And something to drink." I laughed some more, licking my lips from cottonmouth.

Johnny laughed and smiled back. "Okay, man. I got you."

Our pit stop was quick, as I did not like stopping in small towns—nor did I like wasting time. We hopped back in the car, laughing, smiling, and happy to be road-tripping. I turned out of the gas station, and Johnny alerted me of a cop car that was turning onto the road behind us.

"Don't turn just yet!" Johnny said—so that they wouldn't be behind me—but it was too late. I had already begun turning.

I calmly said, "It's all good. They will probably turn into the gas station." Johnny whipped his head around to look back at what the cop was going to do.

"What the fuck, man! Don't look at the fucking cops! I see them in my rearview, man. Don't look at the fucking cops like that," I blurted out at Johnny.

Sure enough, the cop did not turn into the station and followed us onto the entry ramp to the interstate. I was fairly certain the cops racially profiled us. They likely saw two Black kids in the middle of white-town America from a mile away. We were two childhood friends on a road trip. But, to them, they saw two dope dealers.

We weren't on the highway for more than thirty seconds before they flipped their cherries on.

"We're getting pulled over, bro," I calmly said to Johnny.

"*Fuck!*" Johnny cried out.

"It's all good, man. We're clean. No worries," I said, looking at him in the eyes. He looked back at me, wanting to bust out laughing, but saw that I was serious. He really had no idea if we were clean or not. "We're good, bro. Believe me. Just be cool," I stated confidently to him once more.

We pulled to the side of the road. The officer tapped on the passenger window, asking Johnny to roll down the window. Johnny obliged.

"Both of you, get out the vehicle," the cop exclaimed as his hand was already on his gun.

"Hi, officer. Would you like my license and registration first?" I nicely said to the officer.

"I said *get the fuck* out of the car! Don't make me say it again," the officer stated a little louder, but not quite shouting…yet.

"Officer, I have no problem getting out of the car as you directed, but could you please let us know what we are getting pulled over for?" I asked politely once more.

The officer clasped his right hand tightly onto his gun and stated, "I'm not gonna ask you again son. *Get the fuck out of the car!*" He was louder and more aggressive now.

Johnny put his hands up, visually scared now that the officer had his gun clasped and that the officer was angry. "Officer, I am getting out the vehicle." He stated this as the officer was still standing right by his door. "Stan," he whispered to me as he was getting out. "Get out the car, man. It's not worth arguing."

I began to get out of the car as my friend asked me to do. I whispered back to Johnny, "I'm not arguing, Johnny. I know my rights." I obliged the officer's commands and stepped out and to the curbside of the car.

The second officer walked up and politely asked us to sit on the curb.

"My legs are cramped, officer. I would prefer to stand," I stated, mostly because I hated taking commands from cops.

"Okay. That's fine. This shouldn't take long," he said. I was thinking to myself, *What shouldn't take long?* Then, I saw both of them put on gloves as they open both front doors.

"Excuse me, Mr. Officers. You don't have permission to search my car," I shouted to them as the highway traffic zooming by made it hard to hear. They paid no attention, so I walked a little closer. "Excuse me, sir. Sir! Mr. Officer." I was close enough now that I knew they heard me. "I did not give you permission to search my car and you haven't even told us what we did, nor have you taken my ID."

The first cop, who was clearly the dickhead of the two, continued to pay me no mind as he rummaged through my car. The second cop stated politely, "Mr. Andrews, please step back to the curb." I was shocked. How the fuck did he know my name? I didn't care that he pronounced it completely wrong.

They completed the search of the front seats and found nothing. This was good, because we still had two pre-rolled blunts stashed away in the vacuum-sealed stash spot. They popped the trunk and opened the back seats.

"Sir, I did not give you permission to pop my trunk," I stated to the first cop, who began looking into the trunk.

"I just popped it," he said, menacingly staring at me through his aviator highway patrol shades.

"What did we do wrong, sir? Why are you searching us?" I asked politely.

"Listen here, you little punk." The first officer got in my face. "*You* don't ask the questions! *We* ask the questions. You understand that?" he said, turning back to the trunk of the car. "Now sit the fuck on the curb." Disappointed, I sat down as ordered this time, shaking my head in disbelief.

"Do you have any weapons, TNT, explosives, or sharp objects in your suitcases?" the officer asked, but I looked away and paused for a moment.

"No sir, we do not," I stated, despite not wanting to, because I had that right.

"So, where you traveling to with all these clothes?" he asked. I turned away as if I didn't hear him and did not respond.

Johnny jumped in, clearly very scared at this point, and nervously stated, "We are road-tripping to Dallas…"

"Johnny!" I exclaimed. "Don't answer any of his questions. You have the right to remain silent. Anything you say will be purposefully distorted and used against both of us."

The cop laughed a hard chuckle. "We got a college boy, huh?" By this time, they had our clothes dumped all over the highway pavement and were rummaging through the trunk, still not having found anything illegal.

"Well, Mary, Jesus, and Joseph! Look at what we have here." The first cop gently lifted the now-empty suitcase to show to his partner and Johnny and me. "This is a lot of fucking money, son!"

"Holy shit!" said the second cop as his mouth dropped at the sight of several dozen meticulously organized bundles of twenty-dollar bills. "That has to be over fifty grand right there!"

"Whose suitcase is this?" the first cop asked inquisitively.

"My suitcase is the Adidas gym bag…" Johnny blurted out.

"Jonathan!" I shouted to him, looking at him in his eyes. He looked with the face of a child who knew their parents were disappointed in them. I calmly and clearly stated what I said before. "We don't…have to…answer…any of their questions. Please, for the sake of both of us, don't say anything else. Let me do the talking."

The cop laughed at my coaching session. "Jonathan, you guys are both fucked. Your partner here is delusional. You're best to answer all my questions."

"To my understanding, sir, money is not illegal," I stated.

He laughed again. "Carrying fifty grand in the trunk, buried underneath clothes in a suitcase?" He laughed once more.

"What are you holding us for, sir? Have you found anything illegal? You've searched the car up and down," I stated.

"Found it!" The second cop pulled out a wooden one-hitter from Jonathan's Adidas gym bag. "You mean something illegal like this?" He opened it up and turned it upside down as the one-hit pipe slipped out—but no weed.

Johnny whispered to me, "There isn't any weed in it." I looked at him shockingly. One, why was he still talking, and two, we had a stash spot for weed. I asked him if he had anything illegal on him before we rolled out. I knew he didn't lie to me. Johnny never lied to me. I knew that he had either wrongfully thought it was just an empty pipe or he had forgotten it was in there. Nonetheless, paraphernalia is illegal.

"Put your hands behind your backs. You're both under arrest," said the officer. I remained calm and obliged the officer's directives, as did Jonathan. We were placed in the back of the squad car and taken to the Roland, Oklahoma, county jail. This place was a fucking dump. It had dirt floors. The jail cells had the old-school prison bars. There were no lights in the room, only natural light from the small window on the wall. There were only about five jail cells in a dark, dungeon-like basement corridor. There was no one else locked up but Johnny and me.

I could hear some rustling in the corner of my cell. It was a rat foraging through the McDonald's bag that had a half-eaten cold cheeseburger in it. That had been my lunch. This place didn't have a kitchen, so they gave the people locked-up fast food. But this wasn't *fresh* fast food. It was as if they were likely given a bulk amount of unused food and stored a bunch in a fridge, then threw it in the microwave. I took a couple of bites and decided not to eat the rest. But the rats loved it. We had been sitting for several hours before they came and got us for interrogation. They took Jonathan first. He was gone for what seemed like an hour. When he and the officer came back, I made strong eye contact with Jonathan as if to connect by ESP to understand what he had said. I was confident in my right-hand man and in the facial expression he had given me, which was mostly expressionless. But it wasn't one of "I'm sorry man. I fucked up." So that inspired confidence in me.

They unlocked my cage and escorted me to a more lit, normal-looking location of the building where the sheriff's office was. I walked into the room, still handcuffed, and before I could sit down in front of the sheriff's desk, the sheriff looked me in the eyes and unraveled a stack of perforated, old-school printer paper that unfolded across his desk and hung down the front to the ground.

"Do you know what that is, son?" the sheriff said in a voice that closely resembled Clint Eastwood from some Wild West movie.

"Looks like a bunch of old-school printer paper, sir," I told the sheriff.

"That's your fucking rap sheet, boy."

I nodded with an expression of "wow" and said, "Oh. Okay. Was the old-school paper for theatrical effects or are you all still in the Stone Ages here in…where are we?"

The sheriff laughed. "Roland, Oklahoma, son. Listen here, city boy. You're in a whole *heap* of shit. Your buddy Jonathan told us everything." I smirked at him. "He told us that you been selling drugs since a fucking teenager. He pinned all this shit on you."

"Excuse me, sir, sorry to interrupt. Were you finished? Pinned what shit on me? A one-hitter pipe with no weed in it? Is that even a misdemeanor? Did you *read* my rap sheet?" I arrogantly stated.

"You got some fucking balls to talk to me like that, son," he said angrily and in a faster-paced tone, sitting up closer to his desk. "You got twenty-five grand sitting in the fucking suitcase of your fucking car. We each counted that shit twice." He waved his hands over the $25,000, which was pristinely lying on his desk in twenty-five piles of twenty-dollar bills. He continued, "You're a motherfucking convicted felon with money laundering charges, drug trafficking charges, racketeering charges, federal cases, state cases, civil cases. And you think we don't have you by the balls you little…Black…piece…of shit." Both his hands were on his desk and he was glaring at me.

"I'm not talking to you without my lawyer here." I slouched back in my chair. "I'd like to have my phone call now, or you can take me back to my cell."

"Your lawyer, huh?" He smirked back at me. "We'd eat your city-boy attorney alive down here, son." He laughed. "We still got hanging down here on our docket as a form of punishment, boy. We will literally hang your Black ass. Literally!"

I remained slouched, expressionless, and wordless.

After a few moments of silence and staring each other down, he came back with a calmer tone. "Nothing to say. Okay, son. This is how it is. You can decide to say nothing. Call your lawyer. We keep you locked up for God-knows-how-long until official charges are brought on you—could be months. We eventually charge you with *another* case of money laundering, which will be your *second* active case of money laundering, not to mention your active drug trafficking case. You seem to think you have a strong case and a fancy lawyer. Let's say you beat our case. What do you think the judge and prosecutor in your other cases are going to think of you, a convicted drug dealer, having twenty-five grand in his trunk, hundreds of miles from his home city that he's not even supposed to be out of? It won't look good." He looked me in the eye. "You follow me. Now, if you decide to not call your lawyer and you decide to say you have no idea where this money came from, we keep the money as police evidence. We don't file any charges on the money or the one-hitter. And you and your buddy walk out the door free as a bird. How does that sound?"

I thought about it for a long, hot minute, thinking, *These dirty fucking cops.* I nodded my head. "Okay. Deal." And just like that we were free and the Roland, Oklahoma, sheriff's department was $25,000 richer, an early Christmas present. Who said that drug dealers don't pay taxes? A random twenty-five racks being taken out of a suitcase in the trunk of your car by a small-town sheriff's office who threatened to literally hang your Black ass? All part of the game.

❖ ❖ ❖

Days after Roland, Oklahoma, Incident
Jonathan and Jennifer. (c. 2005)

The Good Life

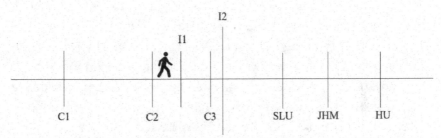

C = arrest that led to conviction; I = sentenced to incarceration; Numbers = number of that event
SLU = Saint Louis University; JHM = Johns Hopkins Medicine; HU = Howard University

"I have my curling iron. My makeup. My toiletries." My girlfriend, Jennifer, was anxiously checking off the list of things she had packed out loud. She was visibly nervous. She had never flown before, and at eighteen and nineteen years old, we were getting ready to fly direct from STL to Jamaica by ourselves.

Jennifer said, "Stan, I'm just nervous. Are you sure these tickets are legit? You were just locked up not too long ago. Are you sure you can leave the country?"

She was rightfully concerned. But, we had made the promise that in order to protect her from having to testify, I would not tell her details of my hustling.

I kissed her on the cheek, smiled, and told her, "Everything is great, baby." Things were everything but great at that point.

"You know I don't like that bitch that you got these tickets from," Jennifer angrily exclaimed.

"The tickets are good, baby." Another half-truth. The tickets were from the mom of a girl that Jennifer vehemently believed I cheated on her with several years back. The girl's mom was a travel agent and their family loved them some Stan. By this point in my life, everyone knew I was a big-time drug dealer, this girl's mom included. I told her I had some arrests and pending charges, so she pulled some strings to get my passport cleared.

It was an amazing seven days: ziplining and hiking in the Dunn's River Waterfall in Ocho Rios; paddle boating deep into the clear blue sea; day cruise and snorkeling near the Grand Cayman coral reef; shopping, buying jewelry and local trinkets; partying until the wee hours of the night in the streets of Negril. I had forgotten all my troubles. Jennifer was as happy as can be. That was what we hustled for, the good life.

Our Jamaica trip was so relieving and normalizing that I decided to take more trips like that. Knowing that shit could hit the fan any moment, making memories was an effective means of money laundering.

✦ ✦ ✦

Not too long after Jamaica, I made a Miami trip. I had been to MIA several times for business, but never for pleasure. I decided to take the crew to MIA: me, Jennifer, Rich, and Jennifer's seventeen-year-old sister Julie, who had a crush on Rich. How I convinced a cop of ten-plus years to let not one but both of his attractive teenage daughters to fly to Miami to party it up on South Beach with two well-known drug dealers is beside me. I have always had a way of getting people to trust me. I was indeed a trustworthy person and man of my word. I was not going to let anything happen to them.

"Drisse! Let's pop open that bubbly," Rich yelled out as he was opening the $300 bottle of Dom Perignon, shooting the top off the side of the balcony of our penthouse suite in the Trump Towers.

Julie laughed as she looked out at the breathtaking view of the ocean from forty stories high. Rich wrapped one arm around Julie's tiny waist as her swimsuit coverup blew in the wind, revealing her two-piece, yellow, polka-dot bikini. "You want a sip of this Don P, baby?" Rich whispered to Julie as he was smirking from ear to ear.

"Richard!" Jennifer jokingly but seriously yelled from inside the room. "You know the ground rules. Hands off my little sister!"

"He's okay, Jennifer," Julie replied as Rich poured the two of them a glass of Don P and continued laying his mack game down. Rich was the only one of us who was twenty-one.

I poured Jennifer and me a glass and wrapped my arms around her bikini-clad body. "So, what do you think?" I whispered in her ear as we both sipped the unreasonably expensive champagne.

"This shit is disgusting." Referring to the Don P. "Make me a glass of Captain and Coke." We both laughed and I proceeded to make her a glass of her favorite drink.

Our six-day getaway was infused with expensive romantic restaurants, videos of us clowning on South Beach, shopping sprees at local malls, and staying up until sunrise partying. The good life.

"I never want this to end," Jennifer said as she was snuggled in my arms and we looked out into the ocean.

"We'll have plenty more vacations like this," I stated, smiling at her.

"No. Not the vacation." She looked me in the eyes with a sense of seriousness and concern. "I mean you and me. I never want us to end."

In this intimate moment, I couldn't muster up a half-truth, half-lie. "You'll always be a special part of me, no matter what. In that sense, this never has to end."

PART TWO

PRISON

"Through valleys of the shadows of death and homicide, I made my way."

DEA Drug Bust—"Think It's Dry Now? Wait until November" (Missouri DEA, 2004)

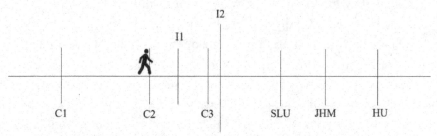

C = arrest that led to conviction; I = sentenced to incarceration; Numbers = number of that event
SLU = Saint Louis University; JHM = Johns Hopkins Medicine; HU = Howard University

We had been in a spell of April showers for weeks. But, on this day, it was the sunniest of spring days, not a cloud in sight. Listening to T.I.'s "24s," anthem music, I wasn't rolling on DUBs like I might usually be. My Grand Prix on DUBs screams drug dealer. I didn't have that option. The Grand Prix had gotten impounded after a high-speed chase months ago. Today, I was in a shiny gold, tinted-out, brand new Infiniti I30.

In my trunk, there was a duffle bag with thirty pounds of dope tucked away. It had been a slow past couple of months. I had closed up shop. One of my stash houses in Florissant had gotten hit up and one of my Fab Five 1.0 had gotten hemmed up. But that was behind us now. Operations had to resume moving. People had to eat. Today was a big deal. I was meeting up with Dominic and Austin in snow-white land. St. Peters was nearly 100 percent white. That was problematic and advantageous, all in one. Problematic because why the fuck is this Black kid in luxurious cars out here in our neighborhood? Snow-white land was lucrative from a business perspective in that I was charging Dominic and Austin twice the amount I was charging my team in St. Louis. I felt like Robin Hood. Stealing from the rich and giving to the poor. Dominic was also getting more weight than others on the team. Getting more product. Paying more money. He was the kind of customer businesses dream of.

I was already counting the stacks in my head. It was finally getting hot outside, so I had jumped in my car wearing only a wifebeater. I was matching as always. Blue tank top, red velour baggy shorts, matching blue briefs showing as my shorts were sagging, and my fresh red, white, and blue Air Forces. Oddly patriotic.

Dominic lived in a wealthy neigh-borhood. As I turned onto his street, which was a cul-de-sac, my mouth immediately dropped. There were at least ten or more cop cars and black SUVs sprawled across his and his neighbor's yards. Dominic's house was at the end of the block. Once I turned onto the street, I had to drive all the way through, or it would look too suspicious. It was the slowest and one of the scariest ninety seconds of my life. I held my breath the entire time. My heart was jumping out of my chest.

As I swerved around the cul-de-sac, I could see several of the officers looking very intently into my car. Although the cops did not recognize me, I saw Dominic and his little brother, handcuffed, sitting on the front porch. Dominic didn't see me. However, his brother and I made direct eye contact. He knew it was me. I could tell by the change in his facial expression. I thought for certain I was about to get flagged. But, to my surprise, the cherries never popped up behind me. I rolled out of the block unscathed but in a complete frenzy.

I was beyond shaken up. I did not know what to do or where to go or who to call. I was certain that they would be coming after me. I was certain that my cell phone was tapped. Driving back to North St. Louis was too far of a drive to ride hot as hell. Then I thought maybe I should lay low to let things cool down and give me time to think. I went with that plan.

I drove to Lindenwood campus and parked my car in a far back parking lot. I walked into the library which overlooked that parking lot and went into one of the tiny study rooms. For fifteen-plus years now, I've tried to remember what I was thinking when I was sitting in that small study room in the Lindenwood Library, but as hard as I try to remember, I can't fully recall what my thought process was. It is literally a solid black hole in my memory. From sitting in that tiny room until days after what I am about to explain to you are mostly black holes in my memory. I do remember praying. I do remember thinking of Jennifer and thinking of my mom and thinking of my little nieces and nephews, my little angels.

But why I decided to go to my stash house...I do not recall the reasoning behind that. What I do recall thinking is that no one that I hustled with had ever been to my stash house except for one person, so I thought it might be safe to simply drop the dope off there. That decision sealed my name being permanently embedded in the criminal legal system.

❖ ❖ ❖

The stash house was in the only low-income area that I knew of in St. Charles. The neighborhood had trailer-park homes and duplexes and primarily college students and elderly white residents. I had bought one of the duplexes in cash and put it under the name of one of the girls on my team. When I turned down the block, the scene was clear.

As I pulled up on the parking pad, hopped out of my car, and began walking to my duplex, a swarm of about five to eight black SUVs pulled up out of the woodwork and in the blink of an eye, I had fifty assault rifles aimed at my head. It was absolutely traumatizing. I thought I was about to die.

"Get down on the fucking ground!" I heard one of the voices yell. I conceded immediately and got down on my knees. All of the officers were in bulletproof vests and SWAT gear. I could see that several of them had

DEA and ATF written across their chests. Why was there a militarized army there to arrest a drug dealer?

I could feel that my knees were bloody as I dropped down so quickly to the gravel that I scraped them up. Several of the officers came running up to me with their rifles still pointed at my head. "I said get down on the fucking ground." Apparently, I misunderstood his command and getting down on my knees was not good enough. As they approached closer, the officer shot a taser gun at me. I jolted in a shock of pain as the voltage rummaged through every single inch of my body. If you've never been tased before, I highly suggest against it. They continued to tase me to the point I felt as if my brain was frying. I thought I was going to die.

One of the officers smashed my face into the gravel as the other dug his knee deep into my spine. They handcuffed my hands and shackled my feet, then picked me up and threw me against my car.

"Where's the fucking *dope!*" one of the officers with DEA written on his chest screamed at me. I didn't respond to him and he instantly hit me with the butt of his rifle. "Where's the fucking *dope!*" he shouted once more.

By this time, the other forty-plus officers that weren't beating the shit out of me began raiding the entire scene. They made everyone get down on their knees with hands behind their backs—even elderly grandmothers were down on their knees. They made an announcement that this was a drug raid and that no one could leave the scene.

Without my consent, the officers had already searched my car and found the bricks in my trunk that were due to be delivered to Dominic and his team. The officer that found the drugs held the bricks and the duffle bag high in the sky as to signal "touchdown" or to signal to all the pedestrians in the area, "See. We got this scumbag. Our drug raid was a success."

They weren't done yet. They kept questioning which house was mine. I didn't reply, so they busted open two doors before getting to the correct duplex. With a heave-ho they swung the giant jackhammer and *boom*—the front door went flying off the hinges and a flood of drug task force officers went swarming in.

They finally found my house. After hearing them bust through walls and tearing open couches, time went by and two officers came out carrying a giant safe. They questioned me about opening it and continued to beat me up. I did not respond to any of their questions. So, right on site, two officers with sledgehammers began pummeling the safe until it burst open, spilling out blocks of dope and stacks of hundred-dollar bills. All in all, they found over seventy pounds of weed, a jar of ecstasy pills, a quarter key of coke, tens of thousands of dollars in all hundred-dollar bills, and an unregistered 9-millimeter Glock. I was fucked.

As they drove me away to the station, I was in and out of consciousness. They continued asking questions and cracking jokes but I continued to not respond to them and fell into a deep, dark daze. I don't even remember being processed, taking my mugshot, or being thrown in my jail cell.

I slept for forty-eight hours straight...or it could have been two weeks. I was exhausted and injured. I was in this black hole. In a way, I felt relieved. No more paranoia. No more looking over my shoulder. Everything was all over. This tragic movie of a life I was living was coming to an end. I didn't eat any food. I don't recall using the toilet. I didn't talk to anyone. I didn't turn on the light in my cell. It was simply darkness, figuratively and literally.

I was awakened by the voice of Dominic. I could hear him excitedly talking in the hallway. He had a very distinctive, raspy voice. Apparently, he was being released. I had not even known he was locked up in the same place. I didn't know where I was. It was a very desolate and lonely feeling. I looked through the little window in my cell door and caught a glimpse of Dominic walking out. He was free, and I was still locked in a cage.

✦ ✦ ✦

After about seventy-two hours, the arresting DEA agents came back and took me into the investigation room.

"Good morning, sunshine. So, are you ready to talk?" The guy who had made the joke several days ago smiled. I didn't crack a smile. I felt like shit. I hadn't eaten in three days. I tried to eat, but I couldn't stomach it. I shook my head no. He looked me in my eyes, shifting his head back and forth as if he were looking deep into my soul to see if I was really the general they were making me out to be. "All right, boss. Back to your fucking cage." He motioned for the correctional officer to take me back.

"I want my phone call. It's been over twenty-four hours," I quietly stated.

He jumped into my face and grabbed me by my orange jumpsuit, grinding his teeth. "We don't have to give you shit. We're the fucking Feds, son. We operate under different guidelines." And he pushed me back into my seat.

I sat back, contemplating. I mustered out, "What's in it for me?"

He laughed again. "Holy shit, man. Do I have to say it again? We're the fucking Feds, mannn. Our conviction rate is like 100 percent. If we want you, we'll fucking lock you up for a long time. And you serve your entire sentence. None of this percentage bullshit they do at the state pen."

"It's a simple question. What's in it for me?" I repeated more boldly.

"Me, me, me. You fucking assholes are so goddamn conceited. How about we start with 'How can I help you, sir?' 'What do you need me to do, sir?'" he said, shifting back and forth with his words. The two agents were dressed in street clothes. The one talking to me had long, Johnny Depp-like hair and was smacking ferociously on his gum.

"How do you think your buddy Dominic walked? Give us a few names. Set up a few pops and that's it." He sniffled as if he were on coke and leaned back in his chair.

I smirked, looked down, and then back into his eyes. "That's it, huh?" I thought to myself about the shootout that just went down with my main man in KC from this most recent pickup and how giving up names like that is anything but "that's it." Giving up names like his was a death wish. I knew giving up his name was out of the question, but I had to play the game.

"This is the last time I will ask. Then, I'm going back to my cell. What's in it for me?" I asked.

"Instead of throwing you away for life in prison, which we certainly can for all that you were caught with, we can make this all go away," the agent said.

"I want that on paper," I stated.

He laughed. "Holy shit. Is that how you think this shit works?" I didn't crack a smile. "Okay, we can put something on paper, but then that would require you telling us what you're giving us."

"My connect," I said, frankly. "But I can't do that locked in a cell. I need to be out on the streets."

"We're gonna need some names before we let you out on the streets," he stated. Through our brief conversations, it was becoming clear to me that there were some huge holes in their understanding of our conglomerate. We had dummy names and numbers of real people that would lead them off our trail.

I provided these names and numbers under the auspices that I would meet back up with the agents in a couple of days to set up a bust. Instead, when I was released, I went into damage-control mode. I alerted the necessary people that shop was closed, not telling them why. I secured the rest of my money for what might be a long vacation. I informed my lawyer of what happened and paid him a large, lump-sum retainer fee. I contacted my family and informed them that I'd be in summer school and summer football camps and to not be concerned. And finally, I completely broke ties with Jennifer. Things were already on shaky grounds after the drug raid on Hazel's house. She gave me an ultimatum and asked me to pick her or the game. Stupid me, I picked the game. Thus, our relationship had dwindled in the past months. She had also been flirting with a guy at her new job. She started dating him for a while. Despite being together four years, the breakup was pretty clean and easy. I told her that we shouldn't talk at all to make it easier.

After getting my ducks in a row, I met up with the agents and told them I had a change of heart. I was not going to provide them any information. So, they locked me back up. I was locked up for over four months without any details being given to me. It was a sort of restful agony. I had no idea what was to come, and that was psychologically very damaging and difficult, but not having the daily paranoia of a deadly drug bust or being killed in a drug deal gone bad or being robbed by jack boys was restful in many ways. I turned my mind off. The only person I contacted was my lawyer. The Feds were still actively investigating my case. One day out of the blue with no reasoning, they let me go. I got out in August 2004, just in time to start my junior year at Lindenwood University.

Losing It All

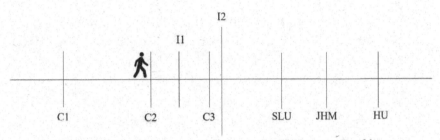

C = arrest that led to conviction; I = sentenced to incarceration; Numbers = number of that event
SLU = Saint Louis University; JHM = Johns Hopkins Medicine; HU = Howard University

To get a clearer picture of how things were crumbling in my life and how I couldn't seem to turn off the self-destruct button, let me take you back to an event just before and then a few events after that fifty-man DEA raid.

Hazel's Raid

"Hello," I recall answering my cell, barely awake, as I lay in my bed at my Lindenwood apartment. It was January 2004, the start of spring semester of my sophomore year.

"Stan, the cops just busted in my house." Hazel's voice was on the other end, crying. "They took the safe."

I hung up, jumped up, and jetted back to North County from St. Charles. Before primarily using the stash house that I bought, I had dope stashed strategically all over the city depending on who that dope was earmarked for—Jeff Bezos-type shit. Hazel's apartment was one of those spots. When it came to supply-chain management and logistics, I was pretty savvy. There were twenty pounds of Mexican weed in the safe from my recent Texas pickup. Hazel had no idea what was in the safe or what the code to get in was. Ironically, pretty much all of it was earmarked for her and her boyfriend. When it was time for them to reup the two to three bricks they moved every week or two, I'd come over, open the safe, and give them their fix.

Hazel was one of my most loyal friends. She loved me more than she loved her boyfriend. She would do anything for me. So, when she called and said she got popped, I wasn't worried about her snitching—I was worried about her boyfriend. I went over to Hazel's to scope the scene.

Hazel's complex was a maze. I crept around the back way, got out of my car, and walked closer to her apartment. As soon as I turned the corner to where her apartment was in view, I saw about three to five cop cars. One of the cops spotted me, pointed, and started running towards me. I ran, hopped in my car, and squirted out. Before I knew it, I had two cop cars behind me. It was like a scene out of *The Fast and the Furious*. I was going at least sixty or seventy miles per hour through a labyrinth of twist and turns. Our tires were squealing like you would hear at a Nascar speedway. You could hear the screeches echoing throughout the complex. It was so loud that neighbors came out to see what was going on. Her complex dumped out into a neighboring subdivision, but the cops had that blocked off. With two cop cars still behind me, I took a hard swerve over the curb into the grass, creating a shortcut into the neighborhood. I had momentarily lost them, but there was only one way out of the sub-division. I slammed on the gas and accelerated past a hundred miles per hour in this tiny neighborhood. I slammed on the brakes and skidded to make the turn for the straightaway that led to the exit of the neighborhood. It was about two to three football fields away. I slammed on the gas, gritting my teeth trying to make it out, and as I was about halfway, three cop cars pulled up, a cop jumped out and rolled out a blanket of spikes, and all six officers pulled out their guns.

"Stop your vehicle now or we will begin to shoot," one of the officers shouted through a megaphone. I slammed on the brakes and screeched to a halt.

"Get out of the car with your hands up." At this point, there were cops in front of me and in back of me. I got out and surrendered. I was slammed up against the car and arrested.

As I am writing this in 2020 and now have (just as the rest of the world has) much more visual evidence of how Black bodies are gunned down in broad daylight at the hands of law enforcement, I can't help but wonder how I am still alive. It requires more than two hands for me to count the number of times I've had multiple guns pointed at my head.

This was my first drug raid. They held me for twenty-four hours then interrogated me—threatening a bunch of bullshit—but I told them I had no idea where that safe came from. They let me go. I was never charged.

I closed up shop for several months. My team was desperate and hungry. They started committing other crimes to eat. The KC shootout was my next pickup. I was going extra big because everyone was hungry. Before I could pop off those hundred bricks, the DEA dropped down on me. I was losing it all. Everything was falling apart. My relationship with my family. My relationship with my girl. My relationship with my life. The number of times I could have died in just the previous year was astounding to me. I wanted it to end, but I didn't know how to get out.

❖ ❖ ❖

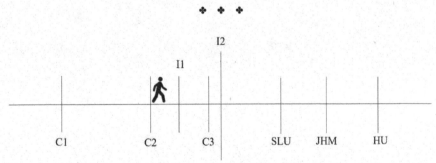

C = arrest that led to conviction; I = sentenced to incarceration; Numbers = number of that event
SLU = Saint Louis University; JHM = Johns Hopkins Medicine; HU = Howard University

As I was recollecting this story, laying in my dorm room at Lindenwood, my phone rang.

"Hello," I answered my cell.

"Oh, my goodness, Stan. Thank you so much for answering," Jennifer said. "I've been thinking about you a lot lately. I know you've been dodging my calls and I get it. That's what we agreed on. But can we talk?"

I didn't tell Jennifer anything about the past four months. I've actually never told anyone in great detail about those four months or about the DEA drug raid or about the KC shootout. Mostly because I was actively still under investigation by the Feds.

"Yeah. We can talk," I told her.

My Infiniti was seized by the Feds, as was the stash house and a large amount of my drug money. But I skipped those details in our conversation. Jennifer and I didn't officially get back on for about another six months, but she reversed her ultimatum. She wanted me to stop selling drugs, but she was not going to flat-out give up on me. I told her that I was working on a plan to get out, but it was not that easy. I asked her to trust me and to maintain our pact of not asking me incriminating questions. She agreed.

❖ ❖ ❖

Not even a week after getting out of jail from being locked up on a federal drug investigation and one day before my junior year started, I rented a car and took a trip out to KC. I needed answers.

"What's up, bro!" Jerome shouted in excitement to see me as he opened the door to his house. "Long time, no see. How you been?" He looked me in the eyes as he was asking.

"I've been cool, man. You know how it is." I started feeling the situation out. Last time I saw him, things were absolutely nuts. He smiled and gestured for me to come to his basement. "Hey!" I waved to his wife and kids and they cordially waved back.

One of his basement walls was a gigantic fish tank with a mini shark and lots of colorful tropical fish. He pointed to the shark. "That's my newest addition right there. We call him Hammer. He's not a hammerhead, though," he said, laughing. "So, to what do I owe the surprise visit? You've been a hard man to reach, my friend."

"Whatever happened with your connect that tried to jack us?" was my first question.

"We took care of that just like I told you we would," he stated very bluntly.

"That's it? No more details?" I asked.

He laughed. "You sure you ain't wearing a wire? It's handled. They won't be a problem anymore." There was an awkwardly long pause. "So where have you been, man?" he asked.

"Shit got too hot, man. I had to lay low," I stated with my head titled to the side, elbows resting on my leg and fingers interlaced, a very calm and comfortable posture. Although inside me questions and thoughts were racing a mile a minute.

He laughed again. "You a cool muthafucka, Stan," he said, shaking his head. "I love how you're able to tell the truth and lie at the same time. But actually, be telling the truth." He laughed again. "And sit there calm as fuck doing it."

I sat back and cracked a smile at his comment. "I'm not following you," I stated.

"Shit has been hot. You have indeed been laying low." He paused. "Annnd the Feds is watching us. Annnd it's hard not to lay low when you're locked up." I shook my head at his response, then he added. "I have eyes everywhere, bro."

I quickly replied in retort to the hint that I may have been being dishonest. "I sent a kite your way, bro. You didn't need special eyes to see that shit." I was angered at his comment.

"Slow down, bro. I didn't mean it like that," he stated. "Did they ask you to flip?"

"Is that even a question?" I said with my eyes squinted in amazement.

"Well?" he said.

"Is *that*…even…a question?" I stated with my head even further tilted to the side. "Would I even be sitting here? Four months after the fact?"

"Maybe you got tired of being locked up. Why would they just let you out?" he said.

"I didn't flip, man. And I don't know why they just let me out," I stated.

"So, what do you know?" he asked.

"I think it was one of my Fab Five," I stated.

"Who?" he asked.

I paused for a second, looking at his shark hunting for food. "Dominic or Austin."

He nodded his head. "Hmmph. Have you put any intel out?" I looked at him in a bit of confusion. "He's got a girlfriend, right? A mom? A brother? Let them fucking know what's up."

Another long pause. I was trying to find my way out of the game, not deeper in. I didn't say anything, but it was a hard pass on that tactic. After being tased, shot at, and having fifty rifles pointed at me, I was starting to condition myself to control that other voice in my head.

"Maybe Dominic or Austin snitched after they got popped. But who snitched on Dominic and Austin?" Jerome made a solid point that I still hadn't figured out. "Remember Colby, white boy with the dreads? He got popped four months ago too. The same exact day that you and Dominic got popped."

I was stunned. "What?"

"I'm heavy in this shit, bro. I put intel out. I've got mouths to feed. Seven to be exact. The people I fuck with got mouths to feed too. This is my fucking job. I'm not a college boy like you." He was clearly angry at this point. I let the shot at me slide, considering that it was true.

"Despite all three of you living in different cities, do you know the connection between you, Colby, and Dominic?" he asked me, looking me in my face.

I shrugged and shook my head as he said, "Missouri Valley College."

"But Coby didn't go to MOVAL," I said. "Colby didn't even finish high school, did he?"

"No, he didn't go to MOVAL, but he did sell dope there," Jay stated. "You know who his main connect was?" I shrugged my shoulder. "Who was your main connect there?"

I was astonished as we both said the name together: "Jake."

I'm not sure exactly what I was hoping to get out of going to KC. I wanted answers. I wanted out. I didn't want to go to prison, but I surely didn't want to snitch because I surely didn't want Jennifer or my family to get hurt or killed. With Colby and me out, Jerome was seriously hurting. Two of his guys that were getting a hundred-plus pickups consistently were out. In more or less threatening words, he basically said that I couldn't get out, not right now. He and his family needed me. His street family and his real family, which were one in the same for him.

I was angry with Jake that he snitched, but I was angrier with myself that I put him in that predicament. From Jerome's intel, Jake decided to expand beyond MOVAL and opened up an operation back in Mexico, Missouri, where he was from. He had a high school kid as one of his main runners. The high school kid got popped with a couple of ounces, snitched on Jake, asked Jake to drop off five bricks to his man, and his man was an undercover. Jake, being a country boy, had his rifle on him when they popped him, so they hit him with distribution and armed criminal action (ACA). He was looking at 85 percent on a ten, so he flipped. Here's where the Feds came in. Jake told them I was the main guy, but Jake never knew where I lived or my real name. He told them StanDrisse from East St. Louis, which is in Illinois. And he told them Colby, who lived in KCK on the Kansas side. Meanwhile, Dominic, the last name he offered, was from St. Charles, Missouri. Thus, three states were involved, which is grounds for calling in the Feds. Colby had already been served his indictment, which included wiretaps, photos of him making transactions, and a DEA raid. The Feds had been watching us for over nine months now. Pretty much right around the time that I had busted into Jake's house when he had been acting erratic and crazy.

He couldn't pay me back not because he had gotten jacked, but because he had gotten popped by the boys.

❖ ❖ ❖

More to my inability to turn off the self-destruct mode, shortly after returning from being incarcerated from my DEA arrest, I was back on the highways managing the movement of large quantities of dope. I like to think that fear of what Jerome might do and providing for my team were my motives. But I would later learn that hustling was itself an addiction and was my addictive drug of choice.

Lil Wayne was blaring out of the speakers of the extended-cab, all-black, tinted-out Yukon Denali rental car as I was racing down I-70 on my second trip to KC in two days. I had just popped off fifty bricks in less than twenty-four hours, made a pitstop to take two exams at school and do my work/study job (as if I needed that), hit the studio up with Dominic and Charlie Hustle to drop a track, and then hopped back in the Denali in the evening after a night class to handle some business. I had maybe one or two hours of sleep in the past seventy-two hours.

Lil Wayne began to serenade my ear drums.

I drifted into deep thought. After the Feds dropped down on us, shit just got crazy. My life was in a spiral.

Just as I was deep in thought, thinking about the drought and now the overflow and all the money that came with it, I drove past the infamous I-70 sign[1] not too far past Wentzville, Missouri: "Think It's Dry Now? Wait until November." This sign was erected shortly after our DEA drug bust. We were infamous. It was February 2005, and many of our cases were coming up later that year. They were preparing to lock up most of the people in the Missouri-Kansas-West Coast conglomerate. I chuckled when I saw it. Drought? My people were in a utopic rainforest right now. I knew I was headed to prison. It was only a matter of time.

Lil Wayne's "Money on My Mind" continued to infiltrate my brainwaves.

I thought to myself, *I don't struggle or fear consequences, even in the face of life or death. I just simply lift the fifty- and hundred-pound backpacks full of dope and "boop" drop them on my shoulder and keep it moving.* I was in a hazy daze with hundred-dollar bills floating in the air. To this day, my wife asks how I can remain in silence so long, but my mind is never silent. It's as if I have a stereo on blast; my thoughts and ideas are constantly entertaining me. I was brought out of this daze when cherries popped up in my rearview.

"Oh shit." I was not in good shape. I had just blazed a blunt. I had another blunt sitting in the middle console and several bundles of cash money tucked underneath my driver seat. I didn't even take the time to stash it anywhere. My eyes squinted in the rearview, glaring through the blinding red-and-blue flashing lights. I quickly threw the full blunt in my mouth and started chomping away until I swallowed it whole. *Why the fuck do I have drugs on me?* I was sloppy. I was flustered. I was losing it.

The officer stated that he smelled marijuana and asked me to get out of the car. After about thirty seconds of searching, he easily found the tens of thousands of dollars bundled up under my driver seat.

"Holy shit, son! This is a lot of money," the officer stated, looking at me in the eyes as I sat in the dark on the cold curb, watching cars zoom by on the highway. "What are you doing with all this money?"

"Am I under arrest? Did you find anything illegal in my car?" I politely asked the officer.

He laughed. "Your car reeks of weed. You have, I don't know, what is this?" He looked at the bundle of money in his hand that he now had in a Ziploc bag. "Thirty thousand dollars of cash money in twenty-dollar bills. You are a convicted felon with a federal drug trafficking case pending." He stopped and looked at me again, laughing. "Do you get where I am going?"

Although I was not charged, he still arrested me and kept me locked up for over a month in the middle of Missouri. I was later charged with money laundering.

❖ ❖ ❖

It was three months after returning from my incarceration for my DEA arrest, November 2004, the middle of my junior year. Jennifer and I were in my mom and pop's family room studying. I was prepping for a calculus exam and she was reviewing for a nursing exam. We heard a knock on the door similar to what a pizza man's knock would be. To my surprise, I opened the door to find three US marshals.

One of them asked, "Is Stanley Andrisse home?"

I considered lying for a split second but told them that was me. They told me I was being arrested by the Feds and charged with drug trafficking in relation to the April 2004 DEA drug raid and that my bail was set at an insane $100,000. Only murderers and rapists get six-figure bails, as the court doesn't want them out on the streets. All the time I had sat in jail over the past summer, there were no official charges brought against me—that's why they released me. It's constitutionally illegal to hold someone past seventy-two hours without charging them.[2] I would later learn that they unofficially charged me, thus were legally able to hold me, then removed the charges, thus why they released me and now were finally officially charging me.

My US marshal arrest was one of the nicest encounters I had with law enforcement. No tasing. No face smashing. No guns drawn. No derogatory language. They gave me the opportunity to go talk to my parents and Jennifer privately to prepare and call my lawyer. My dad was distraught and already thinking about putting up the house for my bail. I told him that I would take care of it. I had recently stashed tens of thousands of dollars with Jennifer just for purposes like this. My lawyer got the court to agree to 10 percent. I was arrested and taken in for booking but before I ever made it to a jail cell, Jennifer and my parents brought ten thousand cash, still smelling like dope, to bail me out.

To share a few words on bail, if I went to all my court dates up until sentencing, my $10,000 would be returned to me. If I missed any of the many court dates I had, $100,000 would become due immediately, and thus I would owe an additional $90,000, and be a wanted fugitive. Most crimes have bails of $250 to $500 and most people can't pay that, forcing them to remain incarcerated for long periods of time leading up to their sentencing. Cash bail criminalizes poverty.[3]

Confidential Informant

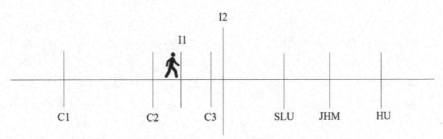

C = arrest that led to conviction; I = sentenced to incarceration; Numbers = number of that event
SLU = Saint Louis University; JHM = Johns Hopkins Medicine; HU = Howard University

It was September 2005. Two days before my court case's eighteenth preliminary hearing, Jake was found fatally injured in North St. Louis City and pronounced dead at Saint Louis University Hospital. He was set to be the primary confidential informant testifying against me, claiming that I was leading a multi-state drug ring. I was astounded and distraught by his death. Many believed that I was responsible for it. We had our altercations in the past and he was set to be one of the primary causes of me being sent to prison for a very long time, but I would never wish death on another person. There is no coming back from that. Still many believed that somehow, I was behind his mysterious death that to this day remains unresolved.

For a while, I was of the assumption that Jerome might have been behind Jake's death, but he gave no indication that he was. To the contrary, he was of the belief that I had "grown a pair" and begun handling business the way he had been hinting and encouraging me to handle business.

For a long time, I believed in death. In the streets, we swear to a code of ethics. And if you violated that code, I truly and deeply felt that you then deserved the results that came with that violation. Loyalty and staying true to one's words were and continue to be one of my top values. You should not have taken an oath that you did not intend to uphold or that you could not uphold. And if you thought you could uphold it, but you could not, that was simply a sign of weakness and more reason for deserving the outcome of the violation, death. This may seem archaic and vile, but this is no different than the death involved in war. If you send airplanes into my towers, I will come after your wife and kids, relentlessly. I will search the earth for you. I will blow up caves, drop bombs, and burn down whole cities filled with innocent women and children, to find you. That's what President George Bush and Barack Obama did. That's what the United States has done on numerous occasions. That's what Rear Admiral William "Deak" Parsons[4] and Colonel Paul Tibbets[5] did as they pressed a button that instantly killed over two hundred thousand civilians. That's what has been done for millennia. When we think about Osama bin Laden and how he took down the towers, no one felt sorry when he died. People felt that the world was a better place with his death. Did anyone for even half a millisecond think what his death might mean to his children and family? No, not at all. When you do something like take down the towers, you lose your right to live.

The way I thought of it (back then), in this game of the streets, if you get killed, it's not the person that killed you that took you away from your family and kids, it's *you* and *your actions* that took you away from your family. You deserved death by doing that action, by playing the game, by rolling the dice. The world is a better place without you. Your family is better off without you. Your children are better off without you. If I killed someone that broke the code, I would feel no remorse in telling that person's mom straight to her face that her son died because he broke the code. I know you may be sad, but the world is better without him. In my eyes, at the time, this was no different than Obama telling the world that Osama was dead.

That's how I thought. That's how I lived. Until death was at my doorstep. Until someone's death was suspiciously directly linked to me. I battled for a long time with whether Jake deserved to die. How was the world a better place without him? Why should his daughter grow up without her father? The other voice in my head would counter this with because he was a coward. Because he willingly chose to enlist in a high-risk profession. He chose that life. He killed himself and left his daughter the minute he chose to engage in this life. This is no different than a soldier choosing to be a solider knowing that he or she may go to war or a cop choosing to be a cop knowing that he or she may get put in the line of fire. This is a dangerous, risky profession. I didn't take Jake away from his daughter. *He* took himself away by taking the oath into the game.

For me, this is why you didn't snitch. I took an oath into this risky business knowing that prison was a highly likely scenario. Loyalty was one of the top values that I lived by and it was being challenged at its greatest level. Did breaking loyalty really have to mean death? Did Jake have to die? I could not bring myself to believe that Jake needed to die. This brought me great grief. And continued to bring me heartache knowing his daughter would grow up not knowing the warm embrace of her father.

After months of investigation into foul play, the detectives ruled the death a suicide. I was distressed yet relieved. The federal charges against me were moved to state charges, the level of the crime was dropped to a lower level, and my case was pushed back several more months. It was a difficult time. It was a win for me at a great loss to many others. This weighed heavy on me for an exceedingly long time. And it still remains to weigh heavy on me. For many nights, months, and years after this, I had nightmares. Nightmares of the tragedy that I brought to this family. Nightmares of whether someone would come revenge his death. Uncertainty if I was indeed the cause of his death. I knew his wife Chrissy and his daughter. I wanted to reach out to them. I wanted to tell them sorry. I wanted to somehow be there for them. But we were adversaries. I once broke into her house and pulled a gun on her husband while their two-year-old daughter was crying in her hands. I could not shake the idea that it was indeed me that killed him. Whether it was suicide or homicide, it was me. It was well known that if he testified against me (and the conglomerate that I represented), there was a strong possibility that his family could be endangered. He may have taken what was in his confused and scrambled head at the time…the noble way out for his family. I know that I had seriously contemplated suicide on several occasions at the thought of having to snitch and endanger my family or not snitch and go to prison for life. The world would be better without me. Only I would die; my family would live. I deserved to die. Many people in my criminal circle knew he was one of the main informants to my indictment. Many in that circle wanted him gone. To this day, this still weighs heavy on my heart.

The pain and trauma that this human experience brings us oftentimes appears to be unbearable. This was one of the heaviest demons of many that began following me. So much so that I, too, began to contemplate my worth and presence in this world. It was a difficult burden to bear, but not more difficult than the losing of that loved one that Jake's family had to bear. May Jake continue to rest in peace.

Help is available. Speak with someone today. National Suicide Prevention Lifeline. 1-800-273-8255.

Jail Tails

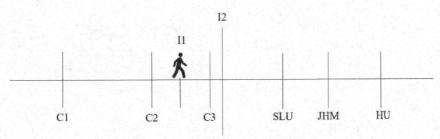

C = arrest that led to conviction; I = sentenced to incarceration; Numbers = number of that event
SLU = Saint Louis University; JHM = Johns Hopkins Medicine; HU = Howard University

From the time I got popped by the Feds in April 2004 to the time of Jake's death in September 2005, I had gone into overdrive with the hustle. For most of that period, I was facing Fed time, and the Feds have a 95 percent rate of successful convictions.[6] I was certain that I was going to prison. At the same time, I was certain that I was done with hustling and thus was setting up my exit from the game. In a six-month period within the beginning of my sophomore year of college, I had experienced a shootout, several hundred-pound-plus pickups, two drug raids with assault rifles aimed at my head, a high-speed police chase, several indictments, and multiple threats on my life. This was not the life I wanted to live.

College was bringing about changes in how I viewed the world, but I was still stuck in the game. With knowing that I was going to prison for a long time, I had two goals: one, stack up a rainy-day fund; and two, successfully step out of the game to where my family and girl would not be in danger of retaliation or death. After the big drug raid, I had essentially lost everything. Before that, I was approaching $500,000 in profits.

By June 2006—the revocation sentencing for my 2004 drug raid—two years had passed since I had fifty assault rifles aimed at my head and bullets flying past me, inches away from tearing into my flesh. I had reacquired some of the money I had lost and I was able to transition my right-hand hustle man, Rich, into a leading role to where I had essentially stepped out of the game without throwing a wrench in the well-oiled machine that I helped create.

I was going through a roller coaster of court appearances. In that two and a half years-plus since that first drug raid on Hazel's apartment, I had seen a sure-shot federal charge turn into a weak and flimsy state case mostly on the shoulders of a dead man (my heart was heavy with sorrow, paranoia, and pain from this); I had lost a federal civil suit that seized two of my vehicles, a house, and a lot of drug money; I had won a state money laundering case that returned tens of thousands of dollars to me,[7] a now-known drug dealer; and I had gone through several rounds of my probation officer sending me to jail for one to two weeks at a time. I was drained from this process. My life was consumed by this process. Somehow, I successfully hid most of this trauma from people closest to me.

On top of all my court proceedings, I was still in college and was still a college athlete for most of that time. I managed to maintain a decent GPA and, despite getting kicked off the football team...three times, I managed to be a good player on a championship Division II collegiate team.[8]

I was battling with college or the hustle since entering college. Since freshman year, I'd wanted to be a different person than I was in North St. Louis. I was hundreds of miles away from my drug dealing days—so I had thought and told myself—but things quickly changed. Despite desperately wanting change, just like an addict, I was constantly chasing the first high. I wanted to be a football star. I was extremely fast and agile. I was really good. I was a natural athlete. Quitting the football team was quitting the idea of college and choosing the hustle.

The hustle had won. I quit because the hustle had grown too big to continue being a college athlete. So, I picked the game over my long-time dream of the game of football. Something I cared so deeply for. I just one day stopped going to practice. I had contemplated quitting school altogether right before the drug bust. I was making so much money. I had, in my young eyes, achieved financial empowerment for myself and my team. I had lost sight of the reality that this was a highly illegal business I was operating. The main reason I continued school was because after the big drug bust, my lawyer's strategy to defend my case was education over incarceration.

❖ ❖ ❖

"Mr. Jangle will see you now," said a young receptionist as she buzzed me in. As I walked through the door to my lawyer's office, he had this deeply concerning look on his face. It was now spring of 2006, two years since the fifty-man DEA raid, and I had accumulated an assortment of new cases, charges, and arrests, most of which I beat. He dropped a stack of legal files about two feet high onto his desk and looked me straight in the eyes as I sat down.

"So, what are we looking at?" I asked.

"Stan, you got caught in butt-fuck Podunk Missouri with $60,000 of cash in all fucking twenty-dollar bills…that reeked of marijuana and dope! And the state had to give it back to you. They wanna hang you by the fucking balls like you were some nigger back in the Ku Klux Klan days. Excuse my language, but we're in fucking St. Charles County, Stan. This is not St. Louis City anymore. They operate like it's still the nineteen-fucking-fifties out this way. Do you know who Emmett Till is? This is how they hang Black people nowadays. The prosecutor wants to sentence you to life in prison!"

"Emmett Till? What? He didn't…listen to that shit. That's ridiculous. I'm a college kid. I make good grades. I go to church with my mom on Sundays. This is fucking weed we're talking about…"

"Stan, Stan, I'm gonna cut you off right there. This is *not* just 'fucking weed' we're talking about." He threw his hands up in a gesture of "oh, who gives a fuck, not a big deal." "You were under investigation by the *Federal. Bureau. Of. Investigation!*[9] The Feds are fucking watching you and you go and get caught with $60,000 of drug money! What the hell were you thinking?" I began to slouch down in my chair even more as I was looking off to the side, sliding into deep contemplation. "Stan, are you still with me? They want…to sentence you…to *life* in prison."

I shook my head in disgust and disbelief. "There has to be something that we can do."

"There is. You have to give up your connect."

"I'm not fucking snitching. We have to think up something else."

"Was I not just clear in anything I just said? Did you not… Are you not comprehending what I'm saying? Hold on, I see, I see. So, how many pounds of weed are we up to now?" He started counting in the air and mumbling under his breath. "Let's see, over seventy-plus on the DEA raid, plus, like, twenty that some girl took the charge for…now this here?"

"I get it. It's a lot of weed. But it's still just weed."

"No, you don't get it. It's not just weed. You are a white-collar criminal now. You've beat *two* money laundering cases. You had a federal forfeiture case that took two cars and a house from *you*…the big-time dope dealer. You have an interstate federal drug trafficking investigation pending against you. They know you're a big-time drug dealer. There's no hiding it. You're not some teenager anymore—"

"I'm not snitching! I can't snitch. They'll come after my girl and my family."

He began to chuckle hysterically, and I gave him a sideways mean mug. "I'm sorry, Stan. I shouldn't have done that. But in all honesty, when you go away, because you will go away if you don't roll on your guy, your girl is gonna be sleeping with another guy before your first shakedown."

"So, because she's going to cheat on me, I should just go ahead and let them off her, huh?" My lawyer sat, still-faced. "You are so outrageous right now." I chuckled and turned the other way and turned back at him as he was still looking at me emotionlessly. "You're serious? Oh, my fucking goodness. I can't believe this." I mumbled to myself, "How did I get myself into this?"

"I don't know the answer to that question. But I do know that at this point, rolling on your buddies is the best option."

"After they go after Jennifer, they'll go after my mom and my dad." I placed my hands on my forehead. "Snitching is out of the question. It's not an option."

"Maybe we should bring your dad into this? He would agree. You have to roll."

"What about money? Can we slide them more money under the table?"

"Stan." My lawyer took a long pause. "It's snitch or go to prison for a very long time."

◆ ◆ ◆

I successfully eluded sentencing for two and a half years. A case that began at the beginning of my sophomore year had trailed all the way to my senior year and college graduation.

Exactly two weeks after the ecstatic excitement of walking across the stage as a college graduate with my bachelor's degree, I was sitting in a courtroom facing decades in prison. While my college peers were still off celebrating their recent graduation, looking for their first jobs after college, and submersed in gifts from family, I was praying that I didn't get fifteen years in prison as my graduation gift.

My sentencing date for my 2004 drug case was June 6, 2006—6/6/6—the devil's number.[10] I knew the court date for about three months in advance. I was dreading it. I was having nightmares about it. I knew this was it.

The prosecutor was the same lady I had been seeing for two years now, Susan Schneider. She was a younger, well-dressed, fairly attractive white junior district attorney. I hated her down to my bones, and I didn't hate very many people. Even the many police officers that used excessive force on me—I didn't dislike them the way I hated Susan Schneider. In the game of cops and robbers, good guys and bad guys, the cops were just doing their jobs. Just as I was doing my job running an illegal drug trade, the cops were doing their job to find me. Their tactics of excessive force were illegal but so were my tactics. We were both *bad* people. But, Susan Schneider…she made my skin crawl just looking at her. I guess I felt that an educated person of the law should be held to a higher standard than a lower-educated street cop or *street thug*. I was wrong. She used just as harsh of tactics as the DEA agent that excessively tased me or that I used when I pulled a pistol on a man in front of his wife and toddler, a man that eventually took his own life. The prosecutor's tactics were not too far removed from these.

She smirked at me as I walked in the courtroom. "Mr. Andrisse, it's pleasant to see you again. You look well."

Expressionless and not responding, I looked at her as I took my seat. This was an odd court date. The judge cleared her entire docket to only have my case for the entire day. Thus, I did not have to come in at 7:00 a.m. and wait hours like I had done on the million other court dates I had had. I came in and the deliberations started as soon as I took my seat.

My mom was there with me. Her lips were quivering, and her eyes were puffy, holding back tears the entire time. She was the only one there with me. She was actually the only person in the entire courtroom besides me and the legal people: my team of lawyers, the prosecution team, the few people providing testimonies (two cops and my PO), the court clerk, and the judge. All these people were on a restricted stage portion of the courtroom. My mom was sitting alone in the back of the audience section of the courtroom.

Susan Schneider stood up and pulled down her perfectly fitting pencil skirt, and her mid-height professional stilettos began click-clacking as she walked to the center of the stage. "Your Honorable, Judge Rauch, we have an extremely dangerous man sitting here with us today. We are not simply dealing with a typical drug case here. Do not let the youthful appearance and recent college degree fool you. This person is an emboldened repeat criminal. We cannot simply give him a slap on the wrist because of his academic accomplishment as the defense is requesting. *We…have…to…*send him to *prison* and we have to send him to prison for a long time."

After some deliberation and my defense attorney offering his opening words, the prosecutor called her first witness, and one of the DEA agents from my drug bust walked into the courtroom.

My lawyer bust out of his seat, saying, "Objection! The federal drug case was thrown out."

The prosecutor retorted, "Your Honor, indeed, due to a man *dying…*" Her voice rose loudly as she emphasized the point of Jake's death. She looked me directly in the eyes, making the presumption that I was the cause of that death. "The federal case against Mr. Andrisse was dropped and most of the evidence acquired in this DEA raid was deemed inadmissible due to illegal seizure, but the drugs for which we stand in this courtroom, which were found in the defendant's trunk, were found by this here officer. We *must* have his testimony."

The judge eventually allowed the agent's testimony but asked that mention of the illegal search not be included. Despite this request, Susan Schneider mentioned the gun and mentioned the coke and the ecstasy and the thousands of dollars.

The judge was not happy with this. This may have played to my advantage. The prosecutor brought in the officer from my money laundering arrest and my PO who had arrested me on multiple occasions.

After hours of deliberation, the judge handed down her sentence. "Mr. Andrisse, it appears that you are caught in between two worlds. I am not quite certain which world has a stronger grasp of you. But I urge you to pull out of the one that is causing you and your family harm. I am not happy with the prosecution's tactics. I understand the picture she is trying to paint, but we have a process that we must abide by. Mr. Andrisse, it appears that you have eluded more serious harm and more serious charges. But I hope that you don't gamble on luck continuing to fall in your favor. I am sentencing you to 180 days shock incarceration in the Missouri Department of Corrections, with five years of SIS probation once you return."

I sighed with relief. Shock incarceration was magnitudes better than the decades in prison the prosecutor was pushing for. SIS stands for "suspended imposition of sentence." This meant that after successful completion of probation, the charge and conviction would be removed from my record. This is opposed to an SES probation, "suspended execution of sentence," meaning after probation, the charge and conviction will remain, even if you were never incarcerated for it.

✦ ✦ ✦

Due to overcrowding in Missouri state prisons, I was ordered to do my shock incarceration in the St. Charles County Jail. Despite being in jail, this was a prison confinement, and I was under the jurisdiction of the Missouri Department of Corrections. I didn't understand or pay much attention to that nuance at this stage in my journey.

The cell block I was in had a heavily wretched smell that lingered in your nostrils and throat to the point that you not only smelled it, but you could taste it. The stench never went away. It was ever-present. At times, I felt that I could see the stench wavering in the distance. It was the smell of years of body odor, smelly feet, urine, and feces layered on top of each other.

The four-inch solid metal doors to the cell block only opened four or five times per day for when a correctional officer would walk through to count their cattle as we stood behind our locked doors. The correctional officers never interacted directly with the animals inside their cages. For chow time, instead of opening the giant sliding metal door to face us human to human, the giant metal door had a hatch in the middle, similar to a dog door. They would slip our food trays through this door during chow time.

The conditions were horrid, the food was inedible, and the despair was palatable. But I did not see any of it as inhumane. I made my bed, and I was okay to be lying in it. I felt that everyone there deserved to be lying in this stench.

I was mostly surrounded by white drug addicts and petty thieves. Being a big-time drug dealer and being a Black person from North St. Louis where real crime took place, I was sort of put on a "don't fuck with me" pedestal. There were a considerable amount of young people and people being locked up for the first time. Mixed in this crowd, there were a few OGs that had been in and out of the system for decades. Many of the younger folks were visibly scared and those same people were extorted for money, food, and other things. I was learning a lot about the system, but I don't recall ever being scared at this time.

The days monotonously began passing by. The only thing to do was play Spades and write raps. I was good at Spades before being locked up, but after playing every day and learning from OGs who'd been playing for decades behind the walls, I became a beast. I went on something like an eight- to ten-week winning spree. I literally never lost. My partner for half of that time was a Black guy maybe in his forties. He had been in and out for some petty stuff. He wasn't a bad person or one of the bullies, but being my partner earned him and me a spot at the power table.

Every couple of weeks the entire wing would pretty much turn over and new blood would be in. This called for the people like me—who had slightly longer incarceration times—to organize another Spades tournament. We'd persuade the newbies on the false hope of winning riches, knowing that they'd never make it past the expert players and teams like my partner and me and this older gentleman we called Ole Skool. The championship games always came down to my team versus Ole Skool and another OG. But not this time. A new Spades team knocked Ole Skool out in the first round and made it all the way to the championship against me. The new team had this light-skinned, Ludacris look-alike Black guy from Wentzville. At this time, Wentzville was probably 95 percent white and super rural. I was 100 percent convinced that there were no gangsters in Wentzville. But here was one right in front of me.

I recall thinking, *Why is this soft-serve ice cream-ass nigga trying to be tough?* Spades is a game of talking shit. I talked very assertively but never aggressively or ignorantly. I was always tactful in my gift of gab.

We were winning in the championship Spades game. It was assumed that I was tougher than the Ludacris look-alike because I was a Black guy from North St. Louis, and he was a Black guy from Wentzville. I don't recall the specifics up to this point, but I flinched my chest at him, lunging my chest and face in his direction from across the table. This is a gesture often used to say, "Lil nigga, stay the fuck in your place." But he was no little guy. He was much taller than me and very lanky. I'm still not sure why I made that gesture. I can't recall if I was making the gesture as a joke because we were winning or if I was seriously telling him, "Lil nigga, stay in your place." But without hesitation, he swung a right hook from across the table that landed smack-dead in the middle of my face, bursting open my lip and my nose all in one punch. Blood went gushing across the room and down my nasal canal and into my throat to where I could instantly taste it. I swallowed the blood, jumped up, and dropped him with a three-piece combo, one to the chin and two toward his chest. He was able to dodge the last two. He put up his dukes, bobbing his head in boxer-style, and jabbed me twice more to the face. I bobbed around boxer-style for a miniature second but quickly realized his advantage with his much longer arms. So, I grabbed a food tray to shield any incoming punches as I charged at him, knocking him in the head with the tray while simultaneously tackling him to the ground. He was taller, but I was far stronger. I was fresh off a college football scholarship. I lifted weights every day. I pummeled his face with the tray until correctional officers came in and broke it apart and locked down the entire wing.

Since no one left the wing in that jail setup, unlike prison, which had its own housing unit for solitary confinement, they put you on room restriction, taking away your ability to leave your cell for recreation time. He and I were put on room restriction for several weeks. People would fly me kites, telling me that he was planning to stab me up when we were released. I wasn't buying it. I still saw him as a wannabe from Wentzville. I was naïve to something that I would later learn: that many murderers were once seen as wannabes. He was transferred to prison before we both got a chance to meet again. This fight taught me that I needed to dial down even more than I already was. I learned to be even more calm, cool, and collected than I already naturally was. This was not the streets. People were on edge here. It was a stressful environment.

✦ ✦ ✦

I was terrifyingly reminded of the tragedy that is heroin addiction one night early in my sentence when my cellmate began screaming at the top of his lungs in the middle of his sleep. His shrills are burned into my memory.

"Aghhh, aghhh, aghhh!" he began yelling as he was tossing and turning in the bunk above me. It was one or two in the morning. My first instinct as his screams woke me were to jump out of bed. But before I had the chance to jump out of bed, he awkwardly rolled off the top bunk, splitting his head open as his skull slammed into the sharp corner of the metal desk in our five-by-eight cell. Blood went everywhere, including all over me.

Despite having a life-threatening gash on his head that was oozing out blood, he was still squirming and screaming on the floor, scratching and clawing all over his body to the point of drawing blood. "Get 'em off me! Get 'em off me! Get 'em off me!"

Correctional officers flooded into our tiny cell in riot gear, thinking that the two of us were fighting, only to find me curled up on my bed, shielding myself with my cover from the blood he was flinging all over the place. I had no idea what was going on. That was my first but not my last exposure to heroin withdrawal. They had purposefully not given him his medication and he nearly died because of it. I am actually not certain if he lived.

At the time, I did not see the tragedy and inhumanity of not providing this person with medication. I only saw a drug addict. A person who made a choice to use an addictive substance. I did not know or understand much about the disease of addiction, although I had been serving it for over ten years. I may have intentionally shielded myself from it. I also primarily sold weed but knew very well that the proceeds from my weed money went into selling heroin, coke, pills, and everything under the sun. My conscience lay deep down under disguise.

✦ ✦ ✦

College Graduation (c. 2006) Two weeks after this photo I was sentenced to my first incarceration under the prior offender guidelines.

CHAPTER 4.5

Relapse

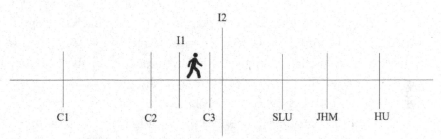

C = arrest that led to conviction; I = sentenced to incarceration; Numbers = number of that event
SLU = Saint Louis University; JHM = Johns Hopkins Medicine; HU = Howard University

I was relieved to be released and away from the crazies of incarceration. I wasn't like *those people*, so I told myself. I had missed all of summer and it had moved into winter now. Jennifer picked me up from jail and brought me to my mom's house where she had decorated my bedroom with a "welcome home" banner that was signed by our close friends and family. I told her that I was done and that I wouldn't leave her again.

After reconnecting with Jennifer, the second person I connected with was my right-hand man, Rich. Sadly, I was just as eager for this connection as I was for Jennifer's connection. Jennifer's and my connection did not skip a beat. More so, our flame grew stronger. On the business side of things, I came to find out that there was trouble in paradise. Due to our phone calls being recorded and mail being read, we never discussed the flip. So, all the past months' problems were dropped on me all at once. The setup was: Rich handled the dope. My cousin handled the money. Rich did not stretch the dope out and sell it slowly, as I had requested.

He popped it off quick and for nearly the regular price, thus creating a drought for the team. My cousin was supposed to have $60,000 for me, of which I was giving him half, just for picking up money with little threat of getting popped by cops because he never even saw the drugs. For all he knew, there weren't any drugs being sold. He just picked up money. He had absolutely zero for me. Not a single dime. He claimed some of it got jacked and the rest of it was picked up by the police as he now had a pending gun charge on him. I knew the system much better than he did. But he simply thought that big cousin could get over on little cousin. I looked his name up on the state's case search and nothing came up. He had no criminal charges pending. He was a war veteran that was licensed to have a gun. His gun charge made no sense. He bought a new truck with twenty-two-inch rims and blew all my money on girls, $60,000-plus, and then his roller coaster came to a crashing end about one year later. When the money was gone, he blamed his financial rout on me. I'm not one for holding grudges, especially with family. I was angrier at myself than him. It was becoming a pattern in my life. Giving people more than I knew they could handle and forcing them into a difficult situation. My cousin, who was already battling PTSD from two tours in Iraq, went on a spiral after I dropped this boatload of free money into his hands. Prior to this, he had a job in finance—which he quit once he had all this free money. It was as if I had the Midas touch. On the surface, I turned everything to gold, but that gold and vanity led to destruction.

I also forever changed Rich's life during this time. The green-eyed monster got the best of Rich. He had hopes on selling the stash I left him, then reupping some more work. Sydney had been running with folks from her hometown that were way too hot. I told Rich to vehemently stay the fuck away from Sydney and her crew. The green-eyed monster sent him to Centralia with Sydney where they both sold to separate undercover cops. Sydney would eventually be included in one of Centralia's biggest drug ring indictments, with over twenty-five people being indicted on conspiracy to sell weed, coke, ecstasy, heroin, guns, and more.[11] She would eventually end up serving a considerable amount of prison time. Rich was also charged, eventually convicted, and placed on five years of probation. He would never see prison, but he would be in and out of jail for the next ten years.

My Wellston-Jennings-East St. Louis connection got caught up in a thirty-plus person federal DEA indictment.[12] This came shortly after him running out of dope from Rich. His East St. Louis connections were hungry to keep the supply chain going. So, he started getting bricks from another dealer in Wellston instead of from us. Jason ended up serving an eight-year federal prison sentence. Jason had a wife and four kids that were thrown deep into poverty and desperation. His two oldest sons ended up selling dope to try and support the family in their dad's absence. One of them was killed in a drug deal and the other ended up getting hit with a life sentence for retaliating against the assailant.

✦ ✦ ✦

I had caused harm to so many people but remained mostly oblivious to taking accountability for the harm I was causing. With Rich gone, I relapsed back into the game soon after returning home. I needed to replace the void that Rich left, so I promoted Bryce to the task of lieutenant general. Not too long after his promotion, he got sent away for several months for a charge that I was not aware of. We had a lot of dope out in the streets, so I politely but insistently asked for him to make his pregnant girlfriend pick up the drug money from the various dope dealers we had around the St. Louis metropolitan area. This was very much the lowest of my lows and I already felt the blood of a man on my hands. I minimized the situation by telling myself she's not selling drugs; she's just picking up money from friends of ours. These are good people. I seemed to skim over the fact that she was picking up tens of thousands of dollars from people who regularly carried guns.

We timed Bryce's release with one of our next big pickups. But then his release was pushed back. So now just picking up money turned into selling a few bricks for his pregnant wife. She insisted she could do it. I was not in favor, but she agreed in writing so that Bryce had proof that this was her idea. So, I let a pregnant woman and her unborn child move the dope. Sadly, I slept very well during this time period. I did not see the wrong in my actions. In fact, I saw the opposite. I was taking care of his girl for him while he was gone. When I'd come pick up the money, I would often bring her favorite foods. She was basically living alone, so I'd sit and watch movies with her. I'd ask her about her doctor's appointments and the baby's progression. Bryce and Karina came from poverty. Everything they had was because of me. They were about to be teenage parents. Karina had just turned eighteen and Bryce was about to turn twenty. I had an eighteen-year-old pregnant teenager and her unborn child selling dope for me. I was the definition of a scumbag and didn't even know it.

Serenity was born soon after Bryce returned. Unfortunately, I brought the opposite of tranquility into their lives. I essentially transitioned the entire operation into the hands of Bryce.

I had finally forged my way out of the game. For the first time in an exceptionally long time, I felt a love for life again. Jennifer and I got engaged after seven-plus years of courtship. We bought a house together. After a number of rejections because of my record, I started a fellowship with this amazing and funny professor at Saint Louis University, Dr. Barrie Bode. I obtained the fellowship most likely because I answered 'no' to the criminal convictions question on the application. I started taking night classes for a business degree. After difficulties stemming from my convictions, I started a full-time nine-to-five job. Jennifer and I were also planning to have a baby. Life was good.

❖ ❖ ❖

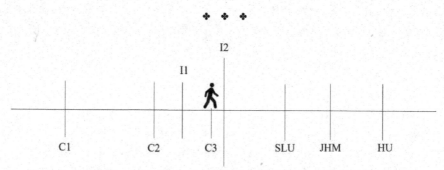

C = arrest that led to conviction; I = sentenced to incarceration; Numbers = number of that event
SLU = Saint Louis University; JHM = Johns Hopkins Medicine; HU = Howard University

By Spring of 2008, I had been back from my first incarceration for a little over a year. I was celebrating two years of sobriety from using drugs as I had stopped smoking weed cold turkey in the midst of my court proceedings, and I was celebrating close to one year of dope dealing sobriety as I had successfully handed the game over to Bryce. It was the Ides of March, known in Roman history as the day Julius Caesar was assassinated by his right-hand man, Marcus Brutus. Living the domesticated life I was now happily living, my duty for the day was to go pick up new, fancy curtains Jennifer had recently ordered. But, after work, I had a free half hour or so to play with before I had to go pick up the curtains and make it home to have dinner with Jennifer as she got off from work. So, in that half hour, I thought I would do a random drop-in on Bryce.

He looked to be doing well. I gave Karina a long, big hug then dapped Bryce up. We chopped it up. He told me business was booming. I smiled at him as I was playing with baby Serenity, who was now a toddler. He said he had to go pick something up and asked if he and I could take a ride. I obliged. We went to the corner store and returned to his house shortly. I went back into the house and talked only a short while longer as my half hour was nearing an end. The world he was in already had started to seem distant to me. And I was happy for that. He seemed happy to be in it and I was happy for that as well. I dropped a few lines of wisdom centered around "this high doesn't last forever." I gave my goodbyes, picking up Serenity and giving her a big hug, and parted ways.

I was now a few minutes late, so I was rushing to my car. I pulled out of his driveway without immediately seeing the cop car ducked off in a corner parking lot at my far two o'clock. The cop car was clearly scoping out Bryce's house. How naïve of me to think that our operation wouldn't still be under investigation, especially considering that they hadn't yet gotten the big drug bust that was right under their noses. I panicked but was reassured by the fact that I didn't sell drugs anymore. But I still couldn't shake the fear and paranoia the cops had struck in my life for over ten years. I drove past the cop, nervously and slowly, trying only to look at his car through my peripheral vision. As I passed him, he quickly turned behind me but did not turn his flashers on. I turned into the convenient store located on my left, hoping that he would pass by me. He did not. He turned into the lot with me, still not turning on his flashers yet. I got out of the car to go inside the store. Then, he flipped on his lights, jumped out of the car, and pulled his gun on me.

I turned in utter and genuine surprise. "Holy shit, officer! What did I do?" I stated with my hands up in the air.

"Put your fucking hands on the car," he shouted at me, walking towards me with his gun pointed at my head. I followed his directives. As he came up, he smashed my face into the car as he patted me down and handcuffed me.

I was completely confused. "Mr. Officer, what did I do? Why are you pulling me over? Why are you handcuffing me?"

"You don't jump out of a car when a cop pulls you over, son. That's not how it works," the cop stated.

"Well, sir, that's not how it happened," I responded politely. "I was out of the car before you turned your lights on to pull me over. And what am I getting pulled over for? Everything on my car is legit."

He didn't respond and simply started searching my car without asking for my permission.

"Sir, you can't search my car without my permission," I stated.

He never opened my trunk. He never opened my glove box. He never opened my middle console. He went straight for the passenger-side back-seat floor and pulled out a black, duct-taped object no bigger than this book. It was *one* brick of weed. How did a pound of weed get in my car? I had been set up. But how? But why?

Everything flashed before me: Jennifer, our wanting to have a baby, our house, our future, my family, my little angels. Then I recalled the words of Judge Lucy Rauch: "If I see you in my courtroom again, it won't be good."

Did Bryce set me up? Or did that brick slip out of his pocket? I was less concerned with finding that out and more broken by breaking my promise to Jennifer.

I sent my cousin down a spiral. I sent Rich down a spiral. I sent Nicole down a spiral. I sent Bryce down a spiral. I sent Jason down a spiral. And in large part, I sent my main connect down a spiral in my absence.

Indictment of KC Connect[13]

Although the federal charges against me were dropped, the federal investigation into the criminal enterprise that I was a part of continued for the next several years until finally coming down on a twenty-two-person, $13 million federal indictment involving five states. Operation Loadrunner, aka "Long Run," resulted in more than $1.1 million in cash seized, more than twenty-two kilograms of cocaine seized (more than forty-eight pounds), and more than 2,500 pounds of marijuana seized. I somehow had dodged a major bullet and eluded this indictment, which would have certainly landed me in prison for the rest of my life as it did for several of the top people that I was closely acquainted with.

Trial

"Mr. Andrisse is a dangerous threat to society with
no hope for change."—Susan Schneider, 2006

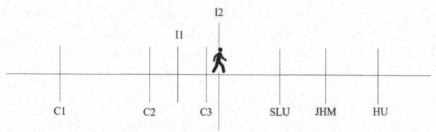

C = arrest that led to conviction; I = sentenced to incarceration; Numbers = number of that event
SLU = Saint Louis University; JHM = Johns Hopkins Medicine; HU = Howard University

It was the spring of 2008 and I was by myself in one of my many court proceedings for my recent and second drug dealing charge. My parole officer had just locked me up for "passing" a drug test. This court date was to determine if I remain in jail or on the streets leading up to my final sentencing court date.

"This is a person with extreme sociopathic tendencies," proclaimed the prosecuting attorney, Susan Schneider. "He shaved his entire body to defy a hair sample drug test."

"Objection! What? He didn't shave his body," my defense attorney exclaimed. "He's a young male that hasn't fully begun growing adult-pattern facial hair and body hair. This is outrageous. Some people are less hairy and Black men in particular regularly keep their haircuts low."

"He impregnated an innocent young lady to use as a defense to not send him to prison," the prosecuting attorney proclaimed.

"Objection, your honor, this is absurd," my defense attorney again burst out in outrage. "The women she is referring to is his girlfriend of eight years and fiancée. And that was an off-the-record comment I made simply informing the prosecutor of her possibly being pregnant. It's absurd to say he intentionally impregnated her. There's no proof of that, not of her pregnancy or any such statement by my client."

"Based on the lack of evidence put forth by the prosecution, the defendant is ordered to be reprimanded on his own recognizance and released," the judge stated. "Ms. Schneider, please keep the blows above the waist."

Very ironically, 3 Doors Down's "When I'm Gone," was playing as Jennifer and I were driving in the car from the courthouse of my billionth court date.

"So, love me when I'm gone,," I mumbled, singing along, holding back the tears in my eyes.

The car ride home was silent, just sniffles as we both stared at objects passing by. When we got home, Jennifer burst into tears as she plopped onto our living room couch, stating, "I don't want you to leave."

I kissed her belly. "I know, baby. I know," I stated, with tears pouring down my cheeks. "Everything will be all right." This was hopeful thinking bordering on being a flat-out lie. With it being my third separate felony conviction and one being a class A felony, the prosecutor was hitting me with the three-strikes law. I was currently facing life in prison.

"Our money can make this disappear, right?" Jennifer asked in an innocent voice. "That's what you said. You told me you wouldn't leave."

❖ ❖ ❖

The months leading up to my second sentencing were an emotional roller coaster like none other I had ever experienced, and Jennifer and I were battling this difficult time all on our own, since we decided to not tell either of our families or friends of my latest conviction. She was all in on the Stan Train. And on most days, I could convince her that things were going to be all right. But, occasionally, the devil got the best of us. In these days, it seemed like Lucifer was all around us. The possibility of me going away for life weighed heavy on our emotional and psychological well-being. This resulted in several heated arguments.

"You fucking asshole," Jennifer shouted out. "Where the fuck have you been?"

"Don't ask me where I've been," I stuttered. "I'm going to bed."

"You stumble in here drunk as fuck at 2:00 a.m., glitter all over your fucking face." She pushed me against the hallway wall. "And you don't think I'm gonna ask you where the fuck you've been." She punched me in my chest as she gritted through her words.

"Jennifer," I stated, taking a deep breath. "Not tonight. Please. Not tonight."

"Where...the fuck...were you!" she yelled at the top of her lungs.

"I was at the fucking East Side with Rich, listening to goddamn Staind and Nickelback. Blowing this fucking tainted drug money. It's no fucking good, baby. It's fucking filthy with blood and sin, baby. I fucking hate myself, baby. I hate me. I hate what I've done to us. I hate what I've done to everybody. You are wonderful and kind and law-abiding. And I introduced you to this fucked-up world. I fucking hate my life. I don't want to do this to you anymore. Fucking leave me, baby. Leave now. Go. Run away." I fell to the bedroom floor in a ball of tears. Jennifer fell to the ground with me, tightly holding me, with tears draping down her cheeks.

Rocking me back and forth attempting to comfort me, she said, "I'll never leave you, baby. I'm not running anywhere. I'm not leaving." We cried in each other's arms for hours until we both fell asleep.

✦ ✦ ✦

I sat in my driveway in my brand-new Lincoln MKZ, bawling, in tears, listening to Jordin Sparks's "No Air," as each word so closely resonated with how each of us felt.

I had Jennifer out in the water so deep. Neither one of us could breathe.

I walked in the door of the house at about 6:00 p.m. to Jennifer sitting quietly at the kitchen table with two letters in front of her. Our house had an open kitchen-family-dining room setup with lots of windows and light. The sunshine was shining on the two letters. One was from an awfully familiar name at this point, Jack Banas, St. Charles County District Attorney's Office. Jennifer left that one unopened. The other envelope had no return address nor stamp on it and simply had "To: Jennifer and Stan Andrisse."

"What's that?" I said, pointing at the mysterious envelope.

Jennifer shrugged angrily. "I'm hoping you can tell me just that." She showed me a polaroid picture of us walking out of the courtroom the other day.

There was a short letter accompanied with the picture. "I hope you and your loved ones are well. We know you will do the right thing. Best wishes, The Family."

"This wasn't delivered by the post office, Stan," Jennifer said in a very demeaning manner. "Someone walked up to our house." She paused before breaking into tears. "And put this letter in our mailbox." She paused again. "Today! Today, Stan."

"It's okay, baby."

"Stan. This is not okay. They could be watching us right now. Our house is full of windows. I've been here by myself, scared to death, Stan." She began bawling as she sank her head into my chest. "I've just been frozen. I literally couldn't move. And I don't know who to call. You told me to never call you and discuss anything related to the case. I can't call my sister or Liz, my best friend or my mom, because none of them know what's going on. I'm so scared. Are we safe, Stan?"

"Jennifer, we are okay. We are not in danger. Trust me." I hated that those words even came out of my mouth. Trusting me meant little anymore. So much was out of my hands at this point. Maybe so much had always been out of my hands and I just couldn't see it.

"Do you know who sent this?" she asked reluctantly. I paused for a long moment. Then she interrupted before I could reply. "You don't have to answer that. You said we are safe. I trust you."

It was clear to me that she knew the truth of the matter without me saying it. "The Family" was my drug conspirators and "doing the right thing" meant don't snitch. And the wording written in invisible ink was "We know where your family and loved ones live."

I thought about confronting my guy, but I knew the Feds were watching us. I also knew that if I didn't snitch, my family and Jennifer would be safe. I was not going to snitch. It wasn't part of my commitment to the game. I was a man of my word. Plus, I knew what my guys and the conglomerate were capable of. Even if I got life in prison, I could rest assured that my family and Jennifer would live. It was a very tough pill to swallow. But, by this point, I had been chewing on the life pill for several months. I was prepared to swallow it.

❖ ❖ ❖

The other letter from Jack Banas was for my trial date, September 6, 2008. This was it. The days leading up to my trial were an absolute whirlwind. Shortly after I had gotten popped this last time in March 2008 near Bryce's house, the district attorney's office was pushing me to roll on some folks. Snitching on my connect was out of the equation. After months of me refusing to snitch, the DA's office vehemently stated they were not going to take any plea deals and that they wanted me to rot in prison.

With the trial date fast approaching and knowing that there was a good chance that I was going to get a life sentence because the prosecutor was charging me under the prior and persistent career criminal guidelines[1] (RsMO 558.016), Missouri's three-strikes law, I began sabotaging Jennifer's and my relationship. More drunken late nights at the strip club. Starting pointless arguments.

Days before my trial, we got into a huge argument. I don't recall exactly what started it, but I know it was an effort to get her to leave me. She was yelling hysterically at me and pushing me out of frustration. In the midst of her argument, I was showing her where all the stash spots of cash were that I was leaving behind for her. In our office from the bookshelf, I pulled out what looked to be a dictionary, turned a couple pages, pressed a few buttons, and opened a hidden safe with $25,000 in it.

She knocked it out of my hand and hundred-dollar bills went fluttering everywhere. "I don't want your drug money, Stan. *I hate your fucking money!*" she shouted at the top of her lungs. "I want *you*. You can't leave." I had just informed her for the first time that there was a real possibility that I might get life in prison.

"Jennifer, listen." I grabbed her by the shoulders. "You're not listening. We have to prepare for this. I'm not asking you to like my money. I'm simply asking you to know where the money is."

"I fucking hate you! I hate you, Stan," she shouted. "You're always so calm. Well, I'm not. I'm a mess, Stan. I don't know how to prepare for the worst. I physically can't do that."

❖ ❖ ❖

The day of the trial had arrived. The new OneRepublic song "Apologize" was playing in my head on repeat. It was much too late to apologize.

Jennifer and I went into that courtroom alone, just the two of us, not knowing if I would walk out. This had been the fourth court date over the past seven months where we were not sure if I was going home with her. After fighting for months to get some type of deal, we conceded. My lawyer convinced me that pleading guilty to the class B drug trafficking charge stemming from the arrest at Bryce's house with the one pound of weed and putting together an argument of mercy would be our best bet. On September 6, 2008, I pled guilty to my third felony conviction. The judge agreed to set my sentencing to October 17, 2008.

To help you with the counting, my first felony (class D tampering) was as a teenager with my good friend Brandon, the white guy who didn't get charged. My second felony was the class A drug trafficking conviction stemming from the fifty-man DEA raid that confiscated over seventy pounds of weed, a quarter kilo of coke, some ecstasy, and a gun, for which I dodged a potential life sentence by eluding a federal indictment of over twenty people that confiscated millions of dollars and thousands of pounds of weed and coke, many of my close conglomerates being sentenced to life, and the reason I dodged that bullet was because someone killed themselves instead of snitching on me. An additional note on that second conviction, for which I was sentenced to 180 days shock incarceration, was that Dominic and Austin, the only two white guys out of the five of us that got popped by the DEA raid, never stepped foot in prison. I guess the prosecutor saw hope in their whiteness and hopelessness in our Blackness. I was now on conviction number three.[2]

We had held out long enough. It was time to tell my family. On September 8, 2008, my birthday, I informed my family of what was going on. I told my mom and dad first. I recall walking into their bedroom and seeing their smiles as they were happy to see me on my birthday.

"I have to tell you something," I said, sitting down with a long face. Their smiles instantly turned serious. They knew what was coming. They were surprised, but not really. My family knew I was on a path of destruction. Oddly, I could very easily be about to tell them I was the new president or that I was about to be sentenced to life in prison. I had that wide range of dynamic to me.

When I broke it down, my mom instantly teared up. My mom and dad were very strong people. They didn't cry much. Although not bawling, each of their eyes had tears.

My dad's first words were *"Il n'est jamais trop tard pour bien faire."* It's never too late to do good.

I told him, "I know." And that I was trying. It was a somber birthday. I told my brothers next. Will was surprised.

"Wow. I thought you had stopped hustling?" Will asked.

"I did. It's a long story," I stated.

"Life in prison for some weed?" he said. "That's crazy."

"Well, it's a little more than just 'some' weed, bro," I explained.

Then I told my sisters, and they were shocked but not surprised. They stated they would be praying for me. After getting home from my tour of telling all my family, I asked Jennifer if she told her family. She did not.

"I don't think they have another straw for you, Stan," she explained. "If you go away, I will tell them. But, if you don't, I likely won't tell them about this, maybe ever."

The next month was spent finalizing my argument for a mitigating sentence. In the months leading up to my trial date, my lawyer would frequently pull me into his office and slap down a stack of files piled two feet high, stating, "You see this? This is all the shit they have against you. We need to build a good pile." This stuck in my head. So, I went to work.

✦ ✦ ✦

For the previous seven months, I had been going to a psychologist, Dr. Bayla Myer. I had gone to her each time I had a legal issue, from back when I was a teenager. We knew each other well.

"So, Stan, tell me how you are feeling," she would open the sessions. "Do you feel depressed?"

I would chuckle and say, "Well, Dr. Myer, that is a loaded question."

Once she asked me, "Wow. You got caught with tens of thousands of dollars again! Stan! What are you doing? That's many people's yearly salary you have in your pocket." I wouldn't respond to those types of questions. It sounded too much like the cops asking. So, she would muse on the conversation. "So, you buy $30,000 worth of drugs. Then, what? You sell it for three to four times that amount? That's a lot of money you're making." I would just remain silent or change the subject.

I worked with her on my other two cases and once the resolution came, I stopped seeing her. Once the new case popped up, I started seeing her again. It was an expensive part of my defense. In total, it was about $10,000 over seven months. But the result was a very strong character letter and psychological evaluation.

My fellowship advisor Dr. Barrie Bode had recently written me a recommendation letter and had provided me an unsigned copy. So, I added this to the good pile. The prosecuting attorney immediately called Dr. Bode.

"Hi, my name is Susan Schneider, with the St. Charles District Attorney's Office. Do you know Stan Andrisse?"

"Ahhh, yea. I know Stan," Dr. Bode replied, confused.

"Did you know that he was a criminal with multiple felony convictions for trafficking drugs? And did you write him a letter stating he was a good person with potential?"

"Well, no, I did not know he was arrested for selling drugs. But, yes, I did write that letter."

"Sir, he was not arrested for selling drugs. He's been convicted multiple times for trafficking drugs, among other things," Ms. Schneider stated as matter of fact.

"Thank you, Ms. Schneider," Dr. Bode replied and got off the phone. That same day. Dr. Bode called me to his office. Dr. Bode was like no one else I had ever met in his position before. He had somewhat of a street swag about him despite being a professor. He leaned back in his chair, stretched his legs as wide as possible, and rested his hands near his crotch. Very much like a D-boy might gangster-lean into a chair.

He nodded his head a few times, motioning for me to close his office door. I knew something was up. He had never asked that before. "So, tell me a little bit about Susan Schneider."

My heart instantly sunk. I looked down at the ground for a second. Then I picked my head up. "She's the prosecuting attorney in my criminal case. I'm looking at life in prison. I likely won't be here long. I'm sorry I didn't tell you."

"Life in prison?" he started to yell. Then mouthed it silently. "Holy shit, Stan!" He then proceeded to tell me his knowledge of the system and how it was fucked up, then ended the conversation, stating, "How can I help? I'm here for you." I thought that was an empty promise, but he ended up rewriting an even better letter directed to the court and agreed to come testify, asking the judge not to send me away.

I ended up getting letters from all four of my siblings and my parents, my church, moms in the neighborhood I grew up in, animal shelters I volunteered at, and the drug treatment program I completed. I included every athletic and academic award I had ever received since kindergarten. All arguing that I was a good kid that made some really bad decisions, but that, with redirection, I could be something great. Ms. Susan Schneider was not hearing one bit of the argument.

The trial date had come. Most of my family was going to be there, except my dad, my brother Will, and all my nieces and nephews who were still under ten or twelve.

We all arrived at the St. Charles Courthouse by 8:30 a.m. Court was set to begin at 9:00 a.m. My case didn't get heard until 2:00 p.m. It was the last case of the day. It was a long day of waiting. Before going into the court room at 9:00 a.m., my family and I held hands and prayed together. Other people that were there looked at us in surprise and bewilderment. It is not common for people who are thought of as "criminals" to have so much support with them on a court date. I had been in these rooms and settings thousands of times and never saw a person with as much support as I had that day.

"Mrs. Andrisse." Dr. Bode showed up right at 8:58 and he shook my mom's hand and pronounced our name correctly. "And future Mrs. Andrisse." He shook Jennifer's hand. He had never met either of them before, but through context knew who they were. "Hello to everyone." He waved to the rest of the family. "Sorry to be meeting you on such a somber occasion." Dr. Bode managed to make successful small talk with my family despite the occasion, further testament to the incredible man that he is.

The judge saw probably twenty cases in the five to six hours we sat in the courtroom before my case. Every single one of them was sentenced to prison. No one was getting probation or shock time or treatment or jail. Everyone was getting sentenced to prison and most of them were Black, despite the district being primarily white. This made me uneasy.

The case right before mine was one of a young, twenty-something-year-old Black kid from North St. Louis who broke into an old white lady's house from St. Charles and stole her big-screen TV. No one was physically hurt in the incident. The lady never saw him in the incident. The TV was apprehended from a pawn shop in North St. Louis. The old white lady wrote a letter to the court and the judge read it. It sounded really bad. The eighty-year-old lady stated being scared to live in her house now and scared to leave the house. And scared of life altogether because of the trauma he imposed. The judge was about to hang his Black ass.

"Although this is a nonviolent C-felony, and no one was physically hurt, your crime was violent. An elderly woman's life is forever changed and traumatized. You have imparted emotional hurt and thus there is a nature of violence. I hereby sentence you to the maximum time for a C-felony, seven years imprisonment in the Missouri Department of Corrections. Bailiffs, please take him away," the judge ordered.

I was thinking to myself, *Wow. Seven years for a $300 TV. This is not good for me. Why did the young Black guy versus the old white lady case have to come up right before mine?* The judge was clearly upset after reading that letter. So much so that the clerk asked if she wanted to take a brief recess before moving into the next case.

She said, "No. This is the last one of the day. The State of Missouri vs. Stan Andrisse." My bones quivered as I looked at my attorney and stood up. I squeezed Jennifer's clammy hands one last time and looked at all of my family as I walked up to the defense table and sat down next to my team of three attorneys.

"Your Honor, we are here today for the sentencing of a dangerous repeat drug offender, Mr. Stan Andrisse," Ms. Susan Schneider stated boldly. "As I mentioned at his trial turned plea hearing, the prosecution is moving to have Mr. Andrisse sentenced under the prior and persistent career criminal law. This court is under jurisdiction to do so as the defendant has three felony convictions, two of which are class A and B drug felonies, respectively." The prosecutor shuffled some paper around. "Under these sentencing guidelines, the defendant's imprisonment range would be moved from five to fifteen years to ten years to life in prison. The prosecution has prepared an argument with witness testimony to recommend twenty years to life in prison for the defendant."

There was a deep audible and visceral gasp in the courtroom.

"Thank you, Ms. Schneider," the judge stated. "The defense may offer opening statements."

My attorney stood up and buttoned his suit jacket. "Your Honor, my client, Mr. Andrisse, is a kid," he stated, pointing back at me. "A college kid. A recently graduated college kid. With a very supportive family that you can see sitting in the front row here. He is a kid with a very bright future ahead of him." My attorney paused. "*If* we can help direct him in the right direction. My client is not dangerous. None of his convictions were violent. My defense team and I are prepared to defend my client with witness testimony, and we recommend a mitigating sentence that *does not* include incarceration in the Department of Corrections."

"Thank you, Mr. Jangle," Judge Rauch exclaimed. After opening statements, for the next one to two hours a litany of witnesses took the stage. First for the prosecution and then my defense. The prosecution brought up arresting officers from all my cases, even ones that did not result in conviction and ones from when I was a teenager.

"Objection, your Honor," my attorney exclaimed. "Why is the prosecution bringing up an officer from when my client was a juvenile? Those documents are sealed."

Ms. Schneider exploded with rage. "Your client failed to make it to the age of eighteen without being rearrested, thus making that juvenile conviction fair game in adult court. Your client has been a criminal since the age of fourteen years old, and that needs to be on record."

Judge Rauch stated, "I will allow the witnesses to testify on the client's juvenile criminal record."

"The next witness of the prosecution is Officer Donald from Roland, Oklahoma, sheriff's office," stated the prosecuting attorney.

"Objection, your Honor!" Mr. Jangle shouted. "This witness is not even on the list. In fact, this officer is from an arrest that never even resulted in charges being brought forward. Moreover, this arrest was filled with police misconduct. If this officer is allowed to testify, I most certainly will be filing prosecutorial misconduct. Ms. Schneider, you know exactly what this sheriff's office did." Mr. Jangle and Ms. Schneider were now together at Judge Rauch's bench, with Mr. Jangle pointing at Ms. Schneider. "Try me and you're going down with them."

"Ms. Schneider, do you mind informing me what Mr. Jangle is referring to?" Judge Rauch asked the prosecution.

"Your Honor, the prosecution will not bring forward the witness from Roland, Oklahoma." Instead her next witness was one of the DEA agents from my 2004 drug raid.

"Objection, your Honor," Mr. Jangle shouted. "Is this a circus or a courtroom?"

"Mr. Jangle, careful," Judge Rauch retorted.

"Your Honor, this agent is from a non-warranted DEA, ATF shenanigan. There was no warrant. The event was illegal. And the findings were thrown out. There is no evidence to be discussed. What part of *illegal* does the prosecution not understand?"

"Ms. Schneider, you are beginning to tread on thin ice," Judge Rauch exclaimed. "If you are trying to refresh my recollection of Mr. Andrisse's history, both evidentiary and non-evidentiary, I can assure you that I remember *all* of Mr. Andrisse's history quite well. So much so that I can remind you that I did not allow the DEA agent to testify on the raid back then, and thus, I surely would not allow him to testify now." Judge Rauch shook her head while taking off her glasses and wiping her eyes.

The objections were starting to make my head spin. We had been in the courthouse for well over eight hours now. So far, we had simply been battling through and objecting to all the bad things. I felt good about them not allowing the DEA to speak and us winning several objections. The judge seemed to be getting upset with the prosecution's tactics.

Although I didn't get convicted of money laundering, getting caught with tens of thousands of dollars on multiple occasions looked really bad. Also, the prosecutor referred several times to the drug raid officers finding a gun in my possession, but this was struck as it came from an illegal search and seizure.

After an hour or more, we took a brief recess before reconvening and jumping into hearing my witnesses. My first witness was a parole officer of mine, Mr. Barry Dorsey. Mr. Dorsey was excellent in that the prosecution was stunned that we got someone supposedly on their side to be on my side. He testified to my excellent obedience of the rules of supervision and that other officers in the office envied him for having me because there was talk of me being the best client the office ever had. This was good, but the prosecution spun it, essentially saying that a rock would be the best client in a predominantly Black St. Louis PO office compared to the prestigious, affluent, and predominantly white St. Charles-area offices.

One of my POs from the St. Charles office, Susan Alagna, testified for the prosecution. Susan Alagna and Susan Schneider were my arch-nemeses. For a long while, I was convinced that I had done something terrible to a Susan in my past life to have these two women so vehemently attacking me. From the day I met Susan Alagna, she had been determined to send me away to prison. She violated me on my very first visit. My skinned crawled when she testified.

My last witness was my psychologist, Dr. Myer. I was feeling good. I felt as if we were winning. I was hoping for Dr. Myer to bring us into the home stretch. Things were going well and then they took a very drastic turn. Her role was to show that I had some personality flaws but was redeemable. Instead, it came across that I had severe psychological issues.

The prosecutor started her closing remarks. "Your Honor, you have heard testimony from an assortment of people and experiences from Mr. Andrisse's life. As we opened up with, the prosecution stands on its recommendation of twenty years to life in prison based on the provided facts and testimonies. As stated by the defense's own expert witness, the defendant is a narcissistic sociopath with no hope for ever changing the way he thinks," stated Ms. Schneider very confidently as she turned to look me in my eyes. "Your Honor, Mr. Andrisse fits the classic definition of a narcissist and sociopath. Yes, he is intelligent. Yes, he is charming. His college degree, many accolades, and beautiful girlfriend are evidence of that. But he is also a conniving budding drug trafficker who's been caught with countless amounts of drugs and tens of thousands of dollars. The fact that several cases could not be discussed in this hearing is only proof that he is getting better at his trade as time progresses."

She paused and looked directly into my eyes. "You know what's worse than a 'street criminal'? An 'educated street criminal.' Mr. Andrisse is a non-empathetic gun-toting thug with controlling tendencies and an extreme grandiose sense of self-importance who clearly exaggerates achievements and talents. The entire defense's argument and testimony further proves that he is a narcissist. Their entire argument is 'Look how good I am.' Well, that's not good enough, your Honor. Mr. Andrisse needs to be sent to prison for life!" Ms. Schneider looked me in the eyes once again. "He can continue pursuing his achievements once he returns from his twenty to life sentence. The prosecution rests."

"Thank you, Ms. Schneider. Mr. Jangle." The judge motioned for my attorney to give his closing remarks.

"Honorable Judge Rauch, you have sat here and watched a circus show by a young prosecuting attorney clearly trying to make a name for herself. Either that or there is some personal vendetta. Or maybe she simply enjoys flirting with debarment." He looked in the prosecutor's direction as she was rolling her eyes. "*Several* of the prosecution's witnesses were unconstitutional, yet she knowingly included them. *Several* of the statements made, alluding to my client being dangerous or a high-level drug dealer, were *illegal*. Thus, unconstitutional. As an agent of law, we must abide by the word of the law. If the word of the law says that certain events can't be discussed, they shouldn't be discussed, nor considered. For clarification, the expert witness stated my client displayed selfish behavior. That is vastly different than being diagnosed with Narcissistic Personality Disorder. And that is not grounds for being medically defined as a sociopath, or Antisocial Personality Disorder. Everything the prosecution proposed was a stretch of the truth. I know you might be angry that you are seeing Mr. Andrisse again. But my client is a bright and intelligent kid. He's made some really bad mistakes but throwing him away for ten to twenty years is not the answer. The defense stands on its recommendation of no imprisonment in the Department of Corrections. At most, we suggest a 180-day treatment program either inside or while on electronic monitoring. The defense rests."

"After hearing both sides of this case, I am prepared to make my decision," Judge Rauch exclaimed.

My head was spinning. The room was completely silent except for the words coming out of the judge's mouth. I can recall looking down on the entire courtroom and myself as if it were an out-of-body experience. My head never turned once throughout the entire proceedings to look at my family's expressions as the prosecutor was painting her Picasso painting of me being a dangerous threat to society. I didn't turn my head mostly out of shame. Most of the things she was mentioning my family had no idea about. The guns. The extremely large sums of money. The arrests that I never got charges from. The charges that never resulted in convictions. All of these were hidden and were now brought to light. Jennifer never even knew about some of them. I felt so small and insignificant. Like a little speck. I felt like the career criminal that I was proclaimed to be. It all seemed to make sense. The dots were connected.

The judge began her sentencing remarks. "Mr. Jangle, I don't personally know Mr. Andrisse. Thus, I am not angry that he is back in my courtroom. I am, however, very frustrated. Mr. Andrisse poses a challenge. On one hand, we have a college-educated young man with a supporting family and a supporting future wife. But on the other hand, we have a repeat offender with a clear history of increasingly reckless behavior. I agree with the defense that we don't have enough evidence to support some of the claims of the prosecution. But I agree with the prosecution that Mr. Andrisse believes he should receive unreasonably special or favorable treatment, thus fostering his increasingly reckless behavior." The judge sighed and paused.

"As such, I am going with the prosecution's recommendation to sentence Mr. Andrisse under the prior and persistent career criminal guidelines." My heart sank and the remaining words of Judge Rauch were a murmured blur. "However..." She paused again for what seemed like a lifetime.

However, what? I thought to myself as I was still in this out-of-body daze. *However, what?*

"I am granting Mr. Andrisse mercy and not going with the prosecution's maximum time recommendation. Instead, I will go with the minimum. I hereby sentence Mr. Andrisse to ten years in the Department of Corrections, to be started immediately. Bailiffs, please take Mr. Andrisse away."

The courtroom burst into an uproar of tears and crying. As I looked back, I saw my brother holding Jennifer as tears were flowing down her face like a waterfall. My eyes went straight to my mom, who was being held by my sister. Both were shivering and crying. As I came back from my out-of-body daze, I immediately asked the judge if I could hug my mother and family one last time. The judge denied me that opportunity. She denied me the civility of a human being and asked the bailiffs once more to handcuff my hands and feet and to take me away. And just like that, I began my ten-year sentence in the Missouri Department of Corrections.

Transportation

A couple of weeks after sentencing, without any prior warning, I was awakened in the middle of the night by the loud click of my jail cell door unlocking and the voice of one of the correctional officers. "Andrisse, pack your shit. It's time to go."

The CO laughed, "You're headed to the big house." I quickly slid the drawer open and snatched up all my letters, notes I had written (I had started a journal), legal documents, personal care items, snacks, etc. I stuffed it all in my pillowcase, threw the pillow sack over my shoulder, and stood outside my cell.

The jail bay door slowly slid open with its ever-so-horribly-memorable sound. Imagine the metal-to-metal clatter of someone dragging a fifty-pound metal chain across a ten-foot metal sewer drain followed by the loud bang of a sledgehammer hitting a bell. The sound resonated in your head.

A group of COs led us out of the bay and walked us through what seemed like a labyrinth to get to the booking area. It was cold outside. But, I had no idea of the actual feel of the temperature. I didn't get to go outside of my bay. There was no fresh air, ever. The bay had a strong stench of sweaty balls, male funk, and all of the different kinds of foul farts you'd ever come across—all mixed in a closed box. There was no ventilation system, and there was really no getting used to the smell.

By the time we reached the checkout area, they had gathered another ten or so people. It was like a mini reunion. Guys that hadn't seen each other in months were sharing stories of fights and lock-up drama and asking about girlfriends and codefendants on the streets. Most of them going upstate with me had been to prison before, so some of the dehumanizing shit taking place was just second nature to them. I was sitting on the cold metal bench silently—each of us had one hand handcuffed to the bench. They processed each of us one by one. It was my turn to be processed.

"Andrisse! Get up here." I was uncuffed and escorted up to talk to the processing officer who stood behind a bulletproof window. "Okay. Ten years for class A drug trafficking to run concurrently with a five-year class B distribution charge. Nice work, son. You'll be heading to bus B headed to the max security R&D prison in Fulton." I walked off with the officer to another room with several other people chained foot-to-foot with each other, sitting on a cold metal bench they were handcuffed to. I now was able to see where the fresh air was coming from. A door to the outside world was open.

"Strip!" I gave the officer a "What the fuck you talking about?" look. "Take your fucking oranges off, you little piece of shit." Several of the chained-up guys looked over at me and chuckled.

"Don't worry, boss, everybody's dick is shriveled up right now. It's cold as fuck in here." A few other incarcerated people laughed at his comment. It was apparent by my sideways look that I had never done this before. I had never been one for showing weakness or being scared. This moment was the same. I looked back at the officer in his eyes with a look of disgust. He smirked at me as I was pulling my pants down, and he blew me a kiss.

"Your balls don't look that big now, Mr. Kingpin." Officer Lee chuckled and yelled over to one of the other officers. "I bet your girl is excited to be riding a big dick finally. She's probably down on her knees right now, deep-throating that big dick. It's probably a white dick too." He laughed at his own joke again. "Put on this fucking cloak, Mr. Kingpin, and go sit your ass over there with the other fuck-ups."

The cloak he was referring to was a thin piece of see-through cloth. It was like the cover-up you get at hospitals, but thinner. This was all we had on in zero-below weather—sitting on a cold metal bench. The other officer came by and shackled my feet together, handcuffed me with my hands behind my back, connected me to the bench, and shackled me to the person next to me.

"All right, I know none of you dumbasses are used to following directions. But I need all of you fuck-ups to stand up at the same time. If you don't stand up carefully and you fall down, it's gonna be like a domino set of criminal convicts falling to the ground. Worst yet, you'll probably have a dick rubbing up in your face. So, be fucking careful." The encouraging and insightful directions of the officer were well heard and adhered to. I did not want anybody's junk rubbing up against me. We were all un-handcuffed from the bench. "Okay, so on the count of three I want all y'all to stand up really carefully." A few of us attentively nodded our heads. "Okay. One, two—oh shit, hold on." Half of the people in the front of the line stood up but the other half did not, causing a couple of them to topple down on the ground. One of the guys fell onto one of the guys still sitting and was immediately forcefully pushed onto the ground by that guy.

All of the officers busted out laughing, one of them leaning onto the other, barely able to hold himself up from the laughter. "Oh, shit, y'all see that? We almost got some dick action there," the officer yelled out to the person who had the other guy fall into him. "Hey Bennett, did you like that white dick in your face? Oh, fucking A, man. That shit never gets old."

The guy shouted back at the officer. "Fuck you, pussy! You real fucking tough when we all got these chains on. Let me see you on the fucking streets."

"Okay, you degenerates, everybody stand the fuck up and start marching. There ain't a goddamn countdown. This ain't the fucking Boy Scouts, fellas. This is fucking prison. March your fucking asses out to that bus." We all carefully stood up. The chains between our legs were only about a foot to a foot and a half, so it wasn't quite a march. We were shuffling. The bus was a long, whitish-gray school-bus-looking piece of junk. It had no writing on it. It didn't say "This way to prison" or "prison bus" on it. But it looked like something that was going to some dark, evil place. I had never really thought about what a prison bus might look like. But here it was, sitting in front of me.

We slowly marched one by one inside of the bus. It was essentially a school bus on the inside with a few modifications. Most notably, the caged fences. About every five rows of seats, there was a caged fence door that locked off that section. I guess the idea might have been that if a fight were to break loose, it could only be between the people in that area. Another notable difference was that the seats were metal, with handcuff slots. We were filed to the back caged sections, un-shackled from each other, and re-shackled, hands and feet, to the seat we were assigned to.

I felt like a zoo animal. Caged up. Shackled up. Talked to in the most disrespectful of ways. The front section of the bus—where the two officers driving were—was sealed off with plexiglass. They had the heat on in that section. But in our section, they actually rolled the windows down. There was snow on the ground. It was below freezing. We were in thin cover-ups. And the windows were rolled down. It was beyond cold.

I tried to think happy thoughts to keep from feeling the cold and the pain from the handcuffs. It had been a couple hours now, and we had made several other stops, picking up more people headed upstate. It was about 3:00 p.m. now. I had been awakened at 3:00 a.m. back in my jail cell. Since then, all I had to eat was a few bites from a soggy bologna sandwich they had given to us while being processed. Too many times, I had found a green slimy layer over the bologna. I couldn't eat that shit. But now I was starving. I arrived at Fulton Prison at about 4:00 p.m.

First Day of Prison

That very first day in prison was unlike any other day in my entire life. The dehumanization started well before I even stepped foot inside the prison walls. It was a cold, blustery, and gloomy November day. We were escorted off the bus still chained together in our chain gang. Stepping foot off the bus, all I could see was a fortress of stone buildings and barbed wires. I was in Fulton, which was about two and a half hours from St. Louis, but it felt like some far-off, distant land in a dystopic dimension of *The Twilight Zone*. The drive was about six to eight hours as we went from jail to jail, county to county, all over the eastern part of the state, adding to our chain gang. In my head, I remembered a fun camping trip I took with Liz and Jennifer back in high school to Fulton. There's not much in Fulton, Missouri. There was a huge nuclear power plant that glowed at night like the one on *The Simpsons*, and there was the Fulton Prison. Those were the highlights of Fulton. I was a low-level drug dealer at that time, but I can recall naively thinking, *Huh, so that's where bad people go.* From that road, the prison was a dot in the distance. Little did I know that would one day be my place of residence.

The chain gang entered the stone structure from a warehouse-like side door. We were marched into what resembled a giant football locker room shower. Everything was stone, and I noticed drains on the floor. Still battling the shivers from coming in from the cold, we were ordered to strip down naked.

"All right, gentlemen, welcome to Fulton Reception and Diagnostic Center. Now, let's see your birthday suits," one of the lead officers said, yelling quite loudly. I and several other newbies to prison hesitated as we thought this was some kind of joke. But I saw some of the more seasoned members of our chain gang obediently taking off their jumpers and stripping naked.

An array of laughter quickly began as the seven to ten officers present began cackling at the dehumanizing experience.

"Oh man, your girlfriend won't be missing that little pecker," said one of the correctional officers to a guy standing near me.

I was still shivering and freezing cold as the door to the outside was still open. If you are familiar with what happens to the male genitalia when it's freezing cold, then you might be able to begin to imagine the sight of thirty adult men standing in line butt-naked with shriveled-up dicks hanging out.

"Oh shit, look at this one. We have a porn star here. It's all shaved up. Even his butthole is shaved." The laughter erupted as they went by, sizing up and making jokes at pretty much all of us.

Soon as we were all naked, they ordered us to first spread our legs and raise our arms in the air as one officer walked down the line of naked men with one of those pump containers that you use to spray and kill weeds in your lawn. Only he wasn't spraying weeds, he was spraying human genitals and arm pits.

It was like a domino effect of uncomfortable grunting and gasps as every man tried to prepare themselves for the spray hitting their genitals. The officer was two men away from me. I closed my eyes and tried to envision a better place. Then it hit me, and I gasped. The ice-cold liquid jolted my entire body from my testicles squeezing in tightly to the muscles in my neck cringing and cramping.

I kept looking forward with a stern face. I did not want to look to my left or my right for fear of someone thinking I might be gay and checking them out and for fear of seeing someone else checking me out, looking for a welcoming sign. I also wanted to maintain some level of respect for my fellow man in this humiliating experience. I thought the worst was over, but the worst was yet to come.

"All right, gentlemen, now bend over while still spreading your legs and cough three times when told." More cackling and laughter continued as the line of thirty men bent over and spread our butt cheeks open.

I thought the humiliating experience was over with the butt spray. Then yet another officer came down the line. This one now had what looked like a power washer that you use to wash your car. We were ordered to again stand, spread our legs, and raise our arms as one by one we were sprayed down with a power washer.

The dehumanizing tactics of stripping naked and making the jokes and spraying you down felt more like a hazing to show that the correctional officers had power over us. They were letting us know that they were above us. We were scum.

Moments after this spraying experience I took my first prison mugshot. If you look into my eyes, you can see emptiness. You can see hopelessness. You can see despair.

The photographer offered the first piece of civility in a long while. He called me by my first name. He oversaw putting the mugshots in the system and confirming our intake info.

"Says here that you were in college as your highest education completed," he stated. "Wow. So, you were trying to bring some good into the world." I took this as a compliment at the time as I was still very heavily in my othering phase. I thought I was different than the "other" people who had committed crimes.

"Class A drug trafficking? Career criminal?" he stated, shaking his head, reading my file in disbelief, looking at my baby face. "But looks like you were also bringing some bad into the world as well." He snapped my picture, then printed a one-page document that had my mugshot on it and my convictions, sentencing information, and custody level score on it. He handed it to me and ordered me to take one of the laundry bags sitting in a pile and to go wait in the next room.

When all thirty-plus of us were completed, we were escorted out of this building and into the yard. I was astounded at the size of this place. It resembled a giant college campus—lots of pristine, big, stone buildings. The main difference was all the tall, barbed-wire fences everywhere and the guard towers with people with AKs sitting in them and no trees and no students reading books or playing frisbee.

❖ ❖ ❖

Walking into the housing unit, I had no idea what to expect. Everything was already quite different than jail. I was told that because there wasn't room to put me in a cell I would be sleeping on one of the bunk beds stationed outside of each of the cells. I was on the top tier. Out of the thirty people I came here with, I was the only one to walk into this wing of the last housing unit in our journey through the prison camp. As I walked in with my laundry sack on my shoulder and single sheet of paper in my hand, I could feel all the eyes looking at me. I walked in with a mean mug, instantly portraying the tough prison persona. Like an evolutionary being designed to live, every cell in my body went into survival mode without me even knowing it.

As I approached my bunk, a middle-aged white gentleman with salt-and-pepper hair politely greeted me with a smile. "Hey! Welcome to paradise!" he stated.

Then a middle-aged, fairly sturdy-looking Mexican man came up to me from behind and stated sternly but politely, "Let me see your paperwork."

I looked at the white guy, then I looked at the Mexican guy, then I looked back at the white guy.

The white guy nodded his head in agreement. "Let him see the paperwork. It's all good, brother." The white guy was inviting, and I got good vibes from him. So, I let the Mexican see my paperwork. I was not sure if I had an option. I was not sure if allowing him to see was the customary thing or if I should have been ready to fight him over not letting him see the document. I was not sure what to do, but I gave him the document.

"Class A drug trafficking! Career Criminal statute? Ten years, sixty-six percent, level four custody," he muttered off to the white guy, who nodded his head in agreement after each statement. "Oh shit, okay. So, you're legit." The Mexican guy looked at me and smiled. "You should hang with us. It's my birthday. I'm making a big feast tonight. You should eat with us. Don't go to dinner. It's a waste of time and it's cold outside."

I just looked at him in the eyes intently and gave him a head nod as he handed me the document back. I neither agreed nor disagreed with his statement. I didn't want to hang with anybody. I didn't want to gang up with any clique. But I was actually bunked with the white guy and the Mexican guy was on the bunk to my right. I never agreed to anything, but I hung with them by default because of my bunk location.

I was treated to world-class prison cuisine. The white guy and the Mexican guy began working on making our dinner feast, which was mixed together in a giant "clean" trash bag. They were making a bunk-sized loaf as the main course and nachos for the appetizer.

"Have you ever had a prison loaf?" the white guy asked me, his head tilted to the side, standing upright like a butler as he handed me a napkin to tuck into my shirt.

The Mexican guy smiled at me again. "We eat civilized over here, bro. Tuck the napkin into your collar so you don't dirty your clothes." I listened and smiled back at him.

The loaf and nachos were big enough to feed ten or more people, but there were about five or six of us eating. The elite leaders of the wing, as I would soon learn. My bunkie, the white guy, did not hold power, money, or rank. He was actually rather poor. A lower-level meth dealer and presumable user, but maybe not, because he was very well shaven and put-together. He was a muse and administrator for the Mexican guy and other elites. At our mock table—my bunkie's bed with the mattress removed—we had the Mexican guy, Ramirez, who was the leader, two bigger muscular guys, one Black and one Hispanic, who I assumed to be enforcers, and two other high-level drug dealers.

"So, tell me about your operation," Ramirez stated inquisitively, wiping his mouth of the sticky chico sauce. After several rounds of laughter and jokes were shared and people were done with their first serving, I guess it was time to talk business.

I looked up at him and grabbed another slice of loaf. "I don't like to talk much about that."

He looked at me and smirked again. "Okay. It's all good, bro. But many of us sitting at this table were traffickers too. We know the statutes. Sixty pounds of weed or more. Five kilos of coke or more. Your paperwork already told us what you do. If you don't want to share specifics now, that's okay."

He then proceeded to tell me the specifics of his operation. He was popped in a large multi-state indictment that landed him six years in the Feds. He showed me his paperwork. This was apparently a thing, showing your paperwork. It felt kind of like whipping out your junk to see whose was bigger. Ramirez had big kahunas. He was moving big-time dope, weed, coke, pills, and heroin from Cali and Mexico to the Midwest.

"Class A ten with sixty-six percent…you will do about eight years on this," Ramirez stated very calmly and bluntly. He chuckled and smiled as he saw the disappointment in my body language and face. "I know the paperwork says sixty-six percent, which is about six and a half years. But listen, you are gonna get into a fight or two; it's inevitable. This is prison; it happens. You will be tested and forced to defend yourself for survival. You will get bullshit violations like out of bounds or grabbing an extra food tray. Dumb shit. But all these minor dumb violations will push your date back. So that sixty-six percent will turn into eighty percent very easily." He could further sense my disdain.

I told him, "Thanks for the advice."

He laughed. "It's not advice, bro. I'm just telling you the real. Make sure you prepare your mind for that shit. It's a long journey. But judging from your rap sheet and your demeanor, you will make it out all right on the other side. And when you do, you should look me up. I'll be out before you. We should link up. He passed along a tiny phone book with his information in it. "This is a gift from me."

"I appreciate that, but I don't need any gifts," I stated, handing the address book back to him.

He shoved it politely back into my hands. "Bro, it's not that type of gift. I don't get down like that. I like your natural instincts, but I guarantee you it's not that kind of gift."

I took it and pondered on all that had just happened in this first day of prison.

That first night, lying in bed in prison, was a night I would never forget. The day was filled with so many different demoralizing and unfamiliar events I was unsure how to process it all. So many new people were being introduced into my life at such a rapid pace, my head was spinning. I stayed up all night, not sure what to expect. Was someone going to come and try to fuck with me while I was sleeping? My bed was out in the open bay, so it was open to everyone else out in the bay. Would someone come and try to test me on the first night? I could not be sure. So, I stayed up all night—boots still laced up tight under my sheet.

✦ ✦ ✦

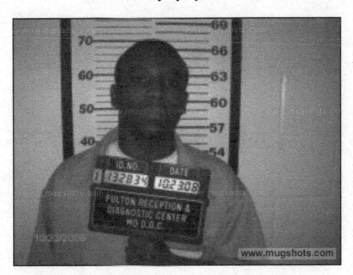

Fulton Reception and Diagnostic Center (FRDC) Arrival (c. 2008)—You can see in my eyes and my slouch that I had just been dehumanized and felt distant from humanity.

LOOSE CANDY		Limit 10
CHICO STICKS	$	0.13
APPLE RANCHER	$	0.17
CHERRY JOLLY RANCHER	$	0.17

BAG CANDY		Limit 2
STARLITE MINT	$	1.33
BUTTERSCOTCH CANDY	$	1.33
SUGAR FREE CANDY	$	1.44

CANDY BARS		Limit 4
PAY DAY BAR	$	0.83
THREE MUSKETEERS	$	0.80
M&M PEANUT	$	0.80
SNICKERS	$	0.80
BUTTERFINGERS	$	0.80
REESE PEANUT BUTTER CUP	$	0.86
HERSHEY'S CHOCOLATE BAR	$	0.84

CHECK AVAILABILITY

MEALS		Limit 6
CAJUN SUMMER SAUSAGE	$	1.49
TUNA - GEISHA	$	1.53

SOUPS		Limit 10
RAMEN	$	0.26

CHECK AVAILABILITY

DRINK MIXES		Limit 2
KEEFE BREAKFAST DRINK JAR	$	1.76
KEEFE LEMONADE JAR	$	1.76
		1.76
POWDERED MILK	$	4.10

SODA		Limit 6
PEPSI	$	0.33
DIET RITE	$	0.33
SIERRA MIST	$	0.33
MUG ROOTBEER	$	0.33
DIET 7-UP	$	0.33

COFFEE		Limit 3
KEEFE COFFEE	$	1.87
FOLGERS COFFEE	$	5.73

TEA AND COCOA		Limit 3
INSTANT TEA PACKET	$	0.55
KEEFE COCOA	$	1.26

SWEETENERS		Limit 1
SUGAR CUBES	$	1.38
SUGAR TWINS	$	1.31

CREAMER		Limit 1
COFFEE CREAMER	$	1.39

BEEF JERKY		Limit 12
BEEF STICK REGULAR	$	1.20
BEEF STICK BBO	$	1.20

CHIPS		Limit 4
C. A. CHEESE PUFFS	$	1.56
NACHO CHEESE CHIPS	$	1.94
PLAIN TORTILLA CHIPS	$	1.64
BBQ CORN CHIPS	$	1.60
RIPPLE POTATO CHIPS	$	1.25
SOUR CREAM & ONION CHIPS	$	1.25
HOT HOT HOT BBQ CHIPS	$	1.25
MICROWAVE POPCORN (LMT 6)	$	0.35

CRACKERS		Limit 3 ea
SALTINE	$	1.30
SNACK CRACKERS	$	1.43

IND. CRACKERS		Limit 16
RITZ CRACKER & CHEESE	$	0.27
RITZ CRACKER & P. BUTTER	$	0.28

CHEESE DIP		Limit 2
JALAPENO CHEESE SPREAD	$	1.40
JALAPENO CHEESE SQUEEZE	$	2.10

PEANUT BUTTER & JELLY		Limit 2
PEANUT BUTTER SMOOTH	$	1.45
PEANUT BUTTER CHUNKY	$	1.45
GRAPE JELLY	$	1.86

CAKES		Limit 6
OATMEAL PIES	$	1.44
NUTTY BARS	$	1.45
FUDGE DIP GRANOLA (BOX)	$	1.94
CHOCOLATE CUPCAKES	$	1.59

****CHECK AVAILABILITY****

SMALL CAKES		Limit 6
HONEY BUNS	$	0.57
ICED HONEY BUNS	$	0.80
APPLE PIE/CHERRY PIE	$	0.82
GLAZED/FRO MINI DONUT	$	0.80

****CHECK AVAILABILITY****

PHONE TIME 10 MIN. UNIT	$	1.00

WRITING ITEMS		Limit 1 ea
PHOTO ALBUM	$	1.50
MANILA ENVELOPE (limit 2)	$	0.13
EXPANDABLE FOLDER BLUE	$	2.90
WRITING PAD (limit 2)	$	0.80
BLUE PEN (limit 3)	$	0.20
BLACK PEN (limit 3)	$	0.20
COLOR PENCIL	$	1.42
STAMP POST CARD(lmt 10)	$	0.30
#2 PENCIL(lmt 3)	$	0.08
STAMPS $.01 (no limit)	$	0.01
POCKET DICTIONARY	$	2.13
SKETCH PAD	$	0.70
STAMPS $.44(lmt 50)	$	0.44
LEGAL ENVELOPE IND(LMT50)	$	0.03

MEDICAL		Limit 1 ea
HALLS (REG/CHERRY)(lmt 2)	$	0.92
ROLAID(REG/CHERRY)(lmt 2)	$	0.90
COLDS RUB	$	1.30
CHAPSTICK	$	1.66
ONE A DAY VITAMIN	$	1.38
COTTON SWABS	$	1.57
MUSCLE RUB	$	1.40
BENZOIL PEROXIDE	$	1.75
CALAMINE LOTION	$	1.31
ALKA SELTZER (limit 4)	$	0.55
BC STOMACH RELIEF	$	2.60
NON ASPIRIN PAIN RELIEF	$	1.63

PERSONAL HYGIENE		Limit 1
SHOWER SHOE (MED)	$	0.99
ANTI FUNGAL POWDER	$	1.72
ODOR EATERS	$	1.65
SHOWER SHOE (L, XL)	$	0.93

TOBACCO		Limit 10
TOP REGULAR	$	2.49
TOP MENTHOL	$	2.49
GPC FULL FLAVOR	$	3.95
GPC MENTHOL	$	3.95
GPC LIGHT 100'S	$	3.95
KOOL KINGS	$	4.39
MARLBORO	$	4.41

TOBACCO ACCESSORIES		Limit 2 ea
ROLLING PAPERS	$	0.33
CIGARETTE ROLLER (limit 1)	$	1.44
LIGHTERS	$	0.13

handwritten:
4 Boxes = 9.44
5 Boxes = 12.46
6 Boxes = 14.94
10 Boxes = 24.90

CANDY BARS,CAKE, AND CHIP SELECTION WILL BE ROTATED - CHECK BOARD FOR CURRENT LISTING

Loaf

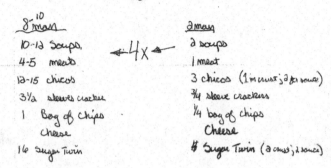

8-10
8 man   2 man
10-12 Soups   ←4X→   2 soups
4-5 meats   1 meat
12-15 chicos   3 chicos (1 in crust; 2 for sauce)
3½ sleeves cracker   ¾ sleeve crackers
1 Bag of chips   ¼ bag of chips
    Cheese   Cheese
16 Sugar Twin   8 Sugar Twin (2 crust; 2 sauce)

FRDC Canteen List—Ingredients to Make
Prison Pizza and Prison Loaf.

French Toast Day—
First Prison Death

R ank and respect meant everything in prison. People on the lower end of the totem pole were constantly targeted, bullied, and abused. This was a sad reality of prison.

Being close with Ramirez was a blessing and a curse. I hadn't yet figured out the curse part, but I was sure it was to come. For that reason, I made it clear that I wasn't part of anything.

Here is a general idea of the prison pecking order.[3] List of highest: cop killers, mob/organized conspiracies, drug traffickers, and armed robbery/murder. List of the lowest: any crime involving a child (this, for the most part, can be a death sentence), rape/crimes against women, law enforcement, domestic terrorists, snitches, and witness protection.

A week had passed, and I still was unable to sleep at night. I literally stayed awake the entire night for several weeks. I was deeply sleep-deprived. I would maybe get a thirty-minute nap during the day here and there. I felt safer sleeping during the day when more guards were patrolling and watching us than at night.

We had already experienced the first snowfall of the season and it was drastically cold at 5:00 a.m. when they woke our house up for breakfast. People like me and Ramirez rarely got up to walk in the cold for the terrible slop they served for breakfast. Since it was 5:00 a.m. and the sun was not out yet and some people stayed in, they never turned on all the lights. They just illuminated the walkways with a dim light for those who wanted to line up for chow—roughly 75 percent of the unit.

There were twenty-five cells on the bottom tier and twenty-five cells on the top tier, each with two people—thus a hundred people in cells. Because of mass incarceration and overcrowding, there were an additional twenty-five bunks on the bottom tier and twenty-five bunks on the top tier positioned right outside of each cell; thus another hundred people slept outside of a cell. One of the reasons I never went to sleep at night was because my bunk was right next to the only bathroom for the hundred people that did not have a cell. Each cell had its one steel toilet, but all hundred people on the outside bunks had to use the one toilet that happened to be positioned right next to my bunk. As a level-five prison (a supermax), we were on twenty-two hours of lockdown per day. We got twenty minutes each for breakfast, lunch, and dinner, then thirty minutes in the morning and thirty minutes in the evening for recreation time. During lockdown hours, people on the outside bunks were in an imaginary cell. We were not allowed to step two feet past our bunk in any direction or else it would be an out-of-bounds violation. The only reason we could leave our imaginary box was if we needed to go use the toilet...that was right by my bunk.

If you've ever been confined and have any level of minor anxiety, confinement gets boring and frustrating real fast. Thus, people would take trips to the bathroom cell simply to leave their five-by-eight confined space. They could do this without fear of a violation, so everyone took advantage of this to pass notes (fly kites), make transactions (drugs, gambling, etc.), and to simply get up and move around. The bathroom cell was also used for smoking. The result of this was literally hundreds of people would pass by my bunk every...single...night. Thus, the reason I never slept.

However, one of the times of the day that I knew I could get a catnap in relatively safely was when the 150-plus people left at 5:00 a.m. to go to breakfast. Every morning it would get real loud as the 150-plus people lined up, then it would get real cold because they opened the outside door to let everyone out, and then it would get real quiet and I would take my power nap.

One particular morning was different. As I would normally do, I had my blanket pulled all the way up to my eyeballs as it was very cold when they opened the doors, but I wanted to see what was going on. Most mornings and all through the night, I would fake as if I were asleep with my eyes half-opened. Ramirez usually stayed asleep, but for some reason he was up this morning, with his state boots on instead of his fresh white tennis shoes he regularly wore. He also had his brown state coat on, which he never wore because he had several clean, fresh jogging pants/sweatshirt outfits. In prison, you had to notice these nuisances. They often meant life or death. I saw him fiddling with his mattress, then reaching in his state coat pocket. Then he quickly went down the steps to the bottom tier. The 150-plus people generally waited in line for a good five to ten minutes before the doors opened, allowing them to leave. Ramirez hopped out of bed, dressed, boots and all. Something was definitely up.

When the notification for chow was made, all the cell doors were immediately unlocked, allowing people to start lining up. As people were lining up towards the door, Ramirez was walking the opposite direction in a steady, nonalarming, but fast pace. He reached the cell of this white guy whom I saw he had a rather heated conversation with just the day prior. I had a clear, bird's-eye view of this person's cell as I was peeking through my blanket. Ramirez walked in the cell and pulled what I discovered was a shank out of his coat pocket, bum-rushed the guy, and began to repeatedly stab him with the shank. He must have stabbed him what seemed like over a hundred times. The guy's shrill screams for help were barely audible over the normal ruckus of the morning breakfast commotion. Watching this scene from a scary movie play out before my eyes from under my sheets, I was bawling in tears—but quiet—for the first and only time while incarcerated.

The entire incident lasted maybe thirty to sixty seconds. Then the guy was no longer screaming, and Ramirez walked out of the room calmly with his hands in his pocket at about the same nonalarming pace he had before. He walked back up to our tier, walked in the bathroom near my cell, went to his bunk, and then came to my bunk. As he approached my bunk, I closed my eyes tightly, wiped my tears, covered my head, and feigned being asleep.

"Andrisse?" he whispered. "Andrisse? C'mon, wake up. I know you don't sleep through this shit." He tapped my shoulder. "It's French toast day. This is the only breakfast day worth going to, bro. C'mon, let's go."

I turned over and peeked through the sheets. To my surprise, he had a genuine smile on his face to match his normal, jovial demeanor. I was perplexed and genuinely scared at the same time. He had just stabbed someone to death. "I'm good. I'm not getting up. Go ahead without me."

"All right, suit yourself. I got some extra trays lined up too," he stated with one last effort to persuade me, then he was off down the steps just in time to jump ahead in line.

When the unit was quiet again, I listened to see if I could hear the dying man. I could not. I presumed he was dead. I was indescribably distraught and terrified. I cried long, deep cries, tucked under my blanket. I prayed to let God take me to a different place. A safe haven. I prayed to let God bring me home from this place. I prayed that I could be in a safe space. Then my breathing slowly began to come back to normal. Then my sobbing slowly began to seize. Then my heart slowly reentered my chest. I took a deep breath as I could finally breathe again.

As I peeked up from under my sheets, I noticed someone had noticed my panic attack from afar. In that moment, I realized the weakness of my vulnerability. I vowed to never let tears come from my eyes again. This was prison. I needed to man up. Death was a reality.

Serious Psychological Distress

T he emotional and psychological distress of prison is daunting and ever-present.[4] This distress is most heightened in the earlier periods of incarceration or in periods of uncertainty. The definition by the Bureau of Justice Statistics states that "serious psychological distress" is measured using the Kessler 6 scale, a tool used to screen for serious mental illness among adults. It asks how frequently in the past thirty days the respondent felt nervous, hopeless, restless, fidgety, so depressed nothing could cheer them up, everything was an effort, and worthless.

Check, check, check, check, check, check, check. I checked all of those boxes. I was not a nervous person by nature. But after witnessing someone get stabbed to death, I had a slight bit of heightened anxiety and nervousness about my surroundings, check. After being assured that I would do eight years instead of six and a half years, I definitely felt a sense of increased hopelessness, check. Right from the jump, I saw some holes in my salient factor score, the metric that determined how long one serves.

What did a "poor" salient factor mean for a person with a ten-year sentence on a class A drug trafficking charge? For that answer, you would have to refer to Appendix G in the MODOC Blue Book.[5] I kept that thing close by my side and read it frontwards and backwards and sideways and upside down. It still said the same thing. With a poor salient factor, a ten, and a Drug A, the guidelines called for me to do 66 percent of my ten-year sentence, roughly six and a half years (see below).

I wrote several elaborate, well-structured, thought-out letters to my institutional parole officer asking for a meeting and explaining how my salient factor score should be reconsidered, due to extenuating circumstances. It took one and a half months to get a meeting with her. Deanna Huff. She was impressed with my writing and my story—college graduate, big-time dope dealer, well-written, and well-spoken. I shaved, wore extra deodorant to try and smell extra fresh, and wore my cleanest of grays for the meeting with her. I wanted to impress her in every aspect.

She was indeed impressed. She helped ease some of my hopelessness in that she confirmed that there was no way I would serve eight years straight (it was against the law) unless I caught a new case. But the only way that happens is if you kill someone. The most gruesome of fights, dismemberment, stabbings, etc., are major violations, but not new criminal cases. She advised me to not listen too closely to prison banter.

"Mr. Andrisse, I've looked at your file very closely. And the arguments you present," she paused and drew out her words, "are very credible—and sensible, even." She paused again, looking through my file.

I had a bit of excitement take over me as it looked like she agreed with what I was saying. Firstly, I argued that a high school diploma should not be weighed equally as a college degree, which according to MODOC, it was. You could have a PhD, MD, or JD, and it would score equally as a high school diploma. I argued that they should consider giving me an additional point for educational attainment. Secondly, I argued that questions one through five all related to recidivism, but only two questions related to positive aspects of one's life. If a person gets a -1 for question one, they will get a negative score for questions two through five as well, thus putting someone in the poor bracket with little chance to get out since there are only two positive questions. And lastly, I submitted a writ of habeas corpus,[6] requesting that all my jail time and confinement to the jurisdiction of the court be included as time served on my sentence. I had calculated one year of time served already (180-day shock incarceration, the four months being held under federal investigation, the multiple one- to four-week jail stints, and the one and a half months on the box—electronic monitoring, ankle bracelet—right before my sentencing).

With my revised calculations, my salient factor score should have been -1 (average), and thus my percent time should be 30 percent, or three years, and if my writ of habeas corpus was accepted, that meant I should spend roughly two years in prison.

She broke her long pause. "Mr. Andrisse, again, all of this is very impressive. You are very impressive. I want to fight for you." She paused again. "But…these salient factor scores and guidelines are in place by state policy. Policy doesn't change overnight. My hands are tied. I can't do anything for you. A college degree should weigh more. But it doesn't. Recidivism does weigh more heavily than positive things, but this is to deter people like you from making multiple poor decisions. Thus, you fall at 66–70 percent on our ten. So, about seven years. I will fight to help you try and get that year knocked off." She sighed and frowned. "I'm sorry. That's where you are at."

❖ ❖ ❖

So back to that checklist—feelings of hopelessness, check! Looking at six to seven years left me feeling very hopeless.

Regarding how frequently I felt restless or fidgety, the answer was constantly. The entire time I was at the level-five max prison in Fulton on the outside bunk, I did not sleep a single solitary minute during the night. I would get thirty-minute naps here and there during the day hours, but nowhere near amounting to anything more than maybe two to three hours per day. The human body is not built to endure this pattern of sleep and I maintained it for six months. In terms of being fidgety, I was not tapping my legs or biting my nails, but I was chain-smoking. I smoked twenty to forty rolled cigarettes per day. I smoked at least twice per hour. It was the only way to calm my nerves.

Regarding depression, I had battled with serious clinical depression before, but this was the lowest I had ever felt in my life. After Jake's death, I had profoundly contemplated my value in this world and whether I deserved or should be in it. Those were thoughts of wanting to die, because I felt I was partly responsible for taking someone else's life. The thoughts I was having now were purely suicidal. I was having thoughts of actively taking my own life.

I have never shared this with anyone except for partly with my wife. I've told her, but never in great detail. There are so many negative consequences associated with sharing these types of thoughts, especially in prison. If you say you're suicidal in prison, instead of getting you medication or psychotherapy, they lock you in an even smaller cage and take you away from any type of human contact, thus increasing your feelings of wanting to take your life. Why do we put humans in this condition? How have we not thought of a better way?

When I would go into the designated "bathroom" cell to smoke, which was right by my outside bunk, I would be alone, as two people were not allowed to go in together. Part of the reason I smoked so much was that it allowed me a quiet, safe haven away from the constant social exposure. As an introvert, I needed my alone time to think to myself. I would go in the "bathroom" cell and peek through the tiny three-inch-by-eight-inch window and daydream of the outside. Daydream of my family. Sometimes this would ease my anxiety, but sometimes it would heighten it. There was a knob mechanism on the window that was this two- to three-inch blunt, metal stub protruding out from the metal window casing. Many days, I would lean with my back against the wall and my head squarely on that blunt, protruding knob.

I would think to myself, *All I have to do is give one solid backwards head bang and that should do. That would end my misery.* I'd sit there with my eyes closed, taking slow drags from my cigarette.

Just do it. Nobody will miss you. All you do is bring pain into people's lives. Just do it.

Ironically, my saving grace was logic. This method would not at all assure my death. It would assure brain trauma. I would always talk myself out of it. But the logic did not stop me from coming in that cell later that same day or the next day and having the same conversation with myself. This was deep depression.

❖ ❖ ❖

Within a little over one month of me leaving, Jennifer was sleeping with another man, an acquaintance of mine.

Jennifer confessed that she had been going out with him just starting that past week, but she stated they had not had sex. She was lonely, and he had reached out to her asking if she was all right, knowing that I had been sentenced to ten years. I had everyone checking up on Jennifer. But none of those people could stay overnight with her, every night. She couldn't sleep, and at nighttime she'd get lonelier and more scared. She was fearful that one of my drug co-conspirators would come after her. So, it started with having Steve spend the night to soothe her loneliness.

That lasted for one week or so. Then one day as we were on the phone, the first thing that came out of her mouth before she even said hello: "I slept with him last night. I'm so sorry, Stan." She cried and explained how lonely she was and that she would try not to do it again, but she stated she was fairly certain it would happen. It did happen again. And again, and again and again. Many times over. She told me she enjoyed it and it made her feel good. It made her feel like a person again. Not a whole person. Still a broken person, but a person. She told me sorry a lot early on. Then soon after she stopped telling me sorry, as I assured her that it was me that was sorry for putting us in this situation.

We decided early on that we both wanted to stay together despite her openly and very publicly sleeping with another man. No one really understood it as it was happening, and I don't expect many people to understand it as I write it now. It was weird, but it was us. We cared more for and about each other's well-being than anything else.

Condition number six, the last one, "feeling of worthlessness," check. My fiancé, who still was wearing her ring, was sleeping with another man and on top of that my father's health had mysteriously and quickly plummeted. I had just gotten word that he'd had a heart attack. This was within weeks of me starting my sentence. I recalled the time he had broken his hard shell and dropped down into deep tears during my juvenile incarceration. I could not hold back the feelings that this heart attack was my fault, due to the grief of absence, and pain of what was to become of his youngest son.

✦ ✦ ✦

When I got back to my housing unit from my meeting with my institutional PO, Deanna, it was only a short while before "rec time." I was due to call Jennifer and tell her the results of my meeting.

I told Jennifer that the PO said seven years with a possibility for a little less, maybe even two to three years, which was a lie.

Jennifer paused. I could tell she was crying as I could hear tiny sniffles. "I'm not doing good, Stan. I'm not doing good at all. I'm having some really bad thoughts. I mean really, really bad thoughts. I…"

Her voice went away.

"Jennifer! Jennifer!" I shouted quietly. My eyes had been closed and my head was leaning against the wall, so I hadn't seen this guy come up from behind me and press the hang up button.

It was a frail-looking white guy, whom I clearly identified as having meth addiction as a part of his journey, as his face had the characteristic cratered skin. He had just come in a few days ago and I also noticed that he was likely dealing with more serious mental health issues as he would quite loudly speak to himself as he would pace the rec area.

"Your fifteen minutes is up," he said, in a shaky but stern voice.

I looked at him, baffled that he would pull such a stunt. Something like this was immediate grounds for fighting.

"My time is not up. It has not been fifteen minutes," I stated calmly and politely.

"Your fifteen minutes is up," he repeated, almost robotically. "Your fifteen minutes is up."

His finger was still on the hang-up button, and then he reached and also grabbed the phone receiver which my hand was also still holding.

"Your fifteen minutes is up," he repeated again, robotically.

I looked him in the eyes, and I could see deep psychological problems. My guards went down, and I let go of the receiver and walked away.

This entire incident had been watched by essentially the entire dorm.

"You a muthafucking pussy, nigga! You gonna let that little cracker treat you like that?" One of the Black guys, who was also relatively new to the dorm, spat out this hatred as I walked by him. I just looked him intently in the eyes as I walked by.

He continued to mutter on as I was almost past ears distance. Laughing with another guy next to him, he stated, "You gon' get fucked when you sent to general population." He continued laughing at his own joke. "I can't believe these pussy-ass niggaz they sending to prison these days."

Everything was a game of logic for me. I wasn't about to fight a meth-head schizophrenic suffering the prison blues who probably wants to call his mom or girl. And the phones are in front of the guard booth, so I wasn't about to fight this loudmouthed, bigoted dickhead in front of the guards. Fighting was a major violation. I had just left the PO's office that day. I could still hear her voice: "Staying major violation-free is one of the best ways to help your argument for earlier release."

But I could feel all the eyes on me too. Logic wouldn't keep me alive from the predators. I sat down at one of the tables in the rec room with my eyes fixed on the TV screen but with my peripheral vison on 20/20.

"Stan-O, fuck them niggaz, man. Don't fall into that I...gotta...be a gangsta shit," the voice of reason, Hadise, stated, sitting next to me as I stared at the TV. He and probably everyone else could sense my frustration.

They might be able to see the frustration. But they could not hear the thoughts. I was so broken at this moment. Jennifer was so broken at this moment. Was she contemplating suicide like I was on a daily basis? What was she about to tell me? What did she mean by really bad thoughts? *I can't believe she's fucking Steve. In my house. In my bed. On my couch. I hate that I lied to her. But I can't possibly tell her the truth—that I'll be in here for seven years. She'd never make it seven years. Will I make it seven years? Will my mom survive seven years? Will my dad be alive?*

"Stan, fuck that shit, bro. You have to retaliate. This is my second bid. I've been through that bullying shit, bro. It's not the way to do your time. You *have* to fight that dude," the voice of survival, Kee-Lo, stated. Keegan (a white, low-level dealer from South St. Louis), Hadise, and I had become close friends.

I did not respond to either of them. I simply remained emotionless, looking at the TV screen for the remainder of the rec period, then went back to my bunk area after another fifteen minutes went by and rec ended.

✤ ✤ ✤

Appendix C

Offense Classifications

Each of the following offense classifications has a corresponding matrix that incorporates the salient factor risk categories. Beneath each risk category is the minimum, guideline, and maximum percent of sentence associated with that category. Beneath each percent category is the number of months to be served based upon the sentence imposed by the court. For a more complete listing of offenses, refer to the Sentencing Advisory Commission's User Guide available at http://www.mosac.mo.gov/ and at http://www.doc.mo.gov

Drug D and E felonies:
NCIC offense of Dangerous Drugs, including Drug Possession
Males: Appendix D
Females: Appendix E

Drug C felony: Appendix F
NCIC offense of Dangerous Drugs, including Sales, Distribution, Manufacturing and Drug Trafficking 2nd degree, Creating a Danger from Drug Manufacturing.
For offenses committed prior to January 1, 2017 use Appendix G or H

Drug A and B felonies:
NCIC offense of Dangerous Drugs, including Drug Trafficking 1st degree
Males: Appendix G
Females: Appendix H

Non-Violent D and E felonies:
Burglary 2nd degree, Arson 2nd degree excluding causing death, NCIC offenses of Stealing, Forgery, Fraud, Gambling, Damage Property, Stolen Property, Obscenity, Family Offenses (excluding those listed in Violent D and E felonies), Obstructing Judicial Process, Liquor Laws, Peace Disturbance, Election Laws, Health and Safety, Tax Revenue, Conservation, Motor Vehicles (other than DWI and BAC), Public Order Crimes, (with the listed exceptions in Violent D and E felonies), Weapons Offenses (with the listed exceptions in Non-Violent C felony and Violent A and B felonies).
Males: Appendix I
Females: Appendix J

Non-Violent C felony: Appendix K
Including Stealing more than $25,000 (for offenses committed prior to January 1, 2017 use Appendix L or M.), Unlawful Possession of a Firearm, Unlawful Possession, Transport of an Illegal Weapon (for offenses committed prior to January 1, 2017 use Appendix D or E).

Non-Violent A and B felonies:
Including Burglary 1st degree
Males: Appendix L
Females: Appendix M

DWI D and E felonies: Appendix N
Driving While Intoxicated when sentenced as a persistent or aggravated offender

DWI A, B and C felonies: Appendix O
Driving While Intoxicated when sentenced as a chronic or habitual DWI offender

Sex and Child Abuse D & E felonies: Appendix P

Appendix B

The Salient Factor Scale

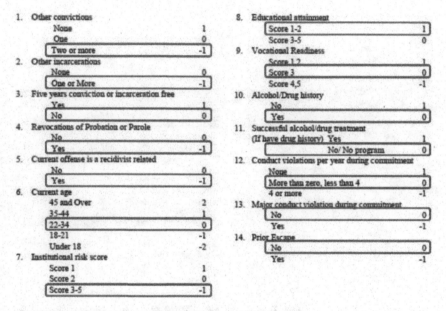

1. Other convictions
None	1
One	0
Two or more	-1

2. Other incarcerations
None	0
One or More	-1

3. Five years conviction or incarceration free
Yes	1
No	0

4. Revocations of Probation or Parole
No	0
Yes	-1

5. Current offense is a recidivist related
No	0
Yes	-1

6. Current age
45 and Over	2
35-44	1
22-34	0
18-21	-1
Under 18	-2

7. Institutional risk score
Score 1	1
Score 2	0
Score 3-5	-1

8. Educational attainment
Score 1-2	1
Score 3-5	0

9. Vocational Readiness
Score 1,2	1
Score 3	0
Score 4,5	-1

10. Alcohol/Drug history
No	1
Yes	0

11. Successful alcohol/drug treatment (If have drug history) Yes
Yes	1
No/ No program	0

12. Conduct violations per year during commitment
None	1
More than zero, less than 4	0
4 or more	-1

13. Major conduct violation during commitment
No	0
Yes	-1

14. Prior Escape
No	0
Yes	-1

Because I was sentenced as a prior and persistent career criminal,
I was given an institutional risk of -1 and considered a recidivist.

Salient Factor Score

Excellent	9 to 4	My score was poor, -4.
Above Average	3 to 2	
Average	-1 to 1	
Below Average	-2 to -3	
Poor	-4 to -11	

Appendix G

Drug A and B felony offenses: Males

According to MODOC guidelines I was due to serve seven years in prison because of my poor salient factor.

Sentence (yrs)	Excellent (9 to 4)			Above Average (3 to 2)			Average (1 to -1)			Below Average (-2 to -3)			Poor (-4 to -11)		
	Min. 25%	Guide 25%	Max. 30%	Min. 25%	Guide 30%	Max. 35%	Min. 30%	Guide 35%	Max. 40%	Min. 35%	Guide 40%	Max. 50%	Min. 42%	Guide 50%	Max. 66%/CR
5	15	15	18	15	18	21	18	21	24	21	24	30	25	30	40
6	18	18	22	18	22	25	22	25	29	25	29	36	30	36	48
7	21	21	25	21	25	29	25	29	34	29	34	42	35	42	55
8	24	24	29	24	29	34	29	34	38	34	38	48	40	48	63
9	27	27	32	27	32	38	32	38	45	38	43	54	45	54	71
10	30	30	36	30	36	42	36	42	48	42	48	60	50	60	84
11	33	33	40	33	40	46	40	46	53	46	53	66	55	66	96
12	36	36	43	36	43	50	43	50	58	50	58	72	60	72	108
13	39	39	47	39	47	55	47	55	62	55	62	78	66	78	120
14	42	42	50	42	50	59	50	59	67	59	67	84	71	84	132
15	45	45	54	45	54	63	54	63	72	63	72	90	76	90	144
16	48	48	58	48	58	67	58	67	77	67	77	96	81	96	132
17	51	51	61	51	61	71	61	71	82	71	82	102	86	102	144
18	54	54	65	54	65	76	65	76	86	76	86	108	91	108	156
19	57	57	68	57	68	80	68	80	91	80	91	114	96	114	168
20	60	60	72	60	72	84	72	84	96	84	96	120	101	120	180
21	63	63	76	63	76	88	76	88	101	88	101	126	106	126	192
22	66	66	79	66	79	92	79	92	106	92	106	132	111	132	204
23	69	69	83	69	83	97	83	97	110	97	110	138	116	138	216
24	72	72	86	72	86	101	86	101	115	101	115	144	121	144	228
25	75	75	90	75	90	105	90	105	120	105	120	150	126	150	240
26	78	78	94	78	94	109	94	109	125	109	125	156	131	156	252
27	81	81	97	81	97	113	97	113	130	113	130	162	136	162	264
28	84	84	101	84	101	118	101	118	134	118	134	168	141	168	276
29	87	87	104	87	104	122	104	122	139	122	139	174	146	174	288
30	90	90	108	90	108	126	108	126	144	126	144	180	151	180	300

Note: The maximum guideline term for offenders with a Poor risk (66%/CR) is 66% of sentence for sentences of less than 10 years and the conditional release date for sentences from 10 to 30 years. Persistent Offenders with enhanced sentences are scored from this matrix.

Length of Sentence Guidelines

AB Boys

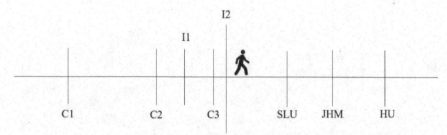

C = arrest that led to conviction; I = sentenced to incarceration; Numbers = number of that event
SLU = Saint Louis University; JHM = Johns Hopkins Medicine; HU = Howard University

I was excited to get out of the level-five, maximum-security, twenty-two-hour lockdown hellhole I had been in for the past six months. I was somewhat "appreciative" of the chained-up, windows-down, cold bus ride to the new prison. My eyes were glued to the outside world—the trees, the birds, the passing cars, the people in the passing cars. I hadn't seen life in what seemed like forever. There were no trees on the prison yard. Birds didn't fly in prison. It was as if they knew that the place was a desolate cage—a no-fly zone. The fresh air was tantalizing and refreshing. The air inside those four prison walls was different. Although most Midwestern prisons are out in the rural, open country, prison air is thick and pungent. Even the bluest, sunniest of days seemed gray when locked inside those walls.

After the dehumanizing spray-down, incoming people were housed in "One House," the holding unit, until housekeeping maids can get your room ready for your extended stay. Walking into this unit was not quite like walking into the unit in the level-five max on that very first day of prison. I walked in with gusto and pride and swag, like I ran that shit. *This ain't my first muthafucking rodeo.* I was actually excited to be at a new prison. The human experience at its rarest nature. Extreme desolation begets excitement at slightly less extreme desolation. I was genuinely happy. I had been told that this place had weights, an indoor and outdoor gym, indoor and outdoor basketball courts, indoor and outdoor tracks, that you could order your own personal TV, and that commissary had more options.

"Andrisse, 1132834. Pack your stuff. You're moving to Seven House."

This prison yard was different than the one I had just left. This place was massive. There were twenty housing units, dormitories of desolation and despair, lined up one after another. Ten on one side (A-yard) and ten on the other side (B-yard). The buildings again resembled those seen on a college campus—massive stone structures. They were rather clean-looking on the outside, likely built in the past ten or so years in the prison boom era.[1] There was a giant arena-looking building in the middle of the yard; I was told that was the gymnasium. As I walked up to and past the gym, I successfully held back the little-kid excitement in me to not appear to be weak with emotions and feelings. Many eyes were watching me. I cannot recall if I was walking alone or with a correctional officer or with a group of newly arriving people. But what I very distinctly remember were all the eyes. So many eyes. Over two thousand eyes, to be quite exact. This "prison camp" had about 2,400 people locked in cages, wrangled onto a people farm, masses of broken down, hopeless humans. Human livestock.

It was moving into summer and was hot outside. This also meant that the sun stayed out late. And the yard stayed open until thirty minutes before sunset. I was genuinely happy to be at this new prison.

❖ ❖ ❖

Excitedly ready to drop my bags and go out and play, I walked into my housing unit, HU-7. I walked into wing B; each HU had four wings. Then, still withholding my excitement, I calmly, coolly, and collectedly walked up the stairs to HU-7B-223, my new permanent residence. I walked into my cell and walked into a wall of the most pungent and decrepit smell of human feces that I had ever encountered. The smell was as if it were repeatedly and viciously slapping me in the face. It invaded my nostrils and went down my throat and into my stomach. I began gagging and threw up a little bit in my mouth and re-swallowed it. My new cellie, an older man in his sixties, did not look pleased with my discomfort. We gave the awkward head nod of new cellies and I walked past him—nearly rubbing chests with him as the cell was literally that small—and set my stuff on the top bunk. He still was very awkwardly looking at me.

"Hey, what's up? My name is Stan," I said, reaching out to dap him up. But he didn't flinch or say a word or give any acknowledgement of welcoming body language. My eyes turned focused and ready. I never turned my back on him, which in itself was awkward because I needed to have my back to him to unpack my stuff. Instead, I just opened my locker, still facing him, put my stuff in, and locked my locker with my lock, awkwardly pausing for a noticeable half second longer with my lock balled in my fist.

"I don't fuck with you young Thundercats. I been doing this shit for a long time, young brother. I done earned my stripes. I done put my work in. I'm tryna lay the fuck back these last few years. Ya understand?"

I paused and looked at him for a second, slightly less threatened now that he had spoken. I smirked and chuckled, "I ain't on no fuck shit, man. I'm wanna do my time and get the fuck outta here too."

"I ain't got no weird muthafucking rules like some muthafuckaz. Only thing I wanna put out up front," he paused. "I got Crohn's disease and that shit straight fucked up my insides. I shit all fucking day and all fucking night."

I nodded my head, seemingly successfully hiding my disgust. "Aight. Cool." Then, I squeezed past him to walk out the door.

"It's Raymond, by the way, young blood."

"Aight. Cool. Raymond." Then, I walked out the door and finally got an opportunity to explore the yard. As a kid, one of the first things I would do when my family and I went on vacations and stayed at a hotel was explore the hotel. I loved looking at maps of hotels and resorts. This was not a resort and there was no map, but I was still eager to explore the "camp."

❖ ❖ ❖

I didn't do anything that first day except walk around the entire A-yard. In each of the individual HU yards was one full outdoor basketball court. Then there was an Olympic-size gravel track. I knew it was Olympic-size because I was a high school track star along with being a trap star. I was excited to begin running every day. Although I ran track, I hated running. I was a sprinter. But, here, I was excited to run laps. Smiling inside, I envisioned myself running three miles every day. Past the track was an outdoor gym. It was jam-packed with super muscular, shirtless, sweaty Black men. I walked past the outdoor gym and on the side of the indoor gym were several handball courts. I had never heard of handball. I am not sure it even exists outside of prison walls. I then walked into the gym and was amazed at the gym facility—a full court, a pretty nice-sized weight room, a calisthenic section. The basketball court had bleachers. I sat alone and watched a few games. Then, close to closing, I walked back to my HU, excited to start my workout plan the next day.

The next morning when I came back from breakfast, Raymond was gone. Completely packed up and out of sight. I didn't ask any questions. Today was going to be my first workout. I was ready and excited. I walked into the indoor weight room full of energy.

I was eager to hit up my new chest exercise that I had designed while sitting in twenty-two-hour lockdown, but to my disdain, all three bench press Smith machines were taken. There was a group of three Black guys with muscles on muscles rotating between the three benches. They were pushing the entire stack on all three presses. Immensely intimidating. But I couldn't show that I was intimidated or scared.

I very confidently, and with a slightly deeper voice, shouted, "Aye, who got next?"

I was pretty cut up from doing calisthenics during twenty-two-hour lockdown. But they still gave me a look like, "Who the fuck are you?" I was incredibly surprised by the very cordial, polite, and rather soft-spoken, "You wanna jump in? We can use a rest between super sets." I guess I may have been expecting him to growl like a grizzly bear instead of sound like a human being.

"Naw. I'm good. I'll wait," I said, thinking to myself, *I can't push a fucking stack.*

"Aight. Cool. I'll get you when we're done."

In this prison as in most prisons, there were no free weights, as they could be used as weapons. There was a regular, an incline, and a decline bench. I had been waiting months to get in a weight room; waiting a little longer wouldn't kill me. Anyway, my new chest workout had six chest exercises with fifty reps each, totaling three hundred reps. I cleverly called it the 300 Workout as it would get you ripped like the guys in the movie *300* and had three hundred reps. So, for the next thirty minutes or less, I started the other three workouts.

The vibe in the weight room was very therapeutic for me. There was music playing. Some people were focused. Some people were talking, joking, and laughing. Some people were in groups. Some were solo. But everyone seemed to have purpose. This was going to be where I lived. This was going to be my oasis. I was a high school and college football star. I spent many hours in the weight room. This was home for me. I didn't have tape player or headphones yet, so I was also inadvertently eavesdropping on conversations. I thought to myself, *I can do this. This is my vibe.*

❖ ❖ ❖

"Yo, young blood. We done over here." The same super solid, soft-spoken Debo look-alike came by and politely mentioned that the bench was free. I walked over to the regular bench, collectedly hiding my excitement, and took the weight down several notches. As I was switching the weight, I felt someone hovering behind and to the side of me—three white guys. Two were younger, and one was much older with a gray handlebar mustache and old wrinkly, leathery skin that was somewhat tightened out because he was fairly ripped for a sixty-plus old man.

"This is our bench, son," said the older gentleman. As he rested his fully tattooed arm on the bench press handle, I could see a swastika tattoo nestled in the array of other tattoos on the back of his hand and on his arm. With this comment, my body went into fight-or-flight mode. Not to add that they were intruding on my personal space; violating personal space in prison is grounds for an instant fight.

I straightened up but didn't back up an inch, as I really didn't have anywhere to back up to because I was pinned against the bench.

I made a mockingly inquisitive face as I saw a few people eavesdropping on us, "Hmmph. I don't happen to see your name on the bench. Mind pointing that out to me?"

He licked his lips and then sucked his teeth for an awkwardly long time as we dove into one of the most prolonged two-second stare-downs I've ever engaged in. He chuckled menacingly and smiled. "That's right. They switched it out about ten years back, when they started getting a bunch of you all up in here."

I stood there, reactionless, at his clearly racist comment and attempt to get me to jump. We stood in yet another awkwardly long, silent stare-down. We were so close that I could not only see the rustling of his nose hairs, but I could also *hear* the rustling. My eyes never left his eyes, but I could feel a growing number of people watching in my peripheral. Although this encounter seemed to last forever and had garnered the subtle attention of others, it did not seem to grab the attention of the guards.

"So, is the weight room history lesson over? Can I get back to lifting weights?" I sarcastically shot back, attempting to both comedically and assertively end this encounter.

He chuckled again, this time less menacingly and more like a real laugh. "Lesson over. Class dismissed. You may proceed as you were." The younger guys began laughing at his comment as if they could tell by his intonation that things had settled down. This was the first peep they had made. They walked away, but my fight-or-flight could not go down. I was scared as shit. I wanted to cry, yell, run, and shrivel up, all at the same time. Instead, I hid all these emotions that were flooding my body and continued my workout as if nothing had just happened. I had seen scenes like this play out before, and they usually ended with someone (or multiple people) lying on the floor—with blood everywhere.

They went over to another area and continued their workout and I continued mine. Once I was done with the bench, I kindly extended the courtesy of shooting them a head nod to acknowledge that I was done. My ex-fiancée's sister, Julie, told me one of the most valuable things that oddly helped carry me through prison: "Just kill them with kindness, Stan." Julie is one of the sweetest and kindest souls that I've ever encountered in my human experience. And on that day, as with many days, I took her advice, by politely offering them the bench when I was done.

I worked out for another hour. I finished my 300-chest workout and I left the gym with a sense of happiness, with a sense of "I can do this." *Seven years, I got this. I'll just get a routine going. Hit this gym hard. Play some ball to pass time.*

Without much of a chance to react, I turned the corner around the gym and *smack*! My eye started gushing blood. I had no idea what had just hit me. I had reacted just enough for whatever just hit me to only have grazed my face. Nonetheless, I could only see out of one eye at the moment as my left eye and entire side of my face was dripping with blood. *Pop*! Before I could even begin to realize what was going on, I felt another blow to the back of my head. That one nearly knocked me down, and I stumbled forward, closer to two blurry figures. I feigned as if I were going to drop to the ground in retreat and instead fired upward and swung a right-hook uppercut with every ounce of my soul and landed a punch directly on one of my attackers' chin. He fell to the ground like a limp sack of potatoes, *thump*! I distinctly remember the sounds of every blow. I backed myself up against the wall of the gym so that they were all in front of me. I had both my fists up, ready to go, as two of them walked up to me. One of them stopped to pick up what I now recognized to be a lock in a sock. That must have been what hit me first. One of the guys charged me and I hit him with a three-piece that stunned him, but then the other one charged me and tackled me as I was fistfighting with the first one. I was taken down to the ground and I wrestled with the two of them. *Crack*! I felt a deep, sharp pain in my side as I could feel my ribs puncturing my insides. The third one was hovering over me swinging the lock in a sock, gesturing for the other two to pin me down. I tried to cover my face in anticipation of what was to come, but my arms were pinned down. My face was a bloody pulp by this time. I closed my eyes and, without evening thinking, my mind went to my family, my little angels, my nieces and nephews, my loved ones. What had I gotten myself into? After what felt like an eternity, to my surprise, I hadn't been hit yet. I heard a different set of mumbles. As I opened my eyes, the guy with the lock in a sock was on the ground, shirt full of blood. And the two holding me down let me go and jumped up. Now I could start to make out what was happening. My heroic liberator had a shank in his hand and was fending the assaulters off like a knight in shining armor swinging a King Arthur battle sword.

As the assailants scampered off, the guy tucked the bloody shank into his crotch and extended that same hand to help me up.

"Kenny-Mo, Derrty. Come on. Let's go. Derrty, let's go. It's about to get too hot." I took his hand and he pulled me up. "Take off your shirt, Derrty. Come on. Take off yo muthafucking shirt and wipe all that goddamn blood off. Come on. Hurry the fuck up. The po-lease gonna be here, Mo."

I took my white shirt off as instructed. Wiped my face and body down with it and stuffed it in my crotch. Kenny-Mo had his gray shirt and his white t-shirt on. He gave me the shirt off his back so that I had a shirt to wear walking back into the housing unit. As best and quickly as I could, I limped back, with the help of Kenny-Mo holding me up. The guards hesitated before opening the door. We were running a little late to lockup. But they let us in without asking any questions. I had never met Kenny-Mo before then. But he saved my life.

✦ ✦ ✦

Northeast Correctional Center (NECC) Arrival. (c. 2009)

It's Gonna Be a Hot
Summer—Homicide #2

"Come feel my pain. And obtain the sickness of the strain. Never use cocaine, but I sell it. In love with Mary Jane. So, come fire up with a killa, that'll come tie 'em up and trigga fuck his daughter and mother for one hunnid thousand bucks!"

"Ohhhhhh, shit!" Everyone started screaming and banging on lockers and bedposts and jumping up and down.

"So, buckle up and stay strapped. Cuz I be a dangerous truck. Life's a bitch. You don't give her a kiss. She'll make you pucker up." Skarr da General, one of my best friends on the inside, hit another punch line.

I walked into the room as SK was holding shop as he always did. It was the weekend, and it was our time to kick it. They had just got done blowing trees. It seemed like everybody in the camp, including the COs, was always high. But when there was weed or new drugs on the block, things were relatively cool. Everyone was laid back and happy.

SK caught me sitting in the doorway of his cell, looking in admiration of his lyrical talent. He stopped mid-flow. "Drizzy! What up, my dude! You just getting off work? You ole scholar-ass nigga." He laughed at his own joke. "This nigga stays in them books." Everybody started laughing.

I walked in and sat on a locker next to my cellie, JoJo. "Here we go again. What the fuck you worried about what I'm doing?" Everybody started chuckling.

JoJo chimed in. "Nigga, you do be in them books all muthafucking day and night. I wake up in the middle of the night the other night, stomach rumbling from eating that bullshit, thinking I'm gonna sneak a shit in real quick. Here this nigga go, like a little mouse with his chin on the edge of the bunk, reading some tiny notecard with only the moonlight shining in through the window. I was like, this nigga got to be crazy!" Everybody busted up laughing again.

By that point I began getting a little bashful, but luckily, I was comfortable enough with that group to show such an emotion as bashfulness. "Can we change the subject?"

SK bust up laughing again. "Hol up, ya. Hol up. The other day we walking the track like we do. We having a heart-to-heart and shit. And this nigga looks me in the face and tell me, 'I'm gonna be a doctor'!" SK started busting up, laughing even harder. "I didn't laugh when we was walking because it was a heart-to-heart…and…and you my nigga…but a doctor?"

Dion jumped in. "Fuck them books, nigga. You need to get back on them muthafucking bricks! Come fuck witchya muthafucking boy!"

Dion was heavy in the game. He would tell me, "I'm several hunnid thousand strong, my nigga" in his stringy hustler's voice. Dion and I had many heart-to-heart conversations, most of which were him trying to convince me to get back in the game. My friends knew that I was hanging up the jersey and retiring from the game.

I was very much an oddball with my closest friends. SK and Kenny-Mo were active gangbangers from the same block, 54 Wren Street Bloods and Rollin' 60s of Walnut Park in North St. Louis. Dion was a certified kingpin that ducked a RICO charge[2] and instead got hit with five years for gun possession. JoJo, my cellie, had twenty twenty-year sentences for twenty armed robberies that were running concurrently. He was on year fifteen when I met him.

I was pretty certain the only reason they all hung out with me was because everyone knew my case. Everyone in the cell block had read it. I was part of one of the biggest drug ring indictments in the state of Missouri. People outside of my housing unit knew me or wanted to get to know me. Being so heavy in the game was my protection. One, they knew that within my indictment were some real killers, so the presumption was that I had easy access to killers and putting hits out. Two, I carried myself with a sense of elegance, intelligence, and fearlessness, like a boss would. The presumption was that I really was still in the game, but I just wasn't one of these "dumb niggas" that go telegraphing that shit. Thus, because of the severity and level of my drug dealing, I was protected.

After Kenny-Mo had saved my life several months back, he and others in his gang attempted quite forcefully at first to get me to join their gang for protection. I came to learn—or at least pondered—that him saving me was only an effort to get me to join the gang. That was my blood in. I guess in prison there are no freebies. But Kenny-Mo and his crew soon came to find out my connections to making large amounts of money, and the attempts halted.

"Ya on some muthafucking bullshit, man. I'm about to hit this phone up." I hopped off of the locker and stepped out of the room.

❖ ❖ ❖

Jennifer and I were not together anymore. After I had gotten jumped, my face was beaten up for a good while. So, I convinced her that she should not come see me and that we should talk less. I didn't want her to see me like this. I was scared for my life. I was certain I was going to get attacked again, and my strong and real fear was that I would not walk away from the next encounter with the AB boys. For me, this solidified that seven years was too long to wait, and that I might not even survive that time.

Jennifer was furious with me. It had been about a year since we had been able to touch each other, and now that I was not at the max-security prison, we could have contact visits. We would be able to hold each other's hands and have one kiss at the beginning of the visit and one kiss at the end, but it could not be tongue-involved because people could potentially exchange contraband and drugs via tongue kissing—the actions of a few detrimentally impacted the masses. We had talked about these visits for months. When you are in a situation like incarceration, you must find every single sliver of silver lining and hold on very tight. We had been holding on to this silver lining for a long time, so, when I told her she couldn't come, she was irate. I went so far as to stop calling her for weeks at a time.

After a year of holding on by a tiny thread, it was truly over. And I was the one who broke it off. I told her that I wanted her to be happy and that waiting seven years for me was not fair to her. She fought me tooth and nail on this. When I stopped calling her, she commenced writing me two or three letters per day. She'd send sexy pictures. She'd send love letters. She'd send letters literally drenched in tears. She'd send scared letters. She'd send depression letters. She even sent near suicide letters. The suicide letters would prompt me to call. She'd cry and tell me she missed me. She'd tell me she was scared to live alone in our house. She'd ask if there was anyone coming after me and if she was safe in our house. She'd tell me how she would go on long, deep spouts of crying uncontrollably for hours. She'd tell me how she'd go on angry spouts where she wanted to break everything, including my face. She'd frequently ask, "Why did you do this to us?" I would frequently hold back my tears on these calls and simply tell her to stay strong. We would small talk, then she'd ask where we were. And I would tell her, "Not together."

We had had visits by this time, but they were very awkward. I was extremely happy to see her and she was incredibly happy to see me. But we were adamantly not together. The first contact visit was unbelievably emotionally difficult for me. I was completely broken inside, completely broken. But I put on my Kanye smile. Seeing her smile and trying to act emotionless was extremely heartbreaking and difficult. She had convinced me that although we weren't together we should at least kiss this one time considering it had been one entire year. So, we kissed and then we hugged for what felt like minutes, but we were only allowed to hug for seconds. I think we both felt something with that first kiss and long hug, but we did not know what to do with that something at that point. It was simply over between us.

One thing was still noticeably clear. We were indeed still close friends. We acknowledged and respected this strong bond and connection and sense of care for each other's well-being. We had always been painfully honest with each other, even before I went away to prison. We tried hard not to lie to each other. None of our friends ever grasped that or understood that about us. For instance, by this time, Jennifer had been sleeping with the acquaintance of mine for some time, even before we broke it off officially. He had been sleeping in my house, in my bed.

My brother saw Jennifer and this guy kicking it at two in the morning at the casino he worked at. My friend Cortney saw them at a club another night. Another friend saw them here or saw them there and heard this about that. All these encounters would get back to me in my prison cell. Everyone loved Jennifer and me. My friends and family. My dope dealing team. We had been together for nine years. She had been through the ups and downs of multiple cases and trials and incarcerations. So, seeing her fucking someone else, everyone was pugnacious and upset. Everyone but me. People assumed she was lying to me and thought that when they were relaying this info to me it was news. They were shocked with disbelief when I would tell them that I already knew.

I understood the pain and depression and the roller coaster she was going through. That I was putting her through. Yet everyone was on my side and seemed to forget that I kept breaking the law and was sent to prison for ten years. I was okay with her sleeping with someone else. So much so that on our visits I would occasionally hit her with super uncomfortable and awkward questions.

She'd be stunned, look at me in the eyes and see if I was serious or joking, and then proceed to answer. There was somewhat of an unfairness in our honesty clause. For her and my protection, it was understood that I would not tell her about anything that could potentially put her in legal danger, such as me telling her about my drug dealing on the outside, but also me telling her about the foul stuff that went on inside prison. Thus, this gave me the opportunity to still be honest within our trust establishment yet not have to tell her about getting jumped and how I deeply feared for my life on a regular basis.

"This is a collect call from the Northeast Correctional Center. To accept this call press one." Beep. I heard the one button get pressed.

"Hi, Stanley."

"Hi, Jennifer."

"What's going on in the world of prison today?"

"You know. Same ole shit. Just got done rapping with SK. He dropped a new single. We're gonna watch the Patriot-Colts game later. Probably whip up a prison pizza for everyone for the game."

Jennifer started giggling about the prison pizza. "You gonna make me one when you get out, Chef Andrisse?"

We continued to small talk. By this time, Jennifer was at a better place with her well-being and as such had broken off the several months-long fling with my acquaintance.

"Drisse! Let's go, bro. Let's go hit this court up, bro!" I heard SK's raspy voice from across the bay.

"Aight, bro. Here I come," I shouted back, covering the receiver of the phone.

SK was right next to me now. "Tell baby I love her too." He giggled waspily as he began blowing kisses into the phone and laughing hysterically. He was still high.

After a short while of catching up with Jennifer, I let her know that I was getting off to go hit the yard and work out. We ended the call on a happy note, wishing each other well for the rest of the day.

❖ ❖ ❖

SK and I hit the basketball court outside of our housing unit. We ran through several pickup games like we were the Harlem Globetrotters. Both of us played competitive high school ball, so those fools were light work.

After running for well over an hour, SK dipped to go take care of something. I was just chilling outside of the housing unit, rapping with some folks on the yard, when I saw three guys walk into HU-7's fences. Keep in mind, it was an "out-of-bounds" violation to walk inside the fences of another housing unit that wasn't yours. There were about two hundred people per housing unit, and I knew the faces of them all. I saw them every day. I had never seen these faces.

In the heat of the August sun, all three were in state-brown, heavy winter coats and state boots. If the winter coats in the height of summer weren't a red flag, I don't know what else was needed. I'm certain that in real life it was not in slow motion, but, as I recall it, each single step of the three men was in slow motion as if it were a scene from a movie. I was thinking to myself, *There is no way the guards are going to buzz these super suspicious guys into the house. Buzzzzz. Cla-clank.* Sure enough, the guards simply let in these three guys, who clearly didn't reside in this housing unit.

Feeling that something was about to go down, my friend and I followed behind the three guys. Just as we walked in the housing unit, I could see that the three guys had already been, once again, buzzed into A-wing, which required yet another security-locked door to be opened by a correctional officer.

The three guys in winter coats in the heat of summer rushed up the steps and continued marching. Before reaching the destination cell the three were headed for, someone popped out of an open cell swinging a lock in a sock like it was a ball and chain from the Roman Empire gladiator days. He connected with the face of the first guy in the winter coat with a fierce blow that sent blood flying across the bay. The blow was so powerful that it sent the guy stumbling. The second lock-in-a-sock blow threw the guy over the second-tier balcony. The guy fell, breaking his back over a chair, then tumbled to the floor motionless, seemingly lifeless.

The lock-in-a-sock guy put up a strong fight but was no match for the two winter-coated guys who pulled out shanks the length of swords. I had never seen anything like them before. The two men repeatedly began stabbing the lock-in-a-sock guy until he lay in a puddle of deep, dark red blood. Everyone in A-bay and all the other bays were glued, watching these two men murder this individual. No one came to this person's rescue. In fact, most people locked themselves in their cells knowing that chaos was about to break loose.

After a short while, COs in military gear rushed in. I and everyone else had been ordered and forced back to our cells and the entire yard had been cleared out. Any given day in prison could be your last.

✣ ✣ ✣

NECC Bike Show. (c. July 2009)

NECC Hot Summer. (c. 2009)

Getting into the Groove— This Is How to Prison

Stay Busy

In order to escape the realities of prison institutionalization, I did every single program and thing that I could do to stay busy. It was summer 2009, and I had been in prison for just about one year. I had found my groove. I had discovered how to survive prison. I had just completed a vocational training course on computer systems. The course was not college-accredited, but it was taught by instructors from a local vocational tech school, thus adding points to my vo-tech salient factor.

I was also hired as a GED teacher. This was my second paid position. It paid pennies, but it felt good to wake up with a purpose. My first position at NECC was a library clerk. One of my favorite places to go was the library. I went every chance I had and would spend hours there. I approached the librarian for a job and became one of the top library workers.

I was simultaneously a GED teacher, a library clerk, and taking the vo-tech class. I would teach GED Monday, Wednesday, and Friday. School hours were similar to what they were on the streets, roughly 8:00 a.m. to 2:00 p.m. Vo-tech classes were similar hours on Tuesday and Thursday. Then I would be in the library for the afternoon shift several days a week. In between all of this, I was training others in my "300 Workout" for a couple of hours per day, five to seven days per week.

On top of school plus two jobs plus being a personal trainer on the side, my good friend SK and I were the team captains of our basketball rec league team. The one season we played together we ended up making it to the championships. It was kind of unfair. I was a college athlete and SK was a high school basketball star from an elite parochial public school. SK was from Walnut Park in North St. Louis but had the opportunity to go to Ladue High via the "deseg program."[3] Aside from the league games, we'd play pickup on the outside basketball courts for hours when I had the time.

In terms of surviving prison, staying busy was one of the key components. I was too busy to take part in the institutionalization that occurred on the yard. I become a sought-after person for knowledge and advice.

Through an integrity acquired via the traumatic experiences of my life, with lived resilience, I was successfully able to dodge recruitment into prison gangs, literally by putting my life on the line. I had come to the point that I was truly *willing to be killed* rather than join a gang for protection and extortion purposes. This level of integrity and resilience cannot be taught in textbooks. By reading this here, one cannot absorb the psychological changes that were taking place within the neurological circuitry of my brain from these lived experiences. Studies have shown that trauma literally changes the physical neuronal connections of the brain.[4]

Why the experiences I had in prison up until this point (fights, deaths, extortion) led me to the direction I was in mentally, as opposed to deeper institutionalization, is a difficult question to answer. I personally believe it was the prosocial connections I had maintained. I would come to find out later that evidenced-based research[5] shows that building prosocial connections such as prison visits, phone calls, and letters from positive people drastically reduces recidivism, even without any educational or vocational programming. I had figured this formula out without the need for randomized control trials or research.

Prosocial Connections

Staying connected to the outside was a way to keep my mind out of prison. I would call Rich and listen to and laugh at his escapades he was having with women in rural Wisconsin. A city boy romping around in rural Wisconsin was hysterical. It was also somewhat healing for me to know that he was no longer in the dope game as it was legal issues that caused him to flee from STL.

Ironically, despite Jennifer and I not talking much, I had built a close relationship with Jennifer's entire family. Despite her dad being a cop, he was very sympathetic and supportive of me. Out of all the people I stayed in contact with—which was roughly two dozen or so—Jennifer's mom, Kate, and I wrote each other the most. We'd write five- or ten-page letters to each other, talking about anything and everything from cooking to daily life. I opened my emotions and feelings to her, and she did the same, telling me stories she had never even told Jennifer and many others. I think I was an outlet for her just as much as she was an outlet for me. It was through Kate that I began to learn the healing power of vulnerability. After Kate, Jennifer's sister Julie and I wrote the second most. Julie was between eighteen and twenty-two years old at the time with a boyfriend that would soon become her husband; thus, it was very surprising that she wrote me as much as she did. She was wise and kind beyond her years. She taught me to fight with my kindness and not with my fist. Kate and Julie were very much a part of my changed perception of integrity and how to do prison.

In addition to Rich, Kate, Julie, and Jennifer, I also stayed in close contact via phone calls and letters to each of my four siblings and parents, and to several close friends—Cortney, Liz, Jonathan, Taron, Brandon, Stephany, and Keisha. My fellowship mentor Dr. Bode had also remained in my life unexpectedly. This rounded up to sixteen to twenty people from the outside that I had a regular rotation of letters and phone calls to, each providing a different aspect of positive support. Julie and Kate were giving me wisdom, kindness, and emotional support. My friends were allowing me to live vicariously through pictures and stories of their escapades of enjoying life as law-abiding mid-twenty-somethings. Liz, who was Jennifer's best friend, was single and enjoying her mid-twenties and telling me all about it—and giving me inside scoops on Jennifer. Cortney was my level-headed logical friend. He kept me grounded as he had always done. Stephany and Keisha were friends and potential options for dating when I returned. They were in and out of being single and enjoying their mid-twenties as well and would often send me provocative pictures of them scantily dressed. For this reason, my photo album was one of the favorite photo albums for my incarcerated friends to frolic through. Stephany and Keisha knew I would let others see the flicks. They were okay with it.

Jonathan, Taron, and Rich, who were a part of my original Fab Five, were no longer hustling the way we were back in the day. We were all over twenty-five years old now. That phase of gregarious drug dealing had dissipated. It is now well established that people "age out of crime" in their mid-twenties.[6] All of us but Jonathan had criminal records. Out of my original Fab Five 1.0 (Jonathan, Rich/Steve, Hazel, Taron, and Anthony), I was the only one sentenced to prison. Out of Fab Five 2.0 (Dominic/Austin, Jason/Carlos, Charles/JP, Pat, and Sydney/Bryce), most of us had ended up in prison or were no longer with us. Out of the five of us that were caught up in the same 2004 federal indictment/investigation, the three of us that were Black (me, Jason, and Carlos) all ended up in prison; the two white guys (Dominic and Austin) never stepped foot in a prison cell.

On top of the letters and phone calls, I would also get visits from many of these people. Someone from my family visited once every month or two, with my mom and sister Sherer visiting the most out of my family. Every time my mom visited, her lips would be quivering, and she'd be fighting back tears. Sherer would be super observant and preoccupied with taking in the disparaging surroundings of prison. This made conversations rather unnatural and a bit awkward, but, nonetheless, it was extremely soothing to me to see family and stay connected.

Cortney, Liz, and Julie each visited at least once during my incarceration. Jennifer's mom never visited me because she said it would be too painful to see me like that. And my dad never visited me because he was too ill to make the long trip. Jennifer, by far, visited the most. Our visits were interesting, to say the least. We would get into detailed conversations of her sexual escapades. We took advantage of the allowed one-second kiss and hug at the beginnings and ends of most of our visits; we eventually stopped kissing but continued to give each other warm embraces. Our conversations were filled with laughs and smiles for the most part. As Jennifer came the most, she somewhat got past the feeling of being in prison, something that my other visitors could not get past.

Years later, Liz told me how after that visit, her, Cortney, and Jennifer went to a diner with hopes of talking and unpacking the prison visit to one of their best friends, but neither could muster any thoughts or words. They simply sat in silence and sadness. Liz said she couldn't sleep for weeks after knowing that she was in a comfy bed and I was in a cage. Similarly, years later, my sister Sherer would recall my sentencing day to me. How my mom fainted from hearing the sentencing, how my dad began bawling, how she nearly burned down her house as she was deep in a daze staring into the distance while her patio was in flames from her cigarette catching a cushion on fire. Her husband had to save her as she'd had no idea the patio was on fire. She was in shock. Prison not only impacts the person but their entire circle of family and friends.

Visits were challenging because you had to go through one of the more dehumanizing aspects of prison, where you stripped naked, bent over, spread your butt cheeks, and coughed, while another man examined your hanging scrotum and butthole, just in order to get to the visit. But the value of the visit overshadowed this dehumanization, as one could ride on the waves of happiness from a visit for weeks, or even months.

With the multitude of these various interactions (letters, phone calls, and visits), I was able to keep my mind successfully and consistently out of prison on a daily basis. Then, when all this was complete, at nighttime I would read and write. Read, read, read, then read some more, then write, then read some more. *This is how you avoid institutionalization.*

Willing to Die, in Order to Live

I began thinking very differently from how I was thinking when I was very depressed and weighted by the feelings of hopelessness and despair at the twenty-two-hour-lockdown max-security prison. A lot had happened since that time; I had witnessed two deaths and had nearly been killed myself. I had a vastly different view on life, death, and dying. At that time, **I had thoughts and feelings of dying because I had lost the will to live. Now I was at a point that I was willing to die in order to live, and that freed my soul to be who I wanted to be.**

There are many examples I could give of this freeing of my soul to live, but I will give two. I explained the most acknowledged prison social order, or totem pole. In almost any rendition of this social order, people with sexual offenses are at the bottom of this pole. They were called "chomos,"[7] short for child molesters. Chomos were targeted, extorted, and abused regularly; associating with them put you at risk for the same. There was a white lifer sentenced for a sex crime against a child that lived five doors down from me. There were not very many white people in my housing unit, as prison was very segregated. Out of the ten housing units at NECC, each with two hundred people, only one was a white housing unit. Thus, white people would be spread sparingly throughout the other housing units. At the max-security prison, I attended all religious services, Muslim, Christian, Catholic, Hindu, Jewish, etc., just to get out of my cage. At this high-medium (level-four) prison, I only attended the Catholic services. Mark, the white lifer with the sex offense down the hall, was one of the devoted Christian followers of this service. I found that many people with sex offenses attended religious services, and Christian/Catholic services may have had the most. In my head, I guessed that they had a deep sense of seeking redemption from the Lord. Mark and I would be the only ones walking to and from our housing unit and our dorm. Thus, we began talking and built a relationship. My Black friends warned me not to hang out with him, for fear that he was luring me into his venomous trap to seduce and rape me. Living without fear of death allowed me to be free in a way that I had never been.

One day after church services, he invited me into his cell. Not thinking twice or hesitating, I walked in the housing unit and went to his cell with him. I could feel the eyes of my friends and haters burning into me, but I didn't care. I was also fairly certain by this time that Mark was openly gay. I learned that Mark had indeed committed a crime against a child some twenty-plus years ago and received a life sentence. That did not stop me from seeing him as a human being. He had been living life like a hermit; no one in our dorm would ever talk to him. He was one of the only white people, gay, older, and a person convicted of child molestation. I was saddened that he was destined to live life with no human interaction. I was saddened that even amongst the "deplorable" he was seen as the *most* deplorable. I would often think about the life of the child that he committed the crime against, and I would think about what I would feel like if that was my child. Even then, I would tell myself that I would still offer him the comfort of human connection. Thus, Mark and I became friends. He'd tell me about his granddaughters and would show me the few pictures he had. After twenty-plus years he did not have many pictures, as his daughters and family had essentially disowned him and never stayed in contact. He was very bubbly, yet soft-spoken, and joyful to have our friendship. Not once did I feel uncomfortable. Not once did he ever give me reason to. We were simply two humans enjoying our human experience together.

The second example of the freeing of my soul to live was surreal. I had become a sought-after mentor and advisor, despite my young age. Much of this was due to the high success of my GED teaching abilities. People that had been lingering for years in the GED program without advancing were all of a sudden completing their GED in record time with my tutelage and teaching. Word around the camp was that if you wanted to pass the GED, you needed to get into Professor Drizzy's class. I was the only incarcerated person to be leading a course. I had a non-incarcerated teacher, but she let me take the reins. I would have lots of people transfer into my section of the GED to fall under my tutelage. I knew how to connect with the criminal mind. I was delivering what academics might call "culturally sensitive curriculum." I would equate algebra problems to selling dope on the streets.

"If you comp five bags of dope for a hundred dollars and you make $2,000 total from selling that dope, how much was your profit?" I would say.

The student would say, "That's easy. $1,500."

"That $1,500 is X. You've now mastered algebra." Relating algebra to the street hustle made people catch on much faster.

In terms of literature, we started reading passages from Tupac, Biggie, and Nirvana, instead of the traditional reads of Shakespeare, *Gatsby*, and *To Kill a Mockingbird*.[8]

It wasn't long before Frank Romano stepped foot into my classroom. The teacher was excited to introduce the two of us, as he was a longtime student of the GED program that just could not pass. When she introduced us, both of our jaws dropped.

She noticed the awkward stares we each had. "Do you two know each other?" she asked.

We both awkwardly muttered and then I managed to get out, "Ahh, yeah, I've seen him on the yard before." He said the same.

She informed him that I was the GED instructor he had heard about and requested and that she'd like for me to work personally with him. He looked at me, awaiting my response.

I nodded my head. "Yeah, that's cool. I will definitely work with him and help him out."

He looked me in the eyes and nodded his head in agreement. Then she went to the front of the class to begin instruction. The two of us sat at a table next to each other.

Frank was the lead white supremacist who ordered the beating that ultimately was to result in my death.

"Frank," I said, looking at his paperwork that stated his educational level and progress.

"Professor," he said, looking at me in the eyes.

"Call me Stan," I said. He began to say something, and I cut him off. "Frank, how bad do you want this GED?"

"Stan, I've been locked up for close to thirty years. I was never supposed to get out, but in a wild turn of events, I recently got a board hearing, and they are considering my release if get my GED. I'm still connected to my kids and grandkids. I just want to get home to my family and live life with my little grandchildren."

I could see the desperation and genuineness in his eyes. I nodded, still looking through his paperwork. "Okay then, well, it looks like we need to get started with algebra," I said.

Frank, a top-ranking white supremacist, eventually asked to get transferred to my housing unit, a primarily Black dorm, so that I could give him personal tutoring lessons.

Just as or even worse than with Mark, the person with the sex offense, the first time I walked into Frank's cell, everyone in the dorm was dumbfounded. I greeted Frank as he first got to the dorm as I knew in advance that he was being transferred. I escorted him to his cell. I was not the only Black person Frank had put hits out on in his thirty years of prison. He was not at all liked by the Black gangs, several of which had top leaders in my dorm. Frank was actually risking his well-being by his relationship with me as well. He had stepped down from leadership in the AB boys. Not formally, but de facto as he moved out of their dorm and disconnected his association with them.

I assured the other Black gang leaders that he was not here as some secret ploy to start some sort of race war. It was not an easy discussion to have and again **I was risking dying in order to live freely**.

Frank was extremely grateful for my assistance. I learned a lot about him in the process of our tutelage. Now that he was in my dorm, we'd have nightly sessions. I insisted that he did not have to pay me, but he did anyway. He'd make large pizzas and loafs to share with me and others. Again, the power of vulnerability showed itself. As was becoming a common thing, people would open up to me things they had never shared before. Frank was incarcerated for a series of bank robberies totaling millions. He claimed that he still had some of this money hidden and that's how he was able to offer rather good pay for his tutoring sessions.

By losing the fear of death and institutionalization, I gained power and the freedom to live freely. Through my experiences, I had moved to this epiphany that I would rather die than not do good.

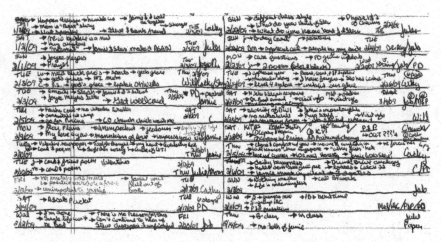

*Letter Writing System. In order to pass time, I would write close to
ten letters a week. I had a rotation of people I wrote to and I kept
detailed notes on what those letters stated. Unlike the easy memory of
an electronic email, there was no memory unless you made one.*

<u>200-300 Rep Workout</u>

<u>Workout</u>   Sets = 8-10 reps (lighter weights)

→<u>Chest</u> (20-30 sets)
 ↳Flat bench (6-7 sets) (260,220,180)
 ↳ Incline (6-7 sets) (200,140,140)
 ↳ Decline (6-7 sets) (240,220,180)
 ↳ Butterflys (6-7 sets) (150,130,110)
 ↳ Pulley Butterflys (6-7 sets) (150,130,110)

→<u>Arms</u> (20-30 sets) (OUTSIDE)
 ↳ Biceps   ↳ Triceps (70,60,50)
  ↳ Upper Pulley curls (7)(40,70,60) ↳ Pulley Pull-down (7)
  ↳ Lower Pulley curls (7)   ↳ Pulley Punch (7)
  ↳ Curl Bar (7)(40,50,70)   ↳ Tricep Pull-down (7)
                    ↳ Forearm Curls (7)
                    ↳ Reverse Forearm Curl (7)

→ <u>Shoulders</u> (20-30 sets) (OUTSIDE)
 ↳ Foreward Thrust (6-7) (30,20,10)
 ↳ Side Thrust (6-7) (30,20,10)
 ↳ Military Press (6-7) (175,150,130)
 ↳ Shoulder Shrugs (6-7)

→ <u>Back</u> (20-30 sets)
 ↳ Lat Pull-down (6-7) (200,180,160)
 ↳ Seated Row (6-7) (135,120,105)
 ↳ Squatted Row (6-7)
 ? ↳ Cleans/Push Jerks (6-7) ?

→<u>Legs</u> (20-30 sets)
 ↳ Squats (6) (460,420,380)
 ↳ Leg Press (6) (895,755,635)
 ↳ Quad Curls (6) } one set
 ↳ Ham Curls (6) } (90,80,70)
 ↳ Deadlift (6)
 ↳ Lunges (6)

→<u>Abs</u> (20 sets) (DAILY)
 ↳ Wheel (5x25)
 ↳ Incline Sit-up (5x25)
 ↳ Weighted Sit-up (5x25)
 ↳ Reg Sit up (3x25) } Night-time in wing
 ↳ Bicycle (3x25)

The 300 Workout

The Hole

C *lick-clank.* The lock to my windowless door unlocked and the door swung open. "Andrisse, it's time for your violation hearing."

"What?" I said, confused, as I began sitting up from lying down on my bunk, looking up at the ceiling, daydreaming. It was the fall of 2009 and I had been in solitary confinement for about one month for a major violation.

"Get the fuck up. It's time for your violation hearing. You heard me."

I wasn't prepared. I had forgotten about my violation case. I had forgotten why I was even in the hole.

I walked in the violation hearing room and was directed to sit in a seat at a table that had four white people sitting down on the other side of it—two older white men, one younger white woman, and one older white woman. The younger white woman was my supervisor in the library, where I had been working when I got the violation.

"Mr. Andrisse, you are in violation of RsMO DOC rule number 8.1, inciting a riot, and rule number 19.4, creating a disturbance. How do you plead?" the oldest-looking white man sitting in the middle stated.

I looked all four of them in their eyes and said, "Not guilty," in a quiet, semi-nervous voice to the point that I had to clear my throat and say it again. "Not guilty," I said louder and more confidently. I had been working in the library for several months. It was paradise for me. Prison rules only allowed a person to have three books in their cell at a time. By comparison, you were allowed twenty boxes of Little Debbie's and ten cans of tobacco, but only three books. It was okay to get diabetes or lung cancer, but heaven forbid you try and get educated. In the library I could read as many books as I could possibly read. I was assigned as the periodical check-out person. People could rent books to take back to their cells for free, but the periodicals had to be read in the library and could not be checked out. To defy the restraint of only being able to have three books and no periodicals in your cell, I would make copies of the books, magazines, and letters I had written and received, important legal documents, etc. This was all fine and allowable. What was not allowable was printing more than one page per printout or printing double-sided. Printing was not free. To save money, I would print four to six pages per printout, double-sided.

"So, not guilty? Okay," said the white man that had spoken before as he was quickly reading through my files. "So, according to these disciplinary action files, you were making four-in-one copies?" he said inquisitively, with his eyes furrowed somewhat in disbelief. I did not respond to his half-question/half-statement. He looked over at the library supervisor and she shook her head in disbelief as well. "And Mr. Andrisse, you were given an inciting a riot and creating a disturbance violation for this?" Again, making a statement question.

I did not respond verbally nor by gesture. By this point in the game, I was well aware that anything you said could and would be used and construed against you. I sat there expressionless and wordless for a short moment of silence, then spoke. "Is that a question, sir?"

He sat quietly reexamining the document then stated, "As written here, this is not inciting a riot nor creating a disturbance. Since the officer who wrote the violation is not present, Ms. Wilson, do you have anything to offer regarding the inmate's conduct while working for you at the library?"

Ms. Wilson looked at me, and I looked at her with eyes of sympathy and desperation. She stated, "I had no other complications with Mr. Andrisse aside from this incident. He was a good worker by all other accounts."

I almost cracked a smile at her comment, but I remained expressionless, awaiting what the white man in power had to say.

"Within the officer's statement, it says that you lied when confronted about the violation. Did you lie to the officer?" the white man stated authoritatively.

I paused and thought before responding, knowing that I hadn't lied to the officer. But also knowing that if I stated I hadn't lied, then they would assume that I was lying now and further put me in trouble. I thought to myself, *Maybe it would be best to say that I lied and that I am sorry and remorseful.*

"You know what? It's okay. I don't need that answer. No matter how you spin it, this is not 'inciting a riot' nor 'creating a disturbance.' Inmate Andrisse shall be released from solitary confinement, effective today, and these aforementioned violations shall be removed from his institutional record. This hearing is adjourned," stated the old white man with the power.

"Thank you, sir," I stated. I was extremely grateful for his kindness and for him seeing the truth and injustice in the situation. At the same time, I felt as if I were a scared slave saying, "Thank you, master, for your kindness and for not subjecting me to thirty more lashes by the whip." Even in my victory, I felt dehumanized. No one in my family or my loved ones knew that I was in this room with these powerful white people. I had no rights to an attorney. I had no rights to make one phone call. I didn't even have access to a rule book while in the hole to learn more about the violation. What I did remember about the violation book was that violations numbered one through five were punishable by a court of law and that violations numbered one through ten could result in up to one year in solitary confinement. Having an 8.1 "inciting a riot" walking into that room, it was a possibility that I could walk out of that room being sentenced to another eleven months in the hole. That very much sounded like and was emotionally and physically worse than thirty lashes by whip. I was indeed a slave of that state.

Despite these heavy emotions of feeling like a slave rushing over me, I did manage to crack a huge smile. I was released back to the general prison population after having served thirty-two days in solitary confinement.

The day I was released from the hole, I got the letter from Jennifer. She did not beat around the bush. Her first sentence said, "Stan, I'm pregnant. I don't know what to do. Please call me."

30 and Out

I had been locked up for about a year and a half at this point. Jennifer was truly gone, but in a better place mentally, so I was genuinely happy for her. I had become content with the fact that I was about to spend seven years in prison. I had never heard back from my writ of habeas corpus requesting my prior incarceration times be included. I had made several visits to my institutional parole officer at NECC, but they were not as kind or impressed with me. They essentially told me, "Fuck off, you're doing 66 percent on your ten." So, I did. I backed off from my fight to get out earlier and began living life in prison.

Jennifer's pregnancy, in a way, freed me from the urgency to get home. Now that she was pregnant and living with someone that cared for her, I no longer felt as heavy of a guilt as when she was depressed and having terrible thoughts.

When I had received that letter after getting out of the hole, I called her immediately. She was in tears and curled up on the couch. Jennifer and Ryan had just started seeing each other less than a couple of weeks ago and weren't even dating. She hadn't told anyone yet, not Ryan, not Julie, not Kate. She had been awaiting my call for two weeks now. That's about how long it took for mail to be received. Holding back my tears, I gave her my approval as I knew that's what she was waiting for before she informed the others in her life. My being okay took a level of weight and guilt off her shoulders.

✦ ✦ ✦

I and everyone else in the dorm had become used to me getting a lot of mail. When it was mail call, I was the envy of the entire dorm. People would sit by their cell doors in anticipation and hopes that a letter would come their way. Most people had a significant other or a girl that was holding them down and, despite the likelihood that they were sleeping around, many would wait weeks or months or years for letters from them. Having twenty different people I was writing to, I got mail literally every day. Everyone thought I was a pimp, because who in prison writes letters about cooking to old ladies? Many on the inside believed that prison letters were to thots talking about sex. To some extent, I purposefully let people think I was a pimp, as I would mostly only let them read and see mail from Keisha and Stephany, girls that would send provocative flicks and write fun-loving letters.

Because of this anticipation, everyone in my dorm would enthusiastically await my mail. This particular day was no different. I had received several pieces of mail, but one stood out to me as it was not in an outside envelope. It was from the NECC Probation Office.

JoJo and I looked at it as he was sipping his midday black coffee. "What you waiting for? Open it up, my nigga."

"Mr. Stan Andrisse, you have been accepted into the MODOC 30 and OUT (Offender Under Treatment) program. This is a six-month intensive institutional treatment program. Upon successful completion, you will be released on parole under supervision."

My mouth dropped in astonishment. I thought out loud: "30 and OUT? That's not…66 percent. I was told very adamantly that I was going to do 66 percent." I was absolutely astounded. I wanted to cry tears of happiness.

JoJo smiled. "You going to treatment, nigga. Pack yo shit up. Let's celebrate! How long you been locked up?" I explained to him my writ of habeas corpus asking for my fourteen months of prior incarceration to be included, but that I had been told it was denied. If my fourteen months were to be included, I would already be at thirty months and an additional six months would total thirty-six months.

"Aww shit. They might went ahead and gave you that shit, bro. Let's celebrate. They gone come get you soon, bro," JoJo stated. His word was pretty credible; he had been locked up for over fourteen years.

The word spread quickly around the dorm as I had become one of the more well-respected people in the unit and on the camp. As JoJo suggested, we celebrated. It was a celebration bigger than the one Ramirez had back at Fulton on his departure. We made two bunk-sized pizzas, one bunk-sized loaf, and nachos. We busted out sodas and drinks. Also, unlike Ramirez's celebration, I invited everyone: my regular crew—SK, Dion, Wonderful, JoJo, and Peo—and my non-regular crew—Frank the reformed white supremacist, Mark, the person convicted of a sex crime, and people that I rarely talked to but noticed never had funds to make big meals like this.

From the depths of darkness, there was light. I would be going home soon. I got advice on how to survive and successfully complete the six-month prison treatment program. I was cautioned that nearly 100 percent of people that get sent to these programs are people that get sent directly from the streets. Thus, it was a different type of jailing going on. The rules of engagement, such as respect and loyalty, at higher-level prisons such as where we were at were not in play.

In anticipation that I might leave soon, I wrote Jennifer that night to tell her the news—and that I may not be able to call her for some time. For the first month of treatment, you were restricted from using the phone. I couldn't help but think, "Had this letter come two weeks earlier, would Jennifer be pregnant?"

"Andrisse, bunk and junk, pack it up. Let's go." The CO popped into my cell at around 3:00 a.m. I hopped out of bed and started packing. JoJo got up as well to help me pack and to talk. I ended up leaving him most of my food items, which was a lot.

"I'm gone miss you, Drisse. In my damn near fifteen years, you were the best cellie I ever had," JoJo said, looking like he was about to tear up.

I smiled at him, pushed him in the shoulders, and then, uncharacteristically to prison life, I gave him a hug. "Man, don't start tearing up on me." I laughed as we embraced.

"All right with all the sentimental shit. Andrisse, pack your shit and let's go," the officer said jokingly. I stuffed the last of my belongings into my mesh laundry sack, threw it over my shoulders, and gave my home of roughly one year now one last look.

"Till next time, brother," JoJo stated.

I smiled at him. "I'll see you on the other side, bro."

As I was walking away, JoJo stated one last thing. "I hope you and Jennifer work everything out, man. She's someone special."

I paused a moment, looking down, thinking what to say. "I appreciate that, man." And just like that, I walked out of the cell into the next chapter of my life.

PART THREE

POST-PRISON

———

"From prison cells to PhD, to Hopkins Med top nominee"

Becoming Senior

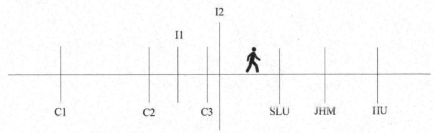

C = arrest that led to conviction; I = sentenced to incarceration; Numbers = number of that event
SLU = Saint Louis University; JHM = Johns Hopkins Medicine; HU = Howard University

I barely even recall the eight-hour, freezing-cold bus ride to the other side of the state. I had made these types of cross-state trips so often now. The stripping naked did not feel as demoralizing. Sadly so, it was me now looking at some of the newbies with the expression of "Grow a pair of balls, this is not the worst part."

As I had been cautioned, treatment was different. I was the only person who had come from prison in my cohort. This made me stand out. As was the case with every facility I moved to, I was very quickly moved to a place of respect and leadership.

Therapeutic communities, as they were called, had a system of leadership and structure designed to facilitate team building and interpersonal growth. In this system, there was a government hierarchy setup where there was a president who was called the senior, and the senior had four cabinet members—a VP, a treasurer, a socials chair, and a disciplinary chair. The previous senior nominated the next senior. I had only been in treatment for one and a half weeks when I was selected. As I was just getting into the swing of things, I was thrown in as the leader of this treatment program.

There were people completing the program every week, and new people coming in every week. After one and a half weeks, I barely knew the people, most of whom had been there ranging from one to five months—and I was now their senior. It was weird, but I ran with it as this was my ticket home. It was made very clear to me that if I were to fail this treatment program, I would go back and complete the remainder of the seven years.

Therapeutic communities utilized something called the pull-up or push-up system. When someone did something good, you pushed them up. Programming started at 6:00 a.m. and ended at 4:00 p.m. We'd have a variety of classes to attend, such as Impact of Crime on Victims one and two, Living in Balance, and Anger Management, to name a few; additionally, we'd do a lot of exercises, assignments, and team-building activities. We started every morning with push-ups. On the flipside, we were required to give out a certain number of pull-ups (someone telling on someone else for doing something they were not supposed to be doing)—in other words, snitching. The therapeutic community was the snitch system. The idea was that you could break someone's criminality and criminal thinking by getting them to do the most fundamental thing that you don't do as a "criminal,": snitch. I would come to find out that these therapeutic communities were grounded in evidence-based studies that wildly showed their success, as it was told by an academic. Noel Vest explains the flaws of this system in this piece from *Nature*[1] that includes the two of us talking about our prison experiences.

The entire pull-up system was a joke. It was all orchestrated. People would collaborate to pull each other up for little things. No one ever pulled people up for serious things. That would get someone kicked out.

I was senior for about two months when I saw Bryce's name on the list of people to pick up. As senior, I was responsible for welcoming the new arrivals. Bryce was my last right-hand man. Bryce was the one I handed my entire operation over to. I gave him access to all my profits but also gave him access to all my problems. Bryce was the one who presumably set me up. He was presumably responsible for the final charge that resulted in my ten-year sentence. Some thought that I was somehow attached to him being sent away—and I was, in that I forced a large number of drugs in his hands and gave him the reins. I also had his pregnant girlfriend sell drugs for me. I was not sure how this encounter was going to go. Was he going to be upset? Were we going to get in a fight? Was I about to get kicked out?

"What the fuck, man! StanDrisssse!" Bryce shouted my name as I used to say it in all my rap songs, ran over to me, dapped me up, and gave me a hug. The incoming people had no idea who was at treatment. He was genuinely flabbergasted.

"What's up, man? How you been?"

I smiled back at him. "I see you got a few new tats." A few was an understatement. Bryce was tatted up nearly head to toe. He had spent some time in Algoa, a level-three prison where, apparently, he decided to dive deep into the prison culture and get a bunch of tats.

"Man, man, man!" Bryce said, looking at me. "I haven't seen you since…" We both paused, laughed, and then smiled at each other. We just shook our heads in agreement. Knowing that the last time we saw each other was my arrest in front of his house. We didn't go into the details of that day, but instead immediately starting reminiscing on the good times.

❖ ❖ ❖

Treatment was moving along well. So well that the end of my senior days was not in sight. I have a unique talent of getting people I barely know to open up their souls to me. In a therapeutic community, this was where the true growth happened. The opening of the soul. I had men crying in front of other men about their wives, daughters, sons, mothers, fathers, homes, jobs, families, friends—you name it and we discussed it and the emotions poured out.

But that love and vibing therapeutic community would soon come to an end. In this facility, everything was open. Our cells were not cells as they did not have locked doors or metal bars. They were open rooms. The doors had been completely removed from the hinges. The rooms were open bays. The showers were open bays. In the higher-level prisons, the showers were single-man showers that had a locked door. You waited in line, if there was a line, until the man in front of you was done with his shower and then the CO had to buzz the man in the shower out and allow the next man to enter. This was done to reduce rape and fighting, as the shower made for a good location for both. Well, in this treatment prison, the showers did not have locked doors, and there were multiple showerheads in an open format like in a locker room. Men that came from the higher-level prisons never showered when there was another man already in the shower. Men that had not done higher-level prison time often showered in groups as if we were a high school football team.

There were cameras everywhere in prison. We were always being watched, except inside the showers. The showers, even here, were still a place for rape and violence. A huge multi-person fight broke out one evening when the counselors Ms. Grace and Mr. Battle had gone home for the day. Every morning I reported to Ms. Grace how things were over the night. The morning after the huge fight there was a big interrogation and investigation undertaken. Everyone's knuckles and faces were being checked for cuts, bumps, and bruises. From this technique, they pinpointed several culprits. If the culprits admitted to fighting, they would be kicked out. A strong contrast from higher-level prisons where the most dangerous people were people with exceptionally long and life sentences, the most dangerous people in this treatment prison were the people with very short sentences. If they got kicked out, many were only looking at an additional few months of prison time, so fighting was not a big deal for them. Being tough was more important. For a person like me who would do another five-plus years if kicked out of the program, fighting was out of the question. In the higher-level prisons, after a fight, you stay in your cell and bed and can successfully hide your bumps and bruises from the cops. Here, that was not the case.

Ms. Grace and Mr. Battle called me into the office that morning and grilled me.

"You are the senior of this community. How is it that you don't know anything about this big incident that took place under your watch?" Ms. Grace was yelling at me.

I had not witnessed the fight, but I had already been told a considerable amount about what had happened and why. "I didn't see the fight, Ms. Grace. And there was no big incident or commotion." This was the truth. There was a royal rumble, but I didn't see it and no cops had been brought to the scene.

"You are still in your criminality. I thought you were different, Mr. Andrisse," Mr. Battle stated.

No one was kicked out as there was a lack of evidence. But after almost two months, I was removed from being senior.

This was a major relief for me. I thought to myself, *Why didn't someone get in a fight earlier?* I had completed many of my treatment courses (certificates below). With light clearly at the end of the tunnel, life felt good. I no longer felt hopeless. I was in a good place. My mind was at ease and starting to switch into release gear.

❖ ❖ ❖

Prison Drug Treatment Program: The cabinet members of my leadership team. (c. 2010)

CERTIFICATE OF

Completion

Awarded to

Stan Andrusse

for successfully completing lessons __1__ - __12__

Pathway to Change Training

on this *18th* day of *June 2010*.

Linda Grace SAC II

Facilitator Signature

MO 591-4894 (9-07)

Missouri Department of Corrections

Certificate of Completion

Substance Abuse Education Program

This is to certify that

Stan Andrisse

has successfully completed the

180 Day Program

at

Western Region Treatment Center

Linda Grace SAC II
Signature

Tracy Reed
Signature

6-18-10
Date

Hours completed: 624

Andrisse, Stan
#1132834

ATTENDED AND PARTICIPATED IN THE

LIFE AFTER RELEASE GROUP

AT

NORTHEAST CORRECTIONAL CENTER

SIGNED _Mona Grote, MSW, LCSW_   DATE _12/16/09_
      Mona Grote, MSW, LCSW

Andrisee, Stanley
1132834

Attended and Participated in the

Coping and Hoping Group

At

Northeast Correctional Center

Signed _Mona Grote, MSW, LCSW_   Date _8-25-09_
    Mona Grote, MSW, LCSW

COPING AND HOPING
MY HOPES

Participant Name: _Stery Andersse_   #: _1132834_   Date: _8-24-09_

Very often, people get caught up in their immediate day-to-day situations and lose focus on the big picture. Take a few minutes to think about what you hope for – not the little stuff like the kind of sandwich you're getting for lunch, but the big hopes – the hopes you have for yourself or the hopes you have for others. Think big. In the *How Likely* column, rate on a scale from 1 to 5 (use the rating system below), how likely it is that your hopes will be fulfilled. Are any of your hopes about staying safe and free from self-injurious or suicidal behaviors?

1 = completely unlikely
2 = somewhat unlikely
3 = neither unlikely or likely
4 = somewhat likely
5 = completely likely

	My Hopes	How Likely
Hopes I have for the next year	1. My hopes for what I want to accomplish: Re-enter into a BioMedical Ph.D. program	4
	2. My hopes for what I want for others: Peace of mind	5
	3. My hopes for how I will be remembered: Calm, cool, & Respectful	5
Hopes I have for the rest of my life	4. My hopes for what I want to accomplish: Happiness & Inner Peace	5
	5. My hopes for what I want for others: Inner Peace	5
	6. My hopes for how I will be remembered: Respectful, Humble, & Driven	5

Treatment Certificates (c. 2010)

Applying for My PhD

After one month at treatment, I was able to make phone calls and I contacted Jennifer, my family, my friends, Dr. Bode—pretty much everyone I had been talking to since I went away—and informed them that I'd be home within six months. It did not soak in immediately for many people, as I had been talking "possibility" nonsense for a long time now. For Jennifer's and my relationship, this discovery came too late. She was three months pregnant now and had moved in with her soon-to-be baby's father.

With release fast approaching, a bigger and scarier question than reconnecting was looming. What was I going to do with my life? What kind of job could I get?

With Dr. Bode stepping in as a mentor of mine, this idea of continuing my education had been brewing for some time. I was extremely fortunate to have Bode in my life. In a way, he was simply one piece, one person in this strong system of support that I had woven together. But, depending on your vantage point, he could easily have been the most integral part of this woven tapestry of support. We had come a long way from the time I was called into his office and he said, "So, tell me about Susan Schneider." I was certain that upon finding out about who I really was he would abandon me. But he did the exact opposite. He dove in deeper than I could have ever imagined, from coming to court and testifying to not to send me away to staying in contact with me during the entire time of my incarceration in prison.

I went into my incarceration just having been told that I was a career criminal. I internalized that and believed it. I had this kind of hate towards the prosecutor, this white lady, but she was a person of authority, so I believed what she said. It's only now that I understand that the brain is not fully developed until the mid-twenties. Adolescent brains are very moldable. And mine had been molded. I was a career criminal. Thus, I went into prison maintaining that thought and fulfilling that prophesy. My mentor, Dr. Bode, saw a different narrative. He saw a different trajectory. And he began investing in my potential from the very beginning—literally investing money and time into my growth.

Father's Inspiration

My dad and I had fallen off as I was making the poor decisions that led to my incarcerations. Almost immediately upon my prison incarceration, my dad's health quickly began to plummet. Piece by piece, over the course of two years, doctors began amputating his lower limbs up to his torso—to the point that he was literally and physically half the man I had known him to be. Before I could reconcile our relationship, he fell into a coma and lost his battle with type 2 diabetes. This was emotionally devastating. Death, suffering, and grief are extremely challenging in any setting. But in a prison setting, emotional challenges such as grief are exacerbated to the highest level. You can't cry in prison. You can't be sad or show emotion in prison.

In prison, you must bottle this emotional pain up. You must tuck it away and hide it someplace deep inside your psyche. Deep inside your bones. Deep inside your soul. For many people, this internal pain matriculates externally by inflicting pain and suffering on others. But, for me, I used this emotional devastation as inspiration. My dad remains my inspiration.

I read my first scientific manuscript on diabetes while I was locked in my cage. I was familiar with diabetes before prison. I knew that my dad had diabetes. I was even familiar with the fact that diabetes occurred more among Black people. But I was completely blind to how the disease could take someone from being relatively healthy to the state of internal deterioration that my dad was in. It was as if his body was eating him alive. I had no idea what diabetic necrosis was. If you've never seen diabetic necrosis of the foot, I don't suggest that you google it. It is not a sight for sore eyes. It looks as if something is eating the flesh, because that is exactly what is happening.

I felt an extreme amount of guilt for my dad falling so ill so quickly after my departure. I combatted this guilt and emotional distress with wanting to know more about the disease that was killing my father. I was deeply driven to learn more about the cellular and molecular processes going on inside the body of someone with diabetes. I wanted to know the mechanisms of these processes, so that I could one day potentially find therapies to keep people like my dad alive longer, so that people like his son could have them in their lives longer to properly help them mature as young men.

With scientific reading, every other word is something that you've never heard of before. Aside from "a" and "the" and "an," every word requires a dictionary. Medical reading is like alphabet soup. There were no medical dictionaries to purchase in prison. The dictionaries available were tiny and useless past third-grade reading.

This is where Dr. Bode stepped in heavily. We would essentially have an in-depth scientific journal club over the course of weeks via short phone calls and long letters. This took place while I was still at NECC before treatment—before knowing I was going to be released. I was learning simply based on the passion for knowledge, learning, and self-growth. Bode had been planting the seed for me to continue my education upon release, but the idea for applying to PhD programs did not come into serious play until treatment. It was a long, difficult, and curvy psychological, mental, and emotional roller coaster to move from the thinking of being a career criminal (as I had thought of myself earlier in my incarceration) to now seeing myself as a scholar with the potential and ability to continue my education. I was ready. I wanted to continue my education.

It was at night that I would engulf massive amounts of scientific articles. I recall the serenity of it. Late at night, with the cage as quiet as it was going to get, me wedged between the thin mattress of my top bunk and the solid concrete of the ceiling. If I bent my legs as I read, my knees nearly touched the ceiling. But I transcended out of the physical space as I read. When I turned on my nightlight and, for hours, immersed myself in scientific terms and envisioned the cellular process of glucose absorption, I was free. I fell in love with science and medicine in my prison cell. I spent hours and weeks just breathing it. While at the high-medium-security prison (NECC), reading scientific articles was one of my primary excitements in life. It was worth the guards shining a light in my face at night to startle me away from my reading. I knew I was about to be exploring new places in my head that would get me out of prison. I would be inside *that* cell—a human cell, not a prison cell.

✦ ✦ ✦

Dr. Bode suggested that I submit at least six to eight applications to various programs of higher education with varying degrees of difficulty regarding admissions. I ended up starting seven applications and submitting to six programs (all in Missouri, as I had to stay in the state): (1) the University of Missouri's School of Medicine's physiology program, (2) the Saint Louis University's School of Medicine's biomedical program, (3) the Saint Louis University's biology program, (4) the Washington University in St. Louis's School of Medicine biomedical program, (5) the Washington University in St. Louis's biology program, (6) the University of Missouri St. Louis's biology program; and (7) Lindenwood's business program.

Jennifer was big pregnant, moved out of our house, and with another man. Yet, she stayed in contact with me and helped me with the applications. We were not together. We had both truly and finally given up the idea of being together. But we were very much still close friends. Some people would have said, "Fuck that cheating bitch. She went and got pregnant behind my back. I don't ever want to talk to her." I didn't think that way. I never had. I had done a lot of growing in prison. But that part of me had always been there—seeing the good in people was always part of me. I am certain that I would not have been able to put the seven applications together had it not been for Jennifer.

There were three big hurdles to submitting the applications. One, all of them *had* to be submitted online. There was not an ability to submit paper applications, clearly discriminating against people in prison as there was no internet access in prison. Finding this one small fact (inability to submit paper applications) alone took several weeks.

Which led to hurdle number two, communications and searching the web. If you've ever applied to anything, then you know that you generally have to click through many pages on that employer's or school's website to find answers to questions that you have. Well, in prison, I could not surf the web for details about the application process. For instance, I was ready to write a personal statement, but who would I address the statement to? Did I have to address it to someone? Would not addressing it to someone make my application look different? Would they be able to tell I'm in prison because of that? Did their application page clearly say, "Address to so and so"? Those tiny nuances added weeks to the process. As these questions popped up, I would write them down. Then I would both write them in a letter to a designated person or I would have to talk to the person on the phone during my limited phone access time. But after that first communication via letter or phone, I would then have to wait for them to go search the web for the answer. Then I'd have to wait to get a letter back or until I talked on the phone again. This was a strong lesson in patience. One simple question, "Who do I address my personal statement to?" could take two to three weeks to get an answer because of poor communication and lack of internet.

All of this led to the third hurdle, the carceral mail system and the carceral values. I would have been able to know the answer to "Who do I address the statement to?" had I been able to receive application packets from the various schools I was applying to. But the prison system saw "big" application and information packets from universities of higher education as contraband. ALL the mail sent by the various universities far exceeded the five-page limit per mail parcel, as many of these packets were information booklets. I fought tooth and nail all the way up to the warden with this. What was the reason and logic behind only allowing five pages? Furthermore, even if there was logic behind not allowing a person's family or friend to send in more than five pages, what was the logic behind not allowing a *school of higher education* to not send in more than five pages? I was trying to better myself and that was literally against the rules. I had so many packets intercepted as contraband that I got a violation for it—which was ridiculous, because a person can't necessarily control who sends them mail.

To overcome this obstacle, I would have the information packets sent to a friend and then have them break the packet down into five-page parcels. If it were an information booklet, they would literally have to rip the book up into individual pages. In some cases, the booklet was fifty-plus pages. Thus, it was mailed to me as ten-plus parcels of mail. Imagine the tediousness of having to do this and to not be doing it for you, but for someone else who was locked up in a cage. On top of that, in all honesty and truth, you thought it was a waste of time because this person was a criminal. He would never get into these programs. Despite many of them believing this, they still spent many tedious hours helping me out. I was supported by some great human beings.

Just to get the information for one program was anywhere from ten to twenty separate parcels of mail. I was applying to seven programs. Seven times twenty is 140 separate parcels of mail. This created another violation. A person is only allowed to keep a certain amount of mail at one time. I was often in violation of having too much mail. The guards knew I was applying to school, so they would search my cell more frequently just so they could find my application materials and take them from me. They would also mock me and call me a nerd, among other things. The additional problem with this system was the mail never came at the same time. When a friend broke down a packet and sent ten-plus parcels of mail to me, I would receive two one day, three the next day, two more the following day, and so forth. Although they sent them at the same time, it would take a week or more to get them and they were not in order—which quickly led to me asking my friends to number the parcels appropriately.

It was a beast to say the least. I could not have accomplished this without my friend factory. To not put too much on any one person, I assigned a different friend to send each application information packet. Jennifer's organization and thoroughness were key factors in this process. Stephany, Keisha, Cortney, Jennifer, and Julie each had distinctive roles. In my head, I knew each of them had a different application they were helping me with. Jennifer was helping me with all of them. Jennifer was recruited to help with one of the most tedious of tasks, typing up all my handwritten statements. Each application called for a personal statement and a research statement. I had no idea how to write a good personal or research statement. This is where Bode stepped into the friend factory. Before the statements were sent to Jennifer for typing, they were sent to Bode for editing. Then Bode hand-edited them (I would double-space my hand-typed letters to allow room for Bode's edits) and sent them back to me. Once back in my hands, after massive editing from Bode, I rewrote them, very neatly, to send to Jennifer for typing. Jennifer typed them up, then mailed a physical copy to me to keep for my records and emailed a copy to the respective person taking care of that application.

The respective person handling that application (Stephany, Keisha, Cortney, Jennifer, and Julie) then began the online submission process. This was another tedious back-and-forth that took weeks. Some of it required me to be on the phone with them as they filled in the online application.

All the applications asked the dreaded question, "Have you ever been convicted of a felony? If yes, please explain." This made my stomach cringe each time. I answered yes on all of them. All of them gave two lines to explain. I cannot even explain one of my convictions in two lines, much less all three of them. Additionally, some of the applications asked for misdemeanors and arrests. Explaining all my arrests would take days. I was not as savvy as I am now with writing up a response to the convictions question. No one in my friend factory had experience with this. But I mustered up some form of remorseful response.

When all was said and done, I successfully submitted six of the seven applications. I was extremely happy and proud and very thankful for my friend factory. It took me months on months to put together each application. But the rejections came within days, one after another, rejection,

rejection, rejection! I applied to six programs. I was rejected from all but one. The one my mentor, Dr. Bode, was on the admission committee for at Saint Louis University. Saint Louis University gave me a second chance. Dr. Bode and my support system helped facilitate that second chance.

This was the last picture I have of my dad and I. It was taken in December 2007, 10-months before my prison incarceration. My dad passed weeks after my return from prison. Although sepsis had taken over his body and he had moved into a comatose state, I was fortunate to be with him and family during his last moments. One of his last wishes was that my siblings and I unite and fly like geese each taking turns leading the way.

Mom and pops. One of my mom's and dad's last pictures together.

Organization of Phone Calls While Applying. I was not nearly as organized prior to prison. I only had five to ten minutes on phone calls, so I made lists well in advance on what I needed to discuss. This list represents about $300 worth of calls over six months. Having the resources to apply the way I did was a privilege most did not have.

Getting Out

In this great nation of America, we incarcerate more people than any other nation in the world. More than two million Americans[2] are locked in cages.[3] We incarcerate at a rate higher than most third-world countries that have extremely heinous punishment systems. In fact, we incarcerate two to four times as much as our closest competitors, places we consider Communist and to have primitive politics, like Russia and China. The US accounts for only 5 percent of the world population[4] but 25 percent of the incarcerated population around the globe.[5] One-fourth of people locked in cages around the globe are right here in this great nation of America.

When I was finally released from prison, it was one of the most joyous days of my life. But, although I was free, I was still shackled. I could walk, but I couldn't run. I was ready to use education to break my shackles.

I still had the remnants of incarceration all over me. I still had to deal with the collateral consequences of incarceration. I was seen as a convict. A felon. A career criminal. A lifetime lowlife. A second-class citizen. I had this mark on me. This scarlet letter. This bracelet of damnation. My shackles. I was free, but I would soon learn that I was still in chains.

Barely anyone ever sleeps the morning they are to be released. In the prison counting system, you never counted the day you were to be released; instead that day was call "the wakeup" because they would release you at, like, three in the morning. So, if you had one week until your release, in prison, we would say, "six days and a wakeup." My wakeup had come.

"Andrisse. Pack it up. C'mon, let's go." The officer came by and got me from my open bay cell.

I followed him to an unfamiliar place along an unfamiliar path. We got to this unfamiliar location and I was handed a bag of clothes and a bus pass, and he pointed me towards the door.

"You're free to go," the officer said.

I looked at him, confused. "Where do I go?"

He pointed to the door once more. The door was a regular door. I had not seen a regular door in so long. I walked out and stepped into the early morning air. It was as if I had never smelled before in my entire life. It was as if I had never breathed before in my entire life. I had literally only taken one step outside the door, but the air smelled different. It smelled fresher and cleaner. It filled up my lungs in a different way. It was as if I could feel every molecule of oxygen being metabolized inside every single cell in my body. It was exhilarating. It was relieving. It was soothing. I was free.

I walked to the shuttle bus and, before I got in, I looked back at the prison. It looked different from this side. It looked like a regular building. It was almost as if it were a mirage, because I knew it was not a regular building. I knew that on the other side it was a stratosphere of dehumanization and hopeless despair. It was a dungeon of individuals whose souls and morale had been ripped out of their chests, whose bodies had been shackled and warehoused, whose minds had been deprived and devalued. Yet, in a very odd way, I felt as if I were leaving home instead of returning home. With this thought, a cold shiver went through my body. I turned and stepped into the shuttle, hoping to have closed this chapter in my story.

I was off to the airport, which was about a forty-five-minute drive to the KC area. I stepped out of prison and, within hours, I was stepping onto an airplane.

My pants and shirt were very baggy. I quickly noticed at the airport that people were no longer wearing baggy clothes. I felt out of place and as if everyone knew I was a convict.

❖ ❖ ❖

The thirty-minute flight finally landed. My brother Will and my not-so-little angels, his twin daughters, picked me up from the airport.

Will hugged me. The girls hugged me. "Uncle Stan! Uncle Stan!"

Will talked a mile a minute the entire car ride. I think I talked back, but I can't recall much. I was having another one of those out-of-body experiences. It had been two years since we'd seen each other.

"I thought you would be bigger with all that working out you said you were doing with that 300 mess," Will commented.

When we got to my mom and pop's house, everyone was there to greet me. Everyone was excited and happy. I was very excited. I felt like I was looking down at myself. There were lots of hugs and laughs and small talk. When I finally came to, after about an hour or more of exchanging pleasantries, I went to go see Jennifer. Jennifer and Julie were waiting at my house to greet me. My family and I invited her over, but she declined, stating that would be too difficult and awkward for her. She was nine months pregnant and due any minute. She had been sending me pictures of her in the earlier days of her pregnancy but had stopped. Before that, I had not gone more than a month without seeing her. But it had now been over seven months. This was the longest time we had gone without seeing each other in over a decade.

❖ ❖ ❖

Will dropped me off at my house, which was a few minutes from my mom and pop's house. He knew I was going to see Jennifer.

"You good, bro? You need me to stay with you?" Will asked, concerned. Will, as well as most other people, was angry at Jennifer.

I chuckled at my brother's comments and the thoughts I knew he was having. "I'm good, bro. We're good." I looked at him with brotherly love. "I swear it, bro. She and I are good. We've moved on, but we're still friends."

He nodded in disbelief, but agreement, and drove off.

I walked in my front door to Jennifer and Julie both screaming, "Welcome home!" Both with huge smiles on their faces. Julie walked over to me first and gave me a big, long hug.

Jennifer hesitated. "Don't mind my ginormous belly." She laughed and smiled as she hugged me, and we embraced for what could have been a very long time or possibly an extremely short time. But however long the embrace was, it ended with both of us feeling a little awkward, as if Julie were looking at us, thinking, "What are you two doing? You're not about to start kissing or crying, are you?" We did not kiss nor cry.

I had mentally conditioned myself for this moment. The conditioning had worked. I did not feel the urge to kiss her nor to cry. But I was very excited to see and hug her.

Jennifer smiled at me a long time as she was looking me up and down, still standing in the foyer where they had rushed up on me. She said softly, "I'm so glad you're home safe, Stan. I'm sorry it's not how we first envisioned it."

"We're past that, Jennifer. It's all good," I mustered.

After these greetings, Jennifer and Julie very excitedly took me on a tour of my own house. Things were rearranged. They had taken my clothes out of storage and placed them back in the closets for me. They had stocked my fridge with food and cleaned the entire house. She then took me on a tour of outside, reminding me of how to maintain the yard, etc. Then she took me to my car and gave me my car keys. I had two cars, both bought with drug money.

I felt guilty that I still had drug money stashed away. That I had a house mostly paid for with drug money and cars paid for with drug money. Over the next few months, I donated my remaining drug money to local charities.

I got home on a Friday morning. I was fortunate to be starting Saint Louis University's PhD program that following Monday. One week from the day I returned home, that next Friday, I would receive my first paycheck from Saint Louis University. A monthly stipend received on the last Friday of the month. Bode and my new mentor Dr. Jonathan Fisher had it arranged that I would get paid for the entire month, despite only working one week. I was blessed beyond blessings. Everyone in my life had helped bring me to where I was that day coming home.

My stipend was $15,000 per year. It was not much—and definitely not what I was used to pre-prison—but it was something and I was extremely happy for it.

"So that's it, Stan," Jennifer said as the tour was over, Jennifer and Julie both still smiling ear to ear.

The departure was once again awkward. I felt the urge to just sit and talk to her, and I could tell she felt the same. But her now-fiancé was waiting for her back at their house. They departed and left me alone at my house. Jennifer and I remained real friends and Facebook friends for a long time (which many thought was weird), commenting on each other's posts and sending congratulations and encouragement to each other for various things. Jennifer's son was born ten days after my return. When she posted on Facebook, I congratulated her. We would text and talk frequently for a while when I first returned, but that eventually dissipated. I would only see her one other time in person after coming home, effectively closing that ten-year chapter in my life.

❖ ❖ ❖

In true Will fashion, Will had planned an extravagant welcome home party. He gave me one week to get myself in order and, the second weekend I was home, after just getting a one-month paycheck, I was on a party bus with nearly forty close friends and family. Drake was the new hot artist and called himself "Drizzy," which is what they were calling me on the inside before Drake came out. His new song was a perfectly fitting theme song for my "Welcome Home, StanDrisse" party. Drake's song "Miss Me" blasted through the speakers, and I sang every single word as if I had written it.

❖ ❖ ❖

Welcome Home Party—I'm on the far right. (c. 2010)

Reconnecting with friends and family—I'm in the bottom middle portion. (c. 2010)

Remnants of Prison—Felony Disenfranchisement

The present carceral system grabs a strong and highly detrimental hold on the human psychology. Studies like "Prevalence of Posttraumatic Stress Disorder in Prisoners" show that nearly 80 percent of people who leave prison have some degree of post-traumatic stress disorder, now classified as prisoner PTSD.[6] As much as I did to keep myself out of the institutionalized way of thinking and behaving while I was on the inside, I was not much different than many others that leave prison. I was extremely damaged, emotionally and psychologically. I thought I had made it through relatively unscathed. I was very wrong, and I would have to come to that difficult realization before I could truly begin my healing.

The remnants of incarceration are diabolical. Angela Davis said it best: "History is a weapon"[7] used against us and we are not even aware of it most of the time. Reflecting on the carceral system after leaving it slightly unveils the masked racism entangled in the intricate web of societal, structural, and systematic racism. Leaving prison results in the uncontrivable new perspective of seeing the world through a new lens. Now, I was seeing the Black achievement gap, which people like Melinda Anderson explain so well, from a different perspective.[8] I was seeing it from an "inside mass incarceration" lens. I was now hyperaware of what new studies were showing: disproportionate imprisonment rates faced by people of color contribute to race-based inequalities in educational attainment. I had just begun reading those studies, but I did not need to read those studies. I lived the truth of these studies. I walked the yard with the fathers who were separated from their children at a young age and heard the stories of their kids then getting entangled in the web, only to soon join their fathers in walking the yard.

I very intimately lived the employment struggle of a formerly incarcerated person with multiple criminal convictions on my record. As the Prison Policy Initiative's report stated, "I was out of prison and out of work."[9] Unemployment among formerly incarcerated people was 27 percent in 2010 when I returned home. This was nearly five times higher than the general public's unemployment and this was moving into the height of the 2010 recession due to the housing market crash. The unemployment rate for formerly incarcerated people was higher than the unemployment rate during the Great Depression of the US. This was considered to be the worst economic time of our country's history.

❖ ❖ ❖

I applied everywhere and every day, it felt like. I applied to grocery stores and department stores. Gas stations and corner shops. I was denied by all of these. One of the most disheartening denials was from my coaching job. My high school basketball coach, Bart Suellentrop, had recently connected with me on Facebook and asked if I would come be the head coach of the JV team for his school. He was now at a small Catholic high school in South St. Louis. I was ecstatic at this opportunity. He stated to me that I was the best defensive player he'd ever coached. I attribute much of my resilience to his coaching philosophy.

I started coaching the team early because he needed me ASAP. I started before all my paperwork had cleared. I told him about my having just got back from prison and all the things I was convicted of.

He brushed it off, stating, "Stan, I know you very well. You were not only my best defensive player ever. You were one of the best people I've coached, period. I've explained your situation to the principal and that I've known you since you were a kid. I told him that I'd trust you with anything in the world. The principal's on board. Don't worry."

So, I began coaching. I poured my heart and soul into these South City fifteen- to seventeen-year-olds. I was in my thirties by this time, but I still looked very much like a teenager. I was still muscular, cut, and very athletic. My players easily related to me. They saw me as one of them. I would often run full court with them, pulling up from five feet behind the arc as I curled around a screen, busting jays in their face like Steph Curry. Shouting out loud in excitement when I hit a tough shot, talking smack to them. I felt my youth again. It was one of the funnest times of my life. I was in school and doing research at Saint Louis University from nine to five but would leave early to rush to the South Side to make it to practice from 4:00 to 6:30 p.m. and the coaches' meeting from 6:30 to 7:00 p.m. Coach Suellentrop gave me nearly complete autonomy, aside from a few offensive plays and structures modeled off of Syracuse. After practices and after my PhD studies and prepping for research, by midnight or so, I would begin poring over online videos of Syracuse's offensive structure and their full-court press. I drafted over thirty plays and I had a coach's clipboard and lanyard whistle. I was official.

The team was a mix of misfits and some skilled players that needed discipline and coaching. They needed discipline on the court and off the court. Some of them had begun entering the street life of South City. I was the perfect on-the-court *and* off-the-court coach. They had my cell number and often called or texted if having difficulty in the classroom or in the streets. I was more than a coach. I was their mentor and friend.

Two days before our first game on the first Friday night of St. Louis-area prep sports basketball—and two months being these kids' head coach and mentor—after seeing them six times per week for roughly three hours per day (Monday through Friday, and Saturday morning practices), I excitedly walked into an extremely quiet and desolate locker room. I had my Nike tear-away pants on with Nike basketball shorts underneath. I had my clipboard with plays and whistle dangling from my neck. I was ready to prep for the final practice before our game.

Coach Suellentrop turned and looked behind him as he saw the kids looking as if they saw a ghost. His back was initially facing me as he was addressing the players.

Coach Suellentrop had a slight stutter when he was angry, saddened, or disappointed. He had the same stutter fifteen years ago when I was his player. "You…you…you didn't get my message, did you?"

I looked at him, shrugging and shaking my head. "No." I was rushing from school and research. I never checked my voicemails.

He stated, "I called you several times and left a message." He walked over and put his hands on my shoulder. "Let's step outside."

He explained to me that not only was the school firing me, but they also had put a restraining order on me and I was not allowed to step foot on the campus nor get within a hundred yards of any of the students under any circumstances. I was dumbfounded and extremely hurt. I was holding back tears as he was telling me this. These were not just my players. They were my mentees, my students, my trainees. We had formed a unique and strong bond.

"I'm sorry, Stan. I thought I could make it work," Coach stated with disappointment as he and a security guard escorted me out of the facility.

I sat in my car in the parking lot and, for the first time in a long time, I cried. Not because of losing the job. I had lost or not gained many jobs. It was deeper than that. I was saddened by who I was, by who society thought I was, by what society saw me as. I was nothing more than a criminal. Always was, as the prosecutor had stated those many years ago, and always would be, as the career criminal stamp on my name indicated.

The carceral system grabs a strong and detrimental hold on the human psyche. I was beaten down more than I had known. Two days later I found myself sneaking into the Chaminade gymnasium where my team was set to play their first game. I thought to myself, *How far is a hundred yards? If I'm in the back of the stands, at the top of the bleachers, that has to be a hundred yards, right?* As I walked in the gym with my hoodie up and sweatpants on, despite being a PhD student at the time, I felt like a criminal. Trying to hide my face from my students or any school staff that might recognize me, I felt that I looked like a criminal. Was I a criminal? Was I breaking the law? I paid to get in and went to the top of the bleachers with my head down. I had already gotten to know the parents, so they would have recognized me. I sat alone in a corner. I felt momentarily safe as no one recognized me. I never moved a muscle from that seat, fearing my criminality. I had to use the bathroom and wanted some popcorn at halftime, but I remained seated the entire game.

My guys ended up winning. I was proud. The smile on my face was magnanimous. I felt good. I felt the risk was worth it. I had done something good. My kids played like warriors. They were scrappy. They perfected the full-court press. They were underdogs but played like champions. They played like ten mini-mes, just as I had coached them to be. As they shook hands and left the court, I stood up and lifted my fist. One of them stared intently at me and smiled. He recognized who I was. I snuck out before anyone else saw me. I never attended any of their other games. I could not bear the feeling of criminality, nor the fear of potentially being sent back to complete my ten-year sentence if I got caught.

The next day they ended up winning the championship game of this opening tournament in a bracket that was two classes above what we were. Chaminade (where Justin Tatum went to school, who now is an NBA star with the Boston Celtics) was the highest class in the state (class 5A). We were 3A, but that weekend we played amongst the Goliaths… and David won.

The players texted me all night that night, proclaiming that they had mounted a petition that had been signed by over a hundred students to get me back. The school only had three hundred students. I was sitting at a local happy hour spot with my good friend Cortney, showing him all the text messages. He was sad for me and proud of me, all at the same time.

❖ ❖ ❖

I would often get cold chills in the middle of the night. I would have these dreams or, more appropriately, nightmares, where I was half awake and could see myself in the bed, but I could not wake up. I would be fighting with all my might to move my body. I'd put all my will into it.

"Stan! Move your arm! Wiggle your toe! *Wake up!*" But I could not move. I was paralyzed. Most of the time, I would be approaching a part in the dream where I was about to die or be re-incarcerated, or I was incarcerated, and I was about to be stabbed or beaten to death. I would often scream in my sleep, but it was only barely audible in real life, as if it were a whimper from a child.

I would have dreams of smoking weed at a real party I had just went to where people were indeed smoking weed. Or I would have a dream where I would be getting caught with bricks in my trunk after really having had contact with one of my past hustle-mates, all of which would result in the very real feeling of me being sent back to prison. This was not an unrealistic fear. I had served 30 percent of my ten-year sentence, three years. I still had seven years left. Being on parole, they could send me back to do the remainder of my time for any little mistake.

After finally waking up and never truly being able to get out of my sleep paralysis,[10] I'd have only a vague memory of having had a dream, meaning I would never actually recall those scary paralysis moments on that day. Thus, I would only wake up thinking, *Did I really smoke last night? Did I really call and talk to my connect?*

I would check my call logs on my cell. I would go inspect the trunk of my car, often spending the entire day frantically and nervously giving it a complete interior detail, all the while worrying that the police were going to swarm up in a brigade of black SUVs with guns blazing. I would be terrified inside but hiding it. Sometimes I would have friends over, watching me in this frenzy, and I was unable to communicate what I was feeling or going through.

Sleep paralysis is deemed harmless by many medical professionals unless it is highly recurrent. In this case, they are likely due to stress, PTSD, high anxiety, or bipolar disorder. Mine were highly recurrent and they affected my entire day—sometimes my entire week. Many times, the only thing that would dampen the fright would be when I visited my PO next, which might be a week or more later, and the PO didn't arrest me. Only then would I begin to feel that the dream was not real.

❖ ❖ ❖

One thing that really soothed my soul and dampened my anxiety and undiagnosed prisoner's PTSD was staying in contact with my prison friends, which coincidentally is grounds for parole violation. I'd send tons of letters and flicks (the name for pictures in prison). The letters would tell of my stories on college campuses and parties and places I'd visit. I'd send pictures of me surrounded by college girls at parties and in bikinis by the pool with headlines such as "This Is College." My close friends Jerry and Rahmari enthusiastically wanted in, they'd tell me.

It seemed that every other month or so I would be welcoming a new friend home. My ritual was standard. I would take them out to dinner at Hooters, which had a good happy hour and scantily dressed women who were paid to flirt with customers. Great wings, fifty-inch, flat-screen, HD sports surrounding the walls, and female attention. It was a combination that resulted in extreme gratitude every single time.

"Stan, you the shit, man!" Dion exclaimed. I paid for Dion as I did everyone else I had treated to the experience. Dion pleaded for me not to pay. Dion was heavy in the game and, despite just getting out, was still sitting on several hundred grand.

"So, you still on that good shit?" Dion asked, smirking as he licked his fingers, with chicken grease and chipotle honey hot sauce all over his lips and face.

I laughed at him and handed him a paper towel. "That chipotle honey is fire, ain't it!" I exclaimed, trying to change the subject.

"I don't need a towel, Drisse. I'm still gutter with it." He laughed, maintaining many of the prison mannerisms I too still had and was fighting to rid myself of.

I laughed again, looking the other direction at one of the Hooters girls, hoping her slim waist, thick thighs, and caramel skin would steal the conversation. It did, but only momentarily. This meeting for Dion was an attempt to beguile me back in the game. It did not work. I told him I was out a long time ago. Dion still received the full treatment of "Stan's Welcome Home Experience."

I still vividly remember picking Dion up that day. Before we left for the night, he picked up his little man and twirled him in the air to an exorbitant number of giggles and coos. His son was very young, just a baby, when Daddy went away to prison for five years. His son, Tray, was happy to be able to talk to Dad without having to go through metal detectors and no longer had to be given some weird explanation on why Daddy couldn't hug or kiss him. I also met Dion's mom, who was standing at the door when I picked him up. Dion was only staying there for a short while until his drug moves were in place. I had heard all about his plans that night as him and I were kicking it.

In the notoriously violent O'Fallon Park neighborhood of North St. Louis, not more than a week after I had been with him and not more than one month since he had been home, Dion[11] was shot twice in the chest and once in the head as his six-year-old son cried hysterically, strapped in his car seat just an arm's reach from his dad's lifeless body oozing out deep red blood. Dion's mom's house was only a few blocks away. This was the neighborhood he grew up in. His mother informed me of his services. I was frightened to even attend. My criminality was in heightened format. What if someone recognized me or thought that I was involved? I attended with an all-black Jay-Z-style coat with my hood up. Again, feeling the criminal all over my body despite being only a short while away from obtaining my PhD. I could not help this feeling when it came over me.

It was not the first time a close friend of mine had been killed since returning from prison. A year earlier, one of my friends and lieutenants, Jason Pruitt, had fallen victim to the streets. He was moving semi-big weight when I met him before prison and then I plugged him, upgrading him to a whole new level. He was shot dead in North St. Louis in a petty street corner deal gone bad.[12] I couldn't help but feel the criminal all over me once more. I felt guilt and responsibility for his death. When he was hustling with me, he wasn't a street corner dealer. He was moving quarter keys and bricks. Deals were made inside nicely furnished houses and apartments. I felt as if it were my fault, that he had moved back to being a street dealer. This was my perverse brain at work. Blaming my criminality for all that was wrong in the world around me. The deaths of J. P. and Dion took a heavy toll on me for a long time—and still do.

Around the same time as J. P.'s passing, my friend Kenny-Mo had returned home from prison. If it were not for Kenny-Mo saving me from the AB boys, I may not be here. Kenny-Mo was gunned down in the streets not too long after he had returned home for the fourth time. He always told me that he would either die in prison or the streets and that he would prefer to die in the streets. He fulfilled his own prophesy, a prophesy that I am quite certain he did not understand, that was bestowed upon him by a force he was not even fully aware of—structural and systematic racism leading to mass incarceration. Yet, he owned that prophesy as his own. I was deeply saddened to see him go.

Felony Disenfranchisement

I once sat at the polls for three long hours, waiting while a nice little old lady called every public official in the state of Missouri to try and help this excited young man vote in the Obama 2012 election. I knew I was a "convicted felon" and I knew I could not vote. But, like many other things in my life, I thought, *Hey, what does it hurt to give it a try?* Twenty-plus calls later and an answer direct from the governor's office: this nice old white lady, who was pushing ninety years old, pulled me to the side and whispered to me, "The governor's office says you are a criminal."

This rejection brought me back to my prison cell. Although I was free, I was still a slave. By this time, I was trusted to make scientific contributions that advanced the well-being of our society, but society did not want me to vote. I was brought back to the euphoric agony of the 2008 historic Obama-McCain presidential election. I was incarcerated at the time; I saw people staring through tiny four-by-six-inch windows on their prison cell doors at a small TV in the common area. I saw cell mates looking through the top three inches and the other person looking through the bottom three inches. This violated the unspoken personal space prison code of ethics, but that night was an exception. That night, we witnessed the election of the first Black US president. In prison, we had a designated light-out time, but the guards made an exception and left the TV on all night so that we could follow the election.

There were four hundred incarcerated people in my unit (90 percent were Black). I will never forget that day and how loud it was. People were banging on the doors in excitement and singing in unison the new song by Young Jeezy, "My President," hopeful that change was coming. It was a euphoric experience, but the agony of thinking that I'd never be able to vote was psychologically painful.

Because of felony disenfranchisement,[13] my home state of Missouri does not allow people convicted of a crime to vote[14] until three years after the end of their supervision. For nearly seventeen years, they took away my constitutional right as a US citizen to vote for the people who will run our country.

Twenty-five percent of the Black population in Florida could not vote[15] at the time of this writing. Disenfranchisement in Florida was at the heart of the infamous 2000 Gore-Bush recount.[16] Disenfranchisement laws were enacted in the 1860s post-Civil War very intentionally to prevent Black people from voting. This is a policy-based extension of slavery. Mass incarceration as a continuation of slavery is explored in the Ava DuVernay documentary, *13ᵗʰ*, titled after the Thirteenth Amendment, which abolished slavery.

Forty-eight states and the District of Columbia prohibit voting while incarcerated for a felony offense. Only two states—Maine and Vermont—permit persons in prison to vote. Thirty-five states prohibit persons on parole from voting. Four states deny the right to vote to all persons with felony convictions, even after they have completed their sentences.

Racial disparities exist. More than two million African Americans, or 7.7 percent of Black adults, are disenfranchised, compared to 1.8 percent of the non-African American population. In three states—Florida (23 percent), Kentucky (22 percent), and Virginia (20 percent)—more than one in five African Americans are disenfranchised.[17]

PhD Years—Unpacking Institutionalization

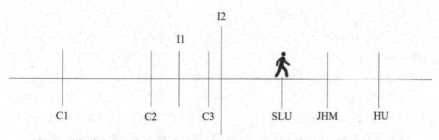

C = arrest that led to conviction; I = sentenced to incarceration; Numbers = number of that event
SLU = Saint Louis University; JHM = Johns Hopkins Medicine; HU = Howard University

"Congratulations, Mr. Stanley Andrisse! You have been accepted into the Saint Louis University Graduate School!" I read the words in the one-page letter probably a hundred times per day. I could not believe it. I could not have imagined this in a million years, not after having received so many rejection letters. Not after having been told it was not possible. Not after all the hurdles I had to go through with putting in the applications.

I was daydreaming of sitting in my prison cell, getting that acceptance letter, as I was sitting in my genetics class. We were taking the last exam of the course. I had been in the biomedical PhD program at Saint Louis University for roughly two years at that point. The PhD program required seventy-two credit hours of coursework, or roughly eighteen courses, before I could be fully advanced to candidacy. After sixty-eight credit hours, or seventeen courses in four academic semesters, I had a 4.0

grade point average (GPA). I had gotten an A+ in all my courses, and in some I had gotten 100 percent. Most of my peers were B and C students, as a C (or 70 percent) was the requirement to pass. .

"Stan, Stan!" I heard my lab mate and graduate student friend, Larry, calling my name. It took me a second to hear him. I was still daydreaming of prison and how far I had come in the two years since release.

"You're walking like a zombie, bro. Did you not hear me?" Larry said, joking but serious. "Don't tell me, you're about to go eat some nuts and berries that you foraged from the forest in Ferguson-Florissant." Larry laughed at his own joke—a joke that he regularly made.

"You're jacked as shit, bro! I dream about having your body, bro. Of course, oiled up in tight-ass boxer briefs, bro! No homo," Larry continued. I cracked a smile at the last one, only because it reminded me of my cellmate, JoJo, repeatedly telling me that I looked like a real-life action figure, walking around the cell block all swelled up.

"C'mon man, that was your last test you'll ever have to take. Let's skip out on lab and hit up happy hour for some drinks. Maybe we'll bump into one of your hot students. Everything is fair game as long as you're not teaching them anymore." Larry laughed again. It was an everyday thing for Larry to have five- to ten-minute conversations with me or anyone—or a wall—without the other person saying a single word, as I had just done.

Larry was a talker to say the least, and a major Facebook stalker and quite the gossiper. It was a lot for me, very quiet, reserved, and fresh out of prison—where Larry's behaviors and loud, sarcastic mouth would have gotten him shanked in the first week, if not the first day. It was a difficult adjustment, but he and I grew to be very close friends.

Despite becoming very close, I never informed Larry of my past. I never told anyone. I was too afraid of what might happen to my career and my well-being. I was certain that, intentionally or unintentionally, a person like Larry would spread the gossip, not necessarily intending harm, but simply because it would be considered a cool story to him. Then the next thing I'd know, I'd be in a room with a bunch of white people with power telling me that I was worthless. I've been in that room many times before. I did not want to take any chances that might lead to me being in such a room again. So, I discussed my past with absolutely no one from my school or program.

I was quite certain that Bode had pulled some type of Harry Houdini trick to get me in. I never once questioned or asked Bode how he did. He never said anything, either.

On top of the fear of being found out and kicked out, the stigma of conviction was all over me. It reeked as pungently as a skunk when I walked in rooms. It laid with me as I would fall asleep every night. It drove with me and grabbed me fiercely every time I would ride by a cop car, or every time I was about to make the decision to speed through a yellow light.

Was I about to get pulled over? Would they send me back to prison? Would they shoot me when they pulled me over, knowing that I was a criminal and that no one would care?"

I lived with the stigma every single day, every single hour, every single minute of the day. It was never not on my mind. It weighed in on and interrupted every single thought I had, always reminding me that I was less than. That I was not good enough to get that A in the class. And that even if I got the A, it did not matter because no one would ever want me or hire me. And that even if I did happen to get this degree and get a job, that did not matter either, because no one would ever want to marry me or be with a criminal. Most of the time, the stigma told me to not even bother putting in that application. I didn't want to face the hurt and embarrassment of what happened in my coaching experience. They didn't want me.

Thus, despite not telling anyone, because of the stench of my stigma, I was sure that everyone knew. It was a contradiction that I was not ready to face. I had a deep gut feeling that everyone could smell the criminal on me. But I refused to tell anyone out of fear of consequences. But, if they all knew, wouldn't the consequences have matriculated? One would think that would be the logic. But this was an illogical phenomenon. It was a deep feeling of guilt and shame. The very real truth was that society regularly sent clear messages that we don't like criminals. It's on the news every night with the wording that is used. It's on the movie screens with the titles and messages and themes of our popular films. It's on the radio in our music. It's on TV shows. The highly negative portrayal of the criminal is very real.

A 2014 report by the National Research Council showed that the experience of prison[1] and its penalties are manifold and long-lasting. The extraordinary upsurge in incarceration rates in the US beginning in the mid-1970s has resulted in hundreds of thousands of people being sent to prison, and many remained there for longer periods of time. Consequently, the amount of people suffering the collateral consequences of incarceration respectively increased. Many of the most negative collateral consequences that undermine reentry remain long after formerly incarcerated persons have been released back into the community.

Over 75 percent of people who leave prison leave with some form of mental health concern. This is intrinsic to the design of the system. They built the prison system like this purposefully. The framers of the system wanted people they saw as scum to remain scum. And if you weren't fully scum at the time of entering prison, then the prison system design will result in you being scum by the time you leave.[2]

I had heard the term "institutionalization" before from media and in conversation, most always jokingly. It had been portrayed in comedies such as *Friday* in its Deebo character. I had heard people tell me how they still took showers with their flip-flops on at their home and in their own bathroom that no one else uses. I had heard people tell me how for months after release they would stand in attention at the doorways to their home bedroom, waiting for a count officer to come by so they could rattle off their institutional number. I had heard of people preferring to make a prison pizza at home instead of ordering Papa John's. Or still putting toilet paper on the seat and on the outside or inside of the bathroom door when going number two. All of these are kind of comical, and they were always stated in a comical light.

Sadly, however, institutionalization is not a laughing matter. I, too, laughed at those jokes at one point in time. But it is difficult for me to stomach such jokes anymore. That is part of the reason it is difficult for me to watch *Orange Is the New Black* or any prison portrait in popular media. These portraits perpetuate the intentional harm and wrongdoing of the system. Again, it was designed to do just that. The process of institutionalization is necessary to help preserve the revolving door of incarceration. These comic portrayals are like the minstrels of the Jim Crow era.[3]

"Let's laugh at these dumb niggas" is what both portraits say. Black people, just as much as or more than white people, love laughing at these caricatures of incarceration.

❖ ❖ ❖

Here is a glimpse at the full iceberg of institutionalization as outlined by Craig Haney's work from the University of California Santa Cruz.[4]

One, there is a dependence on institutional structure and contingencies. The carceral system necessitates that incarcerated people surrender their freedom and autonomy. This setup entails an excruciating modification to most people. Some individuals never acclimate. Yet, acclimation is the goal. The system thrives from people acclimating to the turning off of self-enterprise. The system hopes that the encaged individual becomes severely dependent on institutional authority. This structure leads to people relying on the system and its agenda to coordinate their daily routine. I have witnessed many people lose their capacity to commence actions on their own and the ability to think for themselves, resulting in deeply institutionalized persons who develop an extreme discomfort upon release when freedom and autonomy is returned.

My cellmate and friend JoJo is an example of this. JoJo went in at sixteen years old for multiple cases of armed robbery. He was a young victim of the human trafficking that is the dope game. His judge and jury did not see him as a victim, but he was. He was recruited by an older person in the dope game to be a young enforcer. That would help him prove his ranks in the game and be promoted and advance. We all have a natural desire to be promoted and advance. So did JoJo. His dope dealing affiliates, his job, his company, had been robbed by another dope dealing company—or business. To most people, these companies or businesses I refer to are called gangs. The company JoJo worked at was robbed. Many companies have protocols when such an incident takes place. JoJo's company had a protocol and JoJo was ordered to follow through on that protocol. JoJo defended his company. This resulted in him being convicted of multiple robberies, attempting to get back what was stolen from his company. JoJo wouldn't so much as hurt a fly on the wall. He was not an ill-spirited person. He was a laughing man. He joked all the time. He would never spontaneously rob a random individual. He was no threat to society. He was a loyal employee in a human trafficking business.

I have intentionally worked and conditioned myself to develop the ability to hold both truths in my hand at the same time. JoJo worked for a human trafficking company. A company that was illegal. But, nonetheless, JoJo worked for a company and, furthermore, was very loyal to that company, a quality that most companies would love their employees to have—yet most people do not have this quality in such a strong capacity as JoJo did.

The punishment system forces people to become accustomed to a complex network of boundaries and limits. Violating these boundaries, "stepping out of bounds," results in quick and harsh punishment, even within the already-punishing environment: "jail inside of jail, or the hole" as explained earlier. The vigilant and constant supervision is in place under the auspices of safety, but the underlying result is punishment. A person's internal controls dissipate, or as with many young people (sixteen to twenty-four years old) entering the system, fail to develop wholly as a result of the punishment model of encaging people so vigorously with limits, plunging them so profoundly in a web of rules and regulations, and acclimating them to excessive systems of restriction. The prison system intentionally decapacitates people by making them so reliant on the system that a person loses the ability to depend on themselves. JoJo, for instance, after serving seventeen years on a twenty-year sentence, had become fully reliant on his family and social support systems. He was fortunate at thirty-four years old upon release to have that family structure in place to be reliant on. For many who do not, they return to the punishment system.

Two, institutionalization creates hypervigilance, distrust, paranoia, and suspicion. Most incarceration settings are dangerous by design. Incarcerated people must develop a sense of hypervigilance and constantly remain watchful for hints of threat or harm. As a result, people are primed to exploit vulnerability, carelessness, or inattentiveness. Thus, incarcerated people develop or cast a tough shell or image of violence as an attempt to keep others at bay.

Despite my trying very hard to avoid this aspect of institutionalization, this was true for me to some extent. Within my first weeks of prison, I was involved in a fight that I did not want to get into. I had succumbed to the forces of institutionalization. The next time I was instructed to fight without my wanting to and without it being associated with self-defense (such as after getting jumped and nearly killed), I declined, despite feeling a strong fear for my life. I figured that I would rather die with integrity than live dishonoring my personal values.

A prison study by Richard McCorkle found that fear is the main shaping tool of prison,[5] that nearly 75 percent of incarcerated people had been forced to become violent to avoid harm, and that close to a third of people in prison had access to a "shank" or other weapon to defend themselves.

Three, institutionalization involves emotional over-control, psychological distancing, and alienation. To form this violent-looking outward image, "the tough shell," a person must carefully measure their emotional responses, thus resulting in a constant, minute-by-minute internal battle to manage and conceal emotional responses to *everything*, resulting in emotional over-control. In prison, vulnerability can result in manipulation or even death. A positive result of this aspect of institutionalization is that incarcerated people develop an uncanny ability of self-monitoring and develop a radar for sensing others' emotions and anticipated actions. An incarcerated person is reading you ten steps ahead of your move. This was a survival mechanism. If you encounter a formerly incarcerated person who has escaped the revolving door of incarceration, i.e., "they've survived," it is very likely they have a high-functioning and effective emotional radar and ability to read people. It is one of the top reasons they would be in your presence as a "successfully" returned, formerly incarcerated person.

Without having done any research on the topic, I tried my best to not create this "tough shell." More accurately, it was in prison that I began dismantling the "tough shell" that I had created on the outside. I began this process by *not* using my street name and insisting people use my government name.

Four, institutionalization often encompasses social withdrawal and isolation. Social invisibility creates a safety net. People become disconnected from others. Self-imposed social withdrawal and isolation can be very damaging. It involves a deep retreat into one's self, a general distrust of people and systems, isolation, and living a life of silent despair.[6] This pattern is synonymous with clinical depression.

When my close friend SK recounts stories about me to others, he often projects this institutional aspect upon me. He talks about how I often withdrew and isolated myself and that I successfully stayed away from prison patterns and views. I isolated myself in reading, writing, and studying biomedicine, not necessarily and not intentionally as a safety mechanism. I wasn't scared of the yard. I would argue that I was much less scared of the yard than the people who routinely carried shanks on them. I had a plan, and I kept myself busy with that plan. I am an introvert by birth, so I recharge by living in my head and being alone. Although my isolation was not a safety net, I was indeed clinically depressed, as diagnosed in my pre-sentence investigation right before I was sent to prison—a diagnosis that prison counselors denied, as they did not want to give me medication and did not have the capacity to regularly deliver psychotherapy.

Five, manipulation and exploitation are norms of the prison culture. Informal rules fuel the prison code. These are unwritten but essential. Most prisons like the ones I had been at lack meaningful programming, robbing people of pro-social connections and positive activities. Most prisons don't have access to rewarding employment or educational opportunities. The system intentionally deprives people of the basic needs and desires of human existence. To procreate, to work, to acquire education, to grow, to learn, to love are all prohibited or inhibited intentionally in prison. This intentional setup was designed to drive people into the volatile prison culture.

Six, institutionalization involves a diminished sense of self-value and self-worth. People in prison are deprived of their basic human rights and forfeit control over ordinary aspects of their existence. Most people in the free world take these things for granted. We lived in tiny, deteriorating cages that were no bigger than a king bed (sixty square feet). We had no influence over whom we bunked with, despite having to share very intimate moments like brushing our teeth in the morning and coordinating with your bunkmate on when to shower, urinate, and defecate. We had little choice when to get up or go to bed, when or what to eat, and the list goes on. This continuously reminded us of our second-class social status and stigmatized criminalization. Self-worth and self-value were destroyed in these conditions. Many people, including myself, internalized this feeling of criminality and lived up to the prophesy that was bestowed upon us.

Seven, institutionalization encompasses what has been termed prisoner's post-traumatic stress disorder related to the intentional pains of prison. Incarceration is so psychologically harmful that it embodies a type of traumatic stress sufficient to generate post-traumatic stress once released. But institutionalized people hide their internal state and intimate feelings, thus creating the outward appearance of normality.

I mention all of this because I, too, was battling with the unpacking of my institutionalization more than I wanted to believe. I was constantly comparing people in the free world to people I left back in the incarcerated world. I felt more connected to those from the incarcerated world. I identified more as a person from the incarcerated world than I did as a person in the free world. Society and the system set it up for me to feel this way. I did not truly understand this at this point in my life, leaving me to *not* want to truly form bonds with people in the free world, especially people that did not know me before incarceration, i.e., my academic peers.

✤ ✤ ✤

"So, are you coming out or not?" Larry asked me once more.

I snapped out of my daze. "Yeah, why not? I'll come out for a little bit." I would often fall into these dazes, not knowing exactly how long I was in them. They could have been seconds, or hours.

Unlike the incarcerated person, people in the free world who have never been incarcerated have little understanding of all they are privileged to. This is true of white and Black people—but mostly white people and academic people. I include these groups because they were who I encountered in my personal experience in St. Louis.

My SLU peers were carefree and indulgent. Their worries were laughable and miniscule. Although laughable, I never laughed. I understood even then that everyone's feelings are valid. I also understood that stress level was deeply tied to personal experiences. Many people who've experienced tough situations have a higher tolerance for handling stress. This always reminded me of a 1990s commercial where a military person coming back from combat is asked on a job interview, "How well do you perform under pressure?" and the narrator tells the soldier to try to answer "I have been known to do well" with a straight face as the commercial is B-rolling, showing the soldier carrying one of his wounded comrades on his back through a battlefield, with explosions going off everywhere around him. This was my feeling through almost every single conversation I had in graduate school with my peers.

Most of the time I chose not to go out because I was on parole and still getting urinalyses twice per week, and these tests detected alcohol seventy-two hours after drinking; failing a urinalysis was grounds to be sent back to prison for the remainder of my ten-year sentence. I would often do Friday happy hour at 2:00 or 3:00 p.m., knowing that if I had exactly one or two drinks before 5:00 p.m. I would pass the piss test I had to take on Monday at 5:00 p.m. at my parole office. My academic peers would often coax me into going out Friday night for more fun. I would either find a way to decline or I would go out and order Sprites all night, giving the impression of a vodka Sprite. I rarely ever went out on Saturday because it was too big of a risk. That did not bother me, as I was a natural introvert and, also, I was enthralled in learning more about endocrinology and biomedicine.

More rarely, I chose not to go because I could not stomach the complaints of my peer's miniscule problems. I was often not in the mode for feigning sympathy. I had real problems, like trying to stay out of prison. Once I had a student trainee of mine spend three hours complaining about a C on a test and just that same day I had a call from SK on the inside telling me a friend of ours got stabbed and killed and that SK had been sent to the hole for two months.

My academic peers and many never-incarcerated people were very good at making small problems seem insurmountable. Larry was very good at this. I grew to be more empathetic of these stories instead of them making me uncomfortable. Oftentimes I had suggestions on how to handle the problem, but I rarely offered any comments. This helped me become a very active listener as I mostly just shut my mouth and added confirming comments here and there.

The contrast was not only present in my white and Asian academic peers. It was present in my family and Black friends and less socioeconomically stable friends as well. My first Christmas back home, my cousin and I got into a small altercation over a Spades game. I had become an expert-level Spades player. I won numerous tournaments in prison and, for most Black people in prison, Spades was an essential staple of the experience. A Spades game can get very heated. On the inside, despite the heatedness of the game, it is a requirement that you remain calm, cool, and collected. On the outside, many people get up and dance when they do a good play or yell and taunt their opponent. On the inside, you could very literally lose your life for that type of behavior. I informed my cousin of this as he was dancing and taunting, and he got upset, proclaiming that prison didn't somehow make me tougher than him.

We are a close family and we quickly got over this. But his reaction is a common reaction I get from many "successful" or "well-accomplished" Black people who've never been incarcerated. I am a very unassuming person. Even back in my days of consistently and religiously carrying a weapon, I was still rather unassuming. Many Black people are offended at the idea that I am tougher than them, despite me never claiming to be tougher than them. But they assume me being forthcoming about my prison experience is an attempt to show my toughness, thus compelling them to puff out their chest and proclaim their toughness. This is mostly in the form of "Don't get it fucked up, I'm from the hood too."

I'm not sharing these traumatic and hurtful experiences as some sort of sadistic contest. I relive these hurtful moments of my life because I truly believe they have the power to impact change. I believe this because I've seen it.

✦ ✦ ✦

Obtaining my MBA Degree—Me
and my nieces and nephews.

Falling in Love

By the end of my PhD years, things were starting to come together. I was feeling extremely proud of myself. I thought about and talked to my deceased father pretty much every day. I remember one day being curled up in my kitchen, just bawling for what had to be two to three hours straight. I was switching between talking to my departed dad and God. It was a milestone in my journey. One, I was teaching myself how to feel again, and learning that my emotions were not a bad thing. I hadn't allowed myself to regularly cry in so long. It was as if weights were being removed from my shoulder. I don't exactly recall what triggered the crying bout and emotional outpour; I believe it may have been a call from my godfather, Thomas, who'd known my dad since his teenage years in Haiti. For so long, I was holding on to the guilt that my father's passing was my fault. He was fairly strong and healthy before I went away and almost immediately plummeted when I was sent to prison. In this conversation, the voice of my father told me that I was forgiven, and that the weight of my guilt was ill-inspired. My father's voice told me how proud he was of my resilience and my strength to overcome. His voice told me how he had been watching over me in my moments of weakness. I confessed my deep remorse and sorrow for the pain I caused the family, myself, and others. I confessed the emptiness I felt about him never being able to meet my future children if I were to have any. All the grandchildren loved "Papou," and he adored them. I confessed the pain that my future children would never be immersed in his wisdom and presence. I told him that I had now fallen in love, and that it hurt for him not to know her, and it hurt even more for her not to know him. For he was so much of me and I was so much of him. His voice conveyed to me that he did know her and that he was happy for me. It was a sunny, bright-blue-sky day in the middle of spring 2014. The days were becoming long. I remember crying till nightfall and peacefully falling asleep on my couch, curled up, with his presence all around me.

Yes. You heard that correctly. I had recently fallen in love. This outburst of emotions and relieving of weight may have very likely been building up since meeting this amazing and beautiful lady, my wife Stephanie.

❖ ❖ ❖

It Only Took Six Months, but It Will Last a Lifetime

Here is the story as told by none other than the beautiful and intelligent Stephanie Andrisse herself.

"So, there I was, sitting at the bar.... That's how all great love stories start, right? I had moved in with my sister and her husband about a month prior. I didn't know anyone in St. Louis, so they took me out with them. We were at a bar for a friend's birthday party. Ashley and I were at the bar, snacking and talking, when he walked over and started talking to me. For the life of me, I could not figure out why this handsome stranger was talking to me! I nervous-laughed through the entire conversation, while Ashley just watched me and giggled. I distinctly remember wanting her to jump into the conversation and save me, because to me, I was floundering and certainly wasn't charming anyone. But apparently, I was wrong.

"It wasn't long before I received a Facebook friend request from him. I remember yelling down from upstairs, 'Ashley, he wants to be my Facebook friend!' She giggled again. She does that a lot. Then, he messaged me. It was clear he wanted to take me out, but having just disentangled myself from a rough and very serious relationship, I was not quite ready. He thought I just didn't like him. Seriously. He thought I didn't think he was cute. *eye roll*

"Anyways, with a perseverance anyone could admire, he kept messaging me every so often. *For six months.* And most of the time I did not respond to the advances. If it is not clear by now that I had completely bewitched him, I'm not sure when that's going to hit you. Man was in deep. And I still ask him how I did it, because I do not know. My bet is on the nervous-laugh and clumsy attempt at conversation. I'm sure it was that.

"Then one afternoon, at my sister's diaper party (a coed baby shower), he unexpectedly walked through the door. He was an assistant high school football coach and was still dressed in his uniform. He had not messaged me in a while, and it had been six months since I had seen him in person. He looked devastatingly handsome. He says he saw it written all over me. I would like to think I played it cool, but...well...

"We talked a little, nothing to write home about. A few days later was my birthday. He asked to take me out for dinner. I had a lot of work to do and told him I wasn't sure, that I'd get back to him. Well, papers were graded, and lessons were planned, so I really didn't have an excuse for why I shouldn't let him take me out for my birthday. (To be honest, my exact thought was, *What's the worst that could happen? That he turns out to be a jerk, but you get a free meal out of it?*)

"As it turns out, he wasn't a jerk. He was everything. So, I said yes to every other time he asked me out after then. And when he asked me to be his wife under the Empire State Building on New Year's, I, of course, said yes again.

"It took six months for him to finally get me to agree to go out with him. And there are not enough words in the English language for how thankful I am that he kept at it. I never once asked myself, *What's the best thing that could happen?* But FYI, it's this."

❖ ❖ ❖

My wife wrote that for our wedding. It's pretty accurate. We had an amazing first date—and even better first five dates. Every year since I've made her a detailed photo book of our adventures. She was an angel sent to me from heaven in the exact moment in my life that I needed her.

Difficulties with Dating

By the time, my future wife and I had gone on that first date, I had stopped dating for a little over a year. All my relationships since I had returned failed miserably. All the failures centered around one aspect of me, my felony convictions. In most of the cases, the women ran hard and fast as soon as I informed them or as soon as they found out. But in other cases, it wasn't the felony convictions itself, it was what the felony convictions had done to me. Most of my twenties had been spent caged in a prison cell, held under jurisdiction of a court room, or married to the game—not to mention that I had been in a serious relationship for nine years before prison.

While incarcerated, I regularly conditioned myself for the reality I'd face regarding obtaining employment. In detail, I would envision myself in several scenarios on a regular basis, such as being a line cook at McDonald's or a janitor at a local office building or a garbage man. I would think of these scenarios, and then I would deeply envision *how* they would make me *feel*. How I would feel when people looked at me as "just" a garbage man, or when people cussed at me through the drive-through window, or when people would pass me by every single day of the week and year and never say hi to me but were quick to motion for me to take out their trash. I conditioned myself to be okay with those feelings, if that were to be my life.

So many reentry programs are about employment, workforce development, and housing and drug abuse. **But none of these are focused on happiness or self-worth and value.** I had come to be okay with being a garbageman or janitor. My biggest fear was finding happiness and finding someone to share that happiness. I successfully conditioned myself to be okay with a low-wage job, but in terms of companionship, I was certain that the only women that would want to be with me were those who were actively entrenched in drugs and criminality like I had been.

I may have laid out a self-fulfilling prophesy, but for the first few years I was home this turned out to be true.

My grad school friends nicknamed me Luke, short for Luke Skywalker, as the tag line they had for me was "The force is strong with this one." I am a natural-born hustler. I have the gift of gab. Most people in prison do; unfortunately, it has been used to their detriment. But, if you switch the settings and I'm no longer in the streets, I'm no longer closing large-scale drug deals, and I am instead in a bar or party or barbecue, I still have the gift of gab and the ability to close deals. Talking to people—men, women, old, young, privileged. disadvantaged—is not intimidating to me. It comes easy.

One night we were at a bar. There was a group of attractive women with a group of fittingly attractive men to accompany them. This establishment drew the higher end of the socioeconomic ladder. This group was perfectly fitting for this setting. All the girls were in what was likely very expensive, authentic designer clothing. I looked clean as I always did, but I wasn't wearing designer. My grad student friends, Larry and Sam, were ogling these girls as they normally did. The group was clearly celebrating the girl who Larry and Sam deemed to be the "hottest" out of the group, and the guy next to her was clearly her man. Mostly because I was tired of their ogling and putting this girl on a pedestal, I decided to approach the group at the opportune time, the group picture.

It appeared that I happened to be at the right place at the right time. I asked if they needed me to snap some pics. I shot a few silly pics, got the girls to laugh hysterically, told a few guy jokes and got the men to feel comfortable with me, shot the pedestal girl a few genuine compliments as she was indeed attractive, and then asked if I could take some selfies with the birthday girl. All of a sudden we were in a selfie photoshoot with her making silly-lipped faces and her arms wrapped around me tightly, right in front of her man. I had the best camera phone on the market and my selfie skills were impeccable. The pics looked great. I had the facial smoother on, so she looked even more attractive. She loved them. I complimented them. I complimented her again, enticing her to want the pics. She wanted the pics.

So, I said, "How can I send them to you?" She grabbed my phone and quickly put her number in and texted herself the pics. I now had her name and her number, right in front of her man. She then asked if she could find me on Facebook so she could tag me, and she did.

Thus began my title of "Luke"—because the force was strong with me.

But therein lie my conundrum. I had no problem getting girls. I had problems keeping them once they found out about my past. This led to the outward appearance that I had a lot of women. It looked as if I were getting all these women, probably having sex with them, and then getting rid of them once I got what I wanted. But this couldn't be further from the truth. The girls were dumping and getting rid of me.

For instance, the attractive girl who posted our selfies on Facebook? Nothing ever came of that, mostly because I was vehemently against pursuing girls that had a man. I remember very distinctly that feeling of someone else literally sleeping in my bed. Despite nothing coming of it, for people following my Facebook, it seemed like Stan was up to his shenanigans again.

I didn't really know how to use social media when I first came out. It had blown up when I was away. I slowly learned to dial down on posting the selfies of me with attractive girls in bikinis on social media. Part of the problem was that my friend group from before prison was now in their thirties and had given up doing "immature" stuff like partying with girls in bikinis. Those types of parties were for people in their early twenties, but I had missed that.

But aside from this perception, I happened to start several relationships that lasted several months, all ending abruptly because of my felony conviction. One girl was an SLU pre-med undergraduate student from Colorado. We hit it off extremely well. I was opening in ways I had not done in years. We studied together. We watched similar TV shows. We were four and a half months in when I finally decided to tell her. She was hit completely off guard. It was a lot for her. She came from a white, upper-middle-class, Middle American family. She knew a lot about hip hop, and she could back that ass up to juvenile with the best of them. But she knew nothing about incarceration or the devastation it caused to Black communities. She claimed to not be taken away, but within a week she broke it off, stating she needed space to focus on school.

Why did I wait four and a half months, you might ask? Well, trial and error. I had turned a new leaf of honesty and wanted to be open and honest with everyone, because I knew that being dishonest to loved ones was one of my main character faults. All the girls I dated when I first got out, I'd tell them immediately that I had just gotten out. Those relationships never lasted longer than one to two weeks. Attempting to fulfil this negative prophecy I had for my love life, I even tried dating a stripper, whom I did not meet at the strip club, and she left me once I told her about my past, stating, "I know exactly how you niggaz roll, claiming to be changed. I'm done fucking with worthless niggaz." Yup, I had a stripper dump me and call me a "worthless nigga."

Thus, leaving me to battle with when I should tell a girl about my story. I fell hard and fast for a nurse I met at another restaurant while out with my grad student friends. She had a light mocha complexion with long, wavy hair and a Beyoncé body. As I had done on a regular basis, Larry witnessed me use my force that night and pull her in. We genuinely hit it off immediately. We had so much in common. She grew up in Ferguson-Florissant and went to Hazelwood Central and knew my right-hand man Taron and a lot of other friends. She was an RN studying to be a family nurse practitioner. My sisters were RNs, and my ex was an RN and NP. She loved sports as well. We could talk medicine, sports, or childhood places and be on the same page.

I didn't know what to do. I really liked her, and she really liked me, but every girl I had told up until then left me. It was coming close to Thanksgiving and we'd only been dating for a little over a month, but she invited me to meet her family. Part of my logic was, if she knew Taron and knew I was close to Taron, then she had to know that I was selling dope. Everyone that knew Taron knew he was in the game. Thus, I didn't need to tell her. She likely already knew. I was wrong. She did not know. But she googled me a couple days before Thanksgiving and found out. She broke it off because she felt I had been dishonest.

So, you might be thinking, as I have been asked this question by friends, "I can understand not telling a white girl. But Black people understand incarceration. Why wouldn't you have told the sister?" This is a good question. Thus, when that opportunity arose again, and it arose within a few short weeks, I promised myself to tell the sister.

I met Tanya at an SLU Black Student Lawyer Association event. It was a Black graduate student panel, and I was representing Black biomedical PhD students. I spoke passionately about being one of the only Black people in my program and the importance of helping create more Black professionals. She spoke like a young Angela Davis. She was a strong Black woman. Skin as dark as mine, without a single blemish on her face—even without makeup. She wore her hair naturally and constantly preached about Black empowerment. I was on the same page. I told her about my past immediately. She was unphased, telling me about how her brother was currently serving a Fed bid.

Opposite to how my conviction got in the way with other girls, for Tanya, I wasn't criminal enough. I wasn't thug enough. She wanted someone with more prison mannerisms. I wasn't a real convict because how could I be so smart? How could I be in a PhD program? Convicts like her brother wouldn't ever be in a PhD program. Thus, after a couple months, she eventually ended up breaking it off because I was a "smart convict." Had I just been a smart Black man, I may have had a chance. She ended up marrying a smart Black man who was far from being close to the streets without any convictions.

Before finally hanging up the ropes, I ended up dating an Indian girl from a Hindu family, an Asian girl from South Korea, and many others in between, all of whom left me because of my felony conviction. The Hindu girl was deeply infatuated with me. I was aware of the ethnic barrier. Many Indian families do not like their children dating outside of their ethnic tribe, much less race. She swore this was not the case in her family. But when she found out about my conviction, her reasoning was that her family would never let her date seriously outside her race.

❖ ❖ ❖

This is what happiness looks like. My future wife and I after six months of dating. In my prison journal, I mentioned the number one thing I was looking for, more than a career or employment, was happiness. I found it. (c. Summer 2013)

Dissertation

I want to take you back to when I was nineteen years old. Back to when I was in Texas, linking up with my connect for my first hundred-pack pickup. I walked into the hotel room. Nine tucked in my hip. Tens of thousands of dollars bundled up in rubber bands. There were three Mexican men in the room. Two of them spoke no English, and one of them had a sawed-off shotgun sitting on the table. Finger on the trigger. Looking me in the face. Sitting next him was a big red Rubbermaid bin with one huge hundred-pound block of dope. I've stared down killers eye to eye. Why would I be afraid of a dissertation committee? I was ready for change. I was hungry for change.

Upon release, I was accepted into the Saint Louis University PhD program and I completed my PhD and MBA in four years, at the top of my class. Education was my game changer.

My dissertation in Spring 2014 was a milestone for not just me, but for so many others as well. So many people had been on this journey with me. So many people had their hands in on the success of this day. So many people were to thank for this day. So many people were involved in my journey, the good and the bad. And I invited them all.

All the people that helped put my application together. My Fab Five 1.0 and my Fab Five 2.0 (who were alive and free). People I was incarcerated with. Several of my POs and even Judge Lucy Rauch and Susan Schneider, the prosecutor who stated I had no hope for changing the way I had been thinking as a teenager and young adult. Judge Rauch and the prosecutor never responded to my invitation. I ended up inviting and notifying my judge and prosecutor of all my major life accomplishments. They even later received an invitation to my wedding. They never responded to any of them. I even reached out to them about this book, and they never responded.

The celebration continued strong in their absence. I had over two hundred people in attendance at my dissertation. Most of them not understanding one lick of what I was talking about, but all of them standing in ovation at the completion of my forty-minute talk. I have been to many dissertation defenses in my time; most have five to fifteen attendees. I have never attended one that had anywhere near the amount of people I had. From people in business suits to people with multiple teardrops tattooed on their faces, my friend circle included a little bit of every type of person—white, Black, Asian, Latinx, and much more.

The room was filled with people crying before, during, and after my talk. My PhD mentor, Dr. Fisher, started the crying trend. As he opened the seminar with my introduction, which is common practice for dissertation ceremonies, before he could get through his introduction, he burst into full-form crying, not just tears. He could barely get through his words. He did not directly mention my being formerly incarcerated, but his words leaned in that direction as he told a story of how the cream always rises to the top.

A few weeks after my dissertation celebration, I had a big graduation party where I rented out a banquet room at the Hilton. Not just any Hilton, but my dad's favorite Hilton. This was the Hilton that my dad's funeral reception was at. This was the Hilton that he hosted several Haitian conventions at. I invited my godfather and several other of dad's closest friends, and many other friends and family to celebrate with me. We had a DJ and fancy food and a big dance floor. I had been wanting to prepare a speech for that day, but so much was moving so fast at that time that I did not get the opportunity to fully write the speech until minutes before the start of the event. I wrote it in my hotel room minutes before coming down to greet everyone. I shared it briefly with my girlfriend, Stephanie, and she thought it was perfect.

Soon after everyone was settled into their seats and the servers were coming around with the food, I went up to the podium to deliver an opening welcome to everyone. I had planned for the speech to be a dedication to my dad. My entire dissertation was a dedication to my dad. This book is dedicated to my dad. During my defense just a few weeks prior, I had shared a few words on what he meant to me and how he had inspired me to be where I was. In front of two hundred-plus people, I got through that very well. This day would be different.

I felt him all over me that day. His presence. His light. His wisdom. All were shining down on me in that moment. As I opened my mouth to speak about him, I couldn't. The words were right in front of me on my laptop screen, but I could not get them out of my mouth.

The very first words were "I wish he were here."

It took me five to seven minutes to say that first sentence. "I...I... I...I...wish..." I stuttered out with tears and sniffling. My sisters and mother rushed up to stand beside me. After fifteen minutes, I finally read the half page worth of words that I had written. The room was full of tears by that end. I mentioned how much he had meant to me, how I still felt his presence on a daily basis, and that he continued to be my inspiration.

Telling everyone this, crying in front of everyone, felt liberating. I felt as if I were free. Free from the shackles of my emotional incarceration. Free from the guilt that I held about my father's passing. Just a few months earlier, my father came to me and told me—as I was curled up, crying on my kitchen floor—that I was free from that guilt and that he would always be by my side. But sharing that emotional moment with all my close family and friends gave me complete emotional closure.

✤ ✤ ✤

PhD Graduation and Defense. (c. 2014)

Johns Hopkins

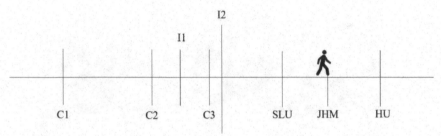

C = arrest that led to conviction; I = sentenced to incarceration; Numbers = number of that event
SLU = Saint Louis University; JHM = Johns Hopkins Medicine; HU = Howard University

"Wow! Who would have ever thought we'd be standing here?" Dr. Bode laughed out loud at my dissertation defense celebration. These thoughts repeated in my head the entire road trip to Johns Hopkins Medicine in Baltimore in July 2014.

Back when I was still nearing the end of my PhD, long before my defense, I asked myself and Bode, "Now that we are here, what do we do?" Crazy as it might seem, I could have completed my PhD even sooner than the four years that it took me. I had met the suggested two-publication requirement by my third year. I was grinding super hard. One reason I decided to prolong the completion was my budding relationship with Stephanie, my future wife. I did not want to potentially move away before our relationship had hit the one-year mark. In addition to this, I was extremely nervous for the end of my PhD. My PhD program gave me job security and purpose. I was proud to be a scientist and I was getting a paycheck. I still had no idea if I was going to be able to get a job after getting this PhD. I had been denied every single job I applied to since returning home, from coaching to working in a department store to working at a gas station. How was I possibly going to get hired as a PhD scientist if I couldn't even get a job at Burger King?

This thought loomed in the back of my head the entire time I was working on my PhD, but now it was front and center. Luckily for me, I had two amazing mentors working tirelessly to assist me. Dr. Fisher had me start the job hunt in year three of my PhD, right after my second publication. He introduced me to multiple people in the field of glucose metabolism and sent me to present my recent publications at conferences, where I got to interact personally with people I might work with. Social settings are where I shine. I have always known that my EQ is much stronger than my IQ. I have the gift of gab. I have had it all my life. Despite being an introvert, I know how to navigate social settings very well.

How does being a social butterfly equate to getting a job as a scientist? Mix social butterfly with being hard-working, very punctual, and thorough and having two great mentors, and you get over ten interviews for postdoctoral scientist positions from top institutions all over the country. I am extremely good at following up with people. From socializing at scientific meetings, I got several interviews. Don't get me wrong; in order to get interviews at the places I had interviews at, you must have a strong science portfolio. I did.

I ended up getting interviews at Harvard Med, Cornell Vet School, University of California San Francisco, Washington University in St. Louis Medical School, and Johns Hopkins Medicine. Four of these schools were in the top five 2014 US News rankings for medical school research institutions.[7] I was offered a position at all of them.

Searching for and applying for a job is a job. Luckily for me, I had grinded so hard the first three years of my PhD, the fourth year was essentially a victory lap. I was able to slow down my grueling pace in the lab and focus more hours on applying to jobs. I had been doing interviews for a couple of months and I had just gotten back from Ithaca, New York, where I visited Cornell's campus. Out of the different offers, this was the one I was most considering.

Moments before sending the acceptance to Cornell, I came across an article stating that Johns Hopkins Medicine was the leading employer of formerly incarcerated people in the state of Maryland.[8]

My mouth dropped when I saw this. I knew that the interview process was not the difficult part for a formerly incarcerated person like me. Nor was getting an offer letter the most difficult part. Academia is different than most other professions. The application process in academia does not involve filling out an application and having to answer the question "Have you ever been convicted of a felony? If so, please explain." Why would that question be needed? Who could possibly be applying to a professorial job as a PhD or MD holder and simultaneously be a convicted felon? That could not be possible, right?

In academia, you simply send in your CV and a research statement (not a personal statement) to the direct boss you would work for. That direct boss reviews your file and decides to move forward on an interview and then has the authority to move forward on sending you an offer. It is not until the offer is made by the direct boss and the department that the applicant is sent to HR to then fill out a form that will ask about criminal history. At that stage, one already has an offer in hand, and it becomes more difficult to discriminate based on criminal history. This was always the game plan. Getting into an Ivy League-caliber academy was also part of the plan. I felt that this would help balance out the strikes against me. Thus, with finding out that Hopkins was intentionally looking to hire people with convictions, I had to apply.

I searched all the job search engines for positions that fit my expertise at Hopkins and, lo and behold, I found Sheng Wu's job posting on the American Physiological Society's Careers page. I immediately sent her my CV and research statement, strategically including the fact that I had an offer in hand from Cornell that I needed to decide on within one week. Being in the endocrinology department at Johns Hopkins, the number one-rated endocrinology department in the country, Sheng had already received over a hundred applications for her position—and it had been open for only a few weeks. Seeing the urgency of my application, she got back to me within days and invited me to a video interview, since time would not permit an in-person interview.

On the strength of having several offers under my belt already, Sheng made me an offer within the same week of me sending in the application. I accepted the offer immediately but did not send my decline letter just yet to the other offers. Hopkins's HR department sent me an application form with the dreaded question. I spent a couple of days drafting the response to the conviction question. I sent it to Cortney and Bode for their review and they provided a few edits, but neither was an expert on this. I had become knowledgeable in this arena since it was now my life. I had searched the web and read a lot on how to respond. **I learned that when they ask you to "please explain," you must explain your changes, not your charges**.

Within a day or so, Hopkins's HR very efficiently got back to me—with full approval. I was now an employee of Johns Hopkins Medicine's Division of Pediatric Endocrinology.

❖ ❖ ❖

I did not sell my house in the Ferguson-Florissant District. Instead, Stephanie moved in. We decided that we would do long-distance.

I packed up and headed to Baltimore in a small U-Haul. I drove straight through the night and made it to Baltimore by early morning. I had to be at Hopkins for my first day at 9:00 a.m. I had not slept one wink of sleep when I first met Sheng. After two hours of introductions to new colleagues, I mentioned to Sheng how I had my U-Haul parallel-parked on the street and that I needed to go put money in the meter.

"What? Did you just get here?" Sheng was shocked and appalled. I did not look the slightest bit disheveled.

From that moment, she knew she had gotten even more than she had bargained for in me. From that action, she could see that I was punctual, hard-working, and did not make excuses. She let me leave work and suggested I take as many days as needed and for me to come back whenever I was ready and settled in.

I came back the next day. I was already settled in. I moved all my belongings into my second-story apartment by myself. I grinded harder at Hopkins than I did at SLU. At SLU, I worked so hard because of fear that they would eventually kick me out once they knew who I really was. At Hopkins, I did not have that fear. I knew why they hired me, and I knew the process. The Hopkins hiring of returning citizens practices were published. Hopkins HR did not recriminalize you. They did not tell your direct boss or supervisor of your past. My past was a secret between me and Hopkins HR.

I worked hard because now this was simply my work ethic. On top of that, I was in a new city by myself, without my girlfriend Stephanie. Because I had a very serious girlfriend, I had no need to go out and mingle. And because that very serious girlfriend was not with me, I had no obligation to go out on dates with her. This freed up my time to work even more. Working fifty to sixty hours per week was Hopkins's culture. People at Hopkins would work well into the night during the week and then also come in on Saturdays. I had already been on that routine at SLU. That's why I finished so quickly.

I was an expert in glucose metabolism, but now I was in a reproductive endocrinology lab. Thus, there was a very steep, uphill learning curve. At Hopkins, every week there were dozens of seminars from Nobel laureates from all over the world. At Hopkins's seminars, shots were fired left and right. People in the audience did not simply ask questions; they took shots, articulately dismantling and challenging the speaker's theories, conclusions, and methods. It was an exhilarating scientific environment.

When I was not cranking away, knocking out several experiments all at once, I was often at a Nobel laureate's seminar, honing my craft of articulately dismantling theories. After work, I would head straight to the gym for an intense workout (after four-plus years, I was still faithfully doing my 300 Workout), then I would continue working by going to the library to read scientific articles for hours upon hours. I would end my day around 10:00 p.m. ET (9:00 p.m. CT) by video-chatting with Stephanie for an hour before she went to bed.

"Hi, Stephanie."

"Hi, Lovey." She'd smile as we started our video chats via an app called Tango. "What's going on in the world of research today?"

"You know. Same routine. Up early. Grind Hard. Workout. Then grind some more." Long-distance was difficult but it helped us grow even stronger. Tango had games and silly reactions and fun virtual backgrounds. We'd put up beach backgrounds and sip drinks on weekend nights or put up a fireplace background and share stories while sitting on the carpet by the fireplace which was one of our favorite things to do in person.

By 11:00 p.m., I might read or write if need be, or go to bed—only to wake up at 4:00 a.m. and be in the lab by 4:45 a.m. I was the first one in the lab by close to four hours. By the time my colleagues came into work, I had already done a full day's worth of work, considering that I would often do two or more experiments at a time. I was also the last one to leave the lab, as I frequently left around 6:00 or 6:30 p.m. and did my evening routine all over again. The result was I had enough data for three publications in the matter of two years. This generally took most other postdoc scientists five to six years.

The remnants of prison were still lurking but were drastically starting to dissipate. I would have less episodes of triggers throwing me into depressive states for hours and days at a time. I was no longer having terrifying bouts of sleep paralysis. I was so busy my subconscious did not have time to terrorize me.

This grueling pace and tireless work ethic are part of the reason I transitioned to a faculty position much faster than most other biomedical postdocs.

❖ ❖ ❖

I was beyond excited to be at Hopkins and to be in the number-one endocrinology department in the nation—and quite possibly the world. Being a formerly incarcerated person, this was simply mind-blowing to me. What I did not love was not seeing another face like mine except for in the janitorial staff. I literally went seven months before meeting another Black PhD or MD holder in a postdoctoral or residence position like mine. When I finally met Dionna and Marc, we hugged and embraced like we were long-lost family members. The three of us co-founded the Diversity Postdoctoral Alliance Committee (DPAC).

Within the first year, we raised over $25,000 to fund the many initiatives we started, such as (1) quarterly diversity town halls to bring issues of diversity in science to the attention of the Hopkins community, (2) DPAC "mentoring families" that created mentor trios including Black and brown grad students, postdocs, and faculty, and (3) an annual diversity research symposium called "Excellence in Diversity," which eventually grew to be the premiere conference for young Black and brown scientists in the DMV area to showcase their research excellence. Marc, Dionna, and I transformed the culture of Hopkins.[9]

By the second year, we had secured several million dollars to fund our biggest initiative—the Postdoctoral Fellowship for Academic Diversity,[10] which eventually became the Provost's Postdoctoral Fellowship program.[11] This award would provide substantial research funding and other supportive resources to create a guaranteed pipeline of transitioning young Black and brown scientists into faculty positions at Hopkins. Hopkins was the worst of the worst when it came to employing Black faculty. Most predominantly white institutions (PWIs) have roughly 5–6 percent Black faculty,[12] which is far less than the 13–14 percent of Black people represented in the public. Therefore, they use the term "underrepresented." Six percent is bad; Hopkins Med was abysmal, employing only 3 percent Black faculty.

We changed that. On a weekly basis, Marc, Dionna, and I were kicking down doors and demanding meetings with deans, provosts, and presidents. We met with all these people. Just as you'd expect from three Hopkins scientists, we came with data to prove our point. I was the organized businessman of the three of us, coming to meetings with pretty packets and having designed engaging PowerPoints to wow our spectators.

Since the implementation of the Provost's Postdoctoral Fellowship program, in just four years from 2016 to 2020, Hopkins had gone from 3 percent Black faculty to nearly 6 percent Black faculty, now on par with other PWIs, but still much further to go.

✦ ✦ ✦

I Made It—First day at Hopkins Med. (c. 2014)

Ferguson and the Baltimore Uprising—the Black Lives Matter Movement

I had only been at Hopkins for one month when unarmed Mike Brown was shot dead in the streets of Ferguson by police officer Darren Wilson. The world watched as my hometown of Ferguson ignited in flames and protests. I remember watching CNN cover the events. It was weird to see streets and buildings I grew up near on national television. I remember watching the CNN map of where the protest was and seeing that they were only a mile or so away from where Stephanie was resting her head in our house we still owned at that time. Stephanie was also a schoolteacher in the Ferguson-Florissant School District.

I had just been introducing myself to people as being from St. Louis. This soon changed to me introducing myself more specifically as being from the Ferguson area. Had the events in Ferguson never happened, there would be no reason for anyone to be familiar with my little part of suburban North St. Louis County called Ferguson-Florissant. But now, everyone will forever remember Ferguson as igniting the Black Lives Matter movement.

Many people would ask me, "Why are your people doing this to their own hometown and community?"

My response would be, "So uninformed people like you can visually see the struggle."

Ferguson illuminated the disparate conditions of Black communities all over the country. Before one year went by, Baltimore was on the national news as riots erupted after the death of Freddie Gray at the hands of Baltimore police.

I marched in both Ferguson and Baltimore protests. I would frequently go back home to visit Stephanie and family at the time. When I did, I would link up with old friends, many of whom had become activists during this time of turmoil.

❖ ❖ ❖

Ferguson sparked a whole generation of new activists, advocates, and non-profit entrepreneurs—me included. I had been home from prison for four years. In that time, I had seen several of my friends from the inside return home. I had tried to encourage all of them to use education to help turn their lives around. I was unfortunately and sadly unable to reach Dion and Kenny-Mo before the streets fatally took their lives. But I was able to help several other friends take this path, including Jerry and Rahmari.

The formula of using education as a therapeutic tool to keep people out of prison worked. By the time Ferguson and Baltimore happened, I had been employing this tool with my friends who were returning home. Another friend that I helped was SK, or Jerry, who returned in 2016.

Jerry spent nine years in prison for armed criminal action, armed robbery, and attempted murder. Music was his passion. He is a hip-hop artist and aspiring producer in St. Louis now. He and I met in 2008 while incarcerated. We promised each other to make a change once we returned. This promise was the inspiration behind From Prison Cells to PhD, Inc.

The conversations that Jerry, Rahmari, and I had were the founding conversations of From Prison Cells to PhD and the Prison-to-Professionals (P2P) program. It started with the conversations in our prison cells before release. Upon release, when I got into SLU, Jerry and Rahmari were in disbelief. I would send them pictures and tell them stories of my adventures as a college student. It inspired them to take that path once they returned.

I remember taking phone calls from Jerry while I was in lab at Hopkins and he was still in prison. These phone calls were a constant reminder of where I had come from. Hearing the operator lady tell me it was a collect call from a prison and the raspy phone connection, I was immediately reminded how I had gotten to the pinnacle of the medical research world. This contrast was not lost on me. How could I get more people like Jerry, Rahmari, and me into places like Johns Hopkins?

At the same time of having these thoughts and conversations, I was actively cranking out research data at an uncharacteristic pace, as well as becoming a diversity leader at Hopkins and in Baltimore. When the Baltimore riots ensued, I reached out to Marilyn Mosby's office and shared my story. Mosby was the Baltimore City state's attorney that had become nationally known by indicting the officers in the Freddie Gray case. She was amazed by my story and immediately drew me into several meetings and speaking engagements.

From these meetings I met Caryn York, who had just recently become the executive director of Job Opportunities Task Force, a mid-sized, Baltimore-based nonprofit that helps poor and disadvantaged people find employment. when Caryn heard my story, she was inspired and began encouraging me to come to Annapolis to testify and share my story publicly. Caryn and I met in 2015. I was not ready to share my story publicly yet. I had every intention of doing so but wanted to do it strategically. I had already begun writing this book back then.

At that time, the writing of this book was a hot topic of debate between my then-fiancée Stephanie and me. By late 2015, Stephanie and I were happily engaged and living together in Baltimore. She had been hearing people tell me I should write a book for quite a while. At first it was coming from close friends like Brandon. Now it was coming from strangers like Caryn York, and more notable people like Marilyn Mosby, Mayor of Baltimore Stephanie Rawlings-Blake, and late US Representative Elijah Cummings.

Stephanie did not quite see the larger vision that I had in mind at that time. Understandably, she was scared on various fronts regarding releasing my story publicly. Everything was fine and inspirational about my vision until it got to the part about me having to spread the vision and what that would entail. That would entail a whirlwind of speaking engagements and events across the nation and globe. That would entail me sharing very intimate and troubling aspects of my past.

From Stephanie's vantage point, this meant, "So, you're not going to be at, or coach, our children's softball games like my daddy use to do for me." Stephanie and I did not have kids at this point but that was her argument: spreading my vision would take me away from our family.

This would then escalate into, "So, you made it out of prison alive and put doctor in front of your name. Why do you think people will care about that? No one cares about that! You're not anyone super special, aside from being special to me. Why do you want to be special to everybody? Why can't you just be special to our family?"

She made a strong point that I have wrestled with throughout the entire writing and releasing of this book. "Why?"

For the record, I never won any of these conversations. But I would attempt to address her thoughts with this:

> "Our child or children will be blessed with two parents who are doing very well for themselves. They will be blessed with being showered with love from us and our large family. I want to provide these blessings to others who are not as fortunate as our children will be. I want to create a support system for people who have been through the legal system like me."

This was a heated debate at our dinner table for some time. But in the long run, Stephanie eventually came around to the vision as she agreed to not only join the board of the nonprofit I would create in 2017, but she also dove deep into learning anti-racist[13] theories,[14] philosophies and practices[15] that shaped, strengthened, and guided the vision and direction of the budding organization. Rounding out that board of directors were my good friends Jerry, whom I was incarcerated with, and Cortney, my childhood friend.

I had spent about two years, from 2015 to 2017, researching the idea of creating a nonprofit. Ferguson and Baltimore sparked and inspired this interest. I eventually built a board of twenty individuals who were founders and directors of similar education-focused reentry or prison programs, fourteen of whom were formerly incarcerated people. In what felt like the blink of an eye, the Prison-to-Professionals (P2P) program was off and running.

Spreading Hope

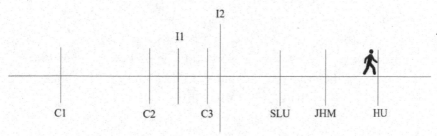

C = arrest that led to conviction; I = sentenced to incarceration; Numbers = number of that event
SLU = Saint Louis University; JHM = Johns Hopkins Medicine; HU = Howard University

After two years of Caryn urging me to come to Annapolis, I was finally ready to share my story. I felt that the time was right. In February 2017, I shared my story as testimony for the Ban the Box for Higher Education bill in the Maryland legislation.[1] Many states had banned the box on employment, but none had moved to removing the criminal conviction question from college applications. We were the first.

Minutes after the testimony, a reporter from the *Washington Post* came up to me, requesting to talk more. The following week I had an entire production team inside my Hopkins lab. To get approval for this, I had to tell my Hopkins boss, Sheng—and her boss—my story. I had never told them prior to this. Sheng's boss responded immediately. Sheng did not respond.

After the *Washington Post* piece came out, I went on a whirlwind of interviews and speaking engagements that have not stopped since that time. Soon I had CBS and ABC[2] camera crews in my workspace and living room.

Several weeks after the whirlwind of camera crews had died down, I finally had the opportunity to talk with Sheng. For the past two and a half years, she and I would see each other and talk every day.

"Hi, Stan," Sheng said, in her still-heavy Chinese accent. "Sorry I have not had the opportunity to talk to you."

I reassured her. "It's okay, Sheng. No worries."

She continued, "I had been wanting to tell you how inspirational your story was and how happy I am that you are sharing it. When I came to this country, I saw that the Black community was very disadvantaged, and I always thought that the Black community needed a person like you. You will inspire many people. I am proud to have been your mentor."

I smiled at her and touched her shoulder. "Thank you, Sheng. But why do you add the 'have been'? You still are my mentor."

She paused and looked the other way, then looked back at me. "Stan, due to Trump being elected and him taking money away from science research, I have to let you go. You have three months left."

I was completely shocked. I had not begun looking for jobs yet. I had not anticipated being on the job market for about another year. Sheng had five people working for her. Three of them were in the same position as I was, a postdoctoral scientist. We were the ones with the highest salary out of her employees. So, I got having to cut one of the highest salaries, but why did it have to be me? I was her first employee, and I was her most productive employee by far. I worked harder than anyone else in our group. But she was getting rid of me because of Trump, and that just so happened to come right after me publicly sharing my story.

She could see the confusion on my face. She continued with, "Your story is very inspirational. Maybe you and I could consider writing a training grant where you share your story and propose to help disadvantaged Black people become scientists."

I thought to myself, *You just fired me, and in the same sentence you are now asking to collaborate with you to use my story to bring you money.*

I maintained my calm and cool demeanor as I always had and told her, "I'll think about that."

I will share more on the unemployment spiral this sent me on in later chapters. But for the next few chapters, I want to take you where my mind was at the time. Although I was sprung into a bout of unemployment and inability to pay my bills, my mind was on something bigger than me and my current situation. My mind was on Prison-to-Professionals and building the vision.

Spreading Hope to Those Deemed Hopeless

Hill Correctional Center is one of the largest high-security-level prisons in the state of Illinois. Roughly 90 of the 1,900 people incarcerated there have life sentences and will never be released from prison.

Shortly after my story appearing in the *Washington Post*, I went on a barrage of speaking engagements, roughly two to four per week. In April 2017, still half-asleep, I woke up at four in the morning to hit the highway for a four-hour drive. I had retired from moving weight. I was now moving words—ones of experience and inspiration. I was headed back to prison for the first time. I'd had a conversation with my mom the night before about me going "back to prison." After her initial gasp, she hit me with the Haitian mom "umpf," showing her concern and doubt, punctuated by "*m ap priye pou ou.*" I told her I was praying for me too.

As a formerly incarcerated person turned postdoctoral scientist at Johns Hopkins Medicine, I had come full circle—from prison cells to PhD—and I was going back to prison to deliver a motivational speech to people on the inside on the importance of education after release. Obtaining higher education reduces the rate of going back[3] to prison from roughly 70 percent to nearly 0 percent. I could not even begin to explain my feelings. I was excited but torn, eager yet uncertain, happy and sad. It's impossible to capture the emotions. Overall, I was inspired and honored to have the opportunity.

When I entered the prison gates and heard the loud clang of the solid iron door slamming closed behind me, I knew there was no turning back. I was politely greeted by the warden, two assistant wardens, and three correctional officers. The warden was a young white lady (maybe forty years old) wearing a very professional navy-blue suit. She was not what I expected the warden of one of the largest high-security prisons in Illinois to look like. In all my years locked up, I had never met a warden. Prisons are comprised of about 70 percent people of color.[4] As I walked the prison yard, a Black man in civilian clothes with two older white men in suits, three white men in uniform, and the head of the prison all had their eyes on me.

I arrived at the activity center and was escorted through more locked doors and past more inquisitive faces. I had a packed room of roughly two hundred incarcerated people. I spoke for two hours straight and had more attentive faces than any college auditorium lecture I had ever delivered. The room was full of tattooed tears and bodies fully covered in art. It was a room bursting with potential, of listeners deeply eager for a second chance. It was truly inspirational.

I took a tour of the grounds. The air in the yard felt like prison, despite being the same rural country air separated by twenty feet of triple-barbed-wire chain fences. Unlike most visitors, I walked through one of the housing units. I saw the cells. I saw the faces I remembered like yesterday. I visited the segregation wing and even hung out in the warden's office talking Illinois politics. The entire day was surreal.[5]

❖ ❖ ❖

Words Matter; I am a Person, Before and After Conviction

I am not a convict. I am not a felon. These are words used by society and the criminal justice system to remind me and you that I am viewed as less than a person. Many people who were close to me were likely not aware or had not really thought about it, but my life had entered an entirely new territory.

Starting in spring 2017, I began having people contact me from all over the country. A pastor contacted me by phone after an interview I had with CBS[6] and told me, "You still look, talk, and smell like a convict."

Wow. What does a "convict" smell like? He continued, "You need Jesus in your life. Back in my day, people were ashamed to have gone to prison. You seem proud. That's what's wrong with you young Black folks." He even threw in a five-minute rant to let me know that I was going to hell.

I tried to not let his words dig too deep. I have been told by many on this journey to let the negative comments and hate fall to the side. I agree. I would not have made it from prison cells to being a PhD scientist at Johns Hopkins if I had let all the people who told me "You can't" get the best of me. But the pastor brought up some points I'd like to address.

First off, I'm not proud to have gone to prison. I'm not proud of things I did that led to my incarcerations. I would not wish what I went through on my worst of enemies. The trauma I endured. The violence I witnessed. The harm I produced. The dehumanizing nature of our criminal justice system.

I am deeply torn, broken, hurt, scarred, and changed by my prison experience. But, also, I grew, improved, learned, endured, battled, fought, strived, and changed for the better through my prison experience. The painful humiliation rang deep in my bones every night, from full to new moons. I fell so deep in my shame that my thoughts would take me to places that no one wants to be. I don't want to live in my painful humiliation anymore. The psychological damage of prison is one of many collateral consequences[7] that are perpetuated by the words and negative views society shares towards people with criminal convictions.

Second, the pastor stated I needed Jesus in my life. In my CBS interview, I mentioned the steps I took to get from prison cells to earning my PhD. I mentioned internal change as the first step to moving forward. What I did not mention, because the interview was only eight minutes, was that my internal change was empowered, envisioned, embedded, and brought out by my faith. Too many times in my journey, the odds were against me. But I prevailed. I consider those moments blessings.

Third, I am a person with a criminal conviction who spent time in prison. I am not a convict. I am not a felon. These are words used by society and the criminal justice system to tell me and remind me that I am less than a person. That I am less than you.

I am not less than you. I am a person. These words are dehumanizing, demoralizing, and derogatory, yet they are embedded in the way we think about people with criminal convictions. We cannot move forward until we leave behind these damaging and stigmatizing words. I urge you to reconsider using this type of language in your conversations on these topics.[8]

❖ ❖ ❖

Cover of The Washington Post. *First time sharing my story publicly. (c. Feb 2017)*

Speaking at the Congressional Black Caucus. (c. September 2017)

Ban the Box—on College Applications

As I was launching the advocacy campaign for the Maryland Ban the Box bill in the summer of 2017, I was reminded of one of the critical moments in my journey back in early 2010.

"This is a collect call from the Northeast Correctional Center," said the operator, as I was thinking to myself how much I hated her voice. I was semi-anxiously waiting for my brother to pick up on the other end. The parole board had recently told me I had only six months left, and I could not wait to share the good news.

"Stan, what's up. Yo, it's not good, lil bro. It's not good," my brother stated. "The infection spread to his brain. Pops is in a coma." Everything he said after that was just a distant mumble. My mind was transcending into that hospital room with my father, outside of those prison walls. The pain rang deep through my bones. Holding back the tears that were just moments away from flowing like a river, I went back and locked myself in my prison cell—my cage. My mind was whirling. I could not cry. Crying was weakness. By then, I had seen things that I would never imagine I'd see in my life. I didn't cry then. I couldn't cry at that point. Instead, I would take hold of my pain and transform it into purpose. It was shortly after this call that I started applying to graduate school.

In September 2017, I visited over twenty student organizations in twenty days. I was spending weeks meeting with student government groups from universities all over Maryland to garner support and spread awareness about the Maryland Fair Access to Education Act of 2017,[9] colloquially called Ban the Box on College Applications. The bill passed with bipartisan support but was vetoed by Governor Hogan and went up for override in January 2018.

Many colleges and universities claim to push towards having a diverse and inclusive student body. However, one piece of diversity never seems to find its way into the conversation of inclusiveness. One single sentence hampers this idea of obtaining a full representation of the spectrum of society. Most people don't remember the box asking about past criminal convictions. But for people like me, that little box is a mountainous barrier to future success.

By requiring applicants to disclose their criminal history, universities impose a barrier to education. This process reduces the applicant to the mere moment (often decades ago) when they incurred a criminal record rather than seeing the full person with all their interests, skills, and experiences.

Studies show checking "yes," that you have been involved in the criminal legal system, greatly lowers your chances of a follow-up to your application. President Obama[10] and the Department of Education[11] supported removing the box. The history of this policy is not rooted in empirical data. Schools that do not have "the box" are equally as safe as those that do. Most of the crimes on campus are by people with no criminal history.[12] The national rate of people returning to prison (recidivism) is 76 percent.[13] For people who obtain a bachelor's degree, that rate drops to 5.6 percent. It's a no-brainer. Statistics support college after incarceration. The "box" is *not* a public safety tactic.

The "box" disproportionately affects applicants of color, due to mass incarceration primarily affecting people of color. The "box" is discouraging to many applicants. Sixty percent of people who check "yes" do not complete the application.[14]

Education is transformative to the person and to the community. Education lowers poverty and progresses public safety. We must open our institutional doors, not create barriers.

❖ ❖ ❖

The Maryland Ban the Box on College Applications went into law in January 2018 after six hard months of advocacy led by me and several others. The Unlock Higher Ed (UHE) Coalition[15] formed partly out of the Ban the Box work I started in Maryland. The P2P co-founder, Jerry Moore III, and I ended up making a music video[16] to promote the Ban the Box work we were doing. This video ended up catching the eyes of several people in the criminal justice reform field, who we ended up linking up with—and some ended up joining our P2P Board.

Our 2017 bill in Maryland landed in the hands of Syrita Steib and Annie Freitas. Syrita was a formerly incarcerated person with college education forging along a similar journey as I was. They took our wording—and materials—and drafted their own bill in Louisiana. Their bill passed in 2017. In November 2017, Syrita, Annie, and I sat on a panel at the National Conference on Higher Education in Prison to discuss our work on Ban the Box. These were the origins of UHE.

The three of us met Noel Vest at this conference. He was inspired by our panel and decided to take our toolkit and use it in Washington. By mid-2018, Washington became the third state to pass this law. In 2019, on the work of one of my organization's scholars, Majid Mohammad, the state of Colorado passed this law. By 2020, we were working with over twenty states to help pass similar laws.[17]

❖ ❖ ❖

From prison cell to PhD

Ex-felon turned endocrinologist wants to 'Ban the Box' on college applications

By Sandra Jordan
Of The St. Louis American

Whether it is the Common Application, used by several hundred colleges and universities in the U.S., or one of their own, most applications for higher education ask about a history of incarceration.

For many, it is an innocuous box to check: "No." You probably don't think about it if you have never served time behind bars. However, if you have, you think about that box a lot. Every time you apply for a job and, in this case, every time you apply for school. If you just ignore the

See BANBOX, A7

Ferguson native Stan Andrisse (left) and his friend, Jerry Moore III of St. Louis want to remove the stigma of persons who have been incarcerated. Upon release from prison Andrisse earned advanced degrees at Saint Louis University and is now a post-doctoral fellow and endocrinologist at Johns Hopkins University in Maryland.

STL American (front page, c. 2017) I was not a fan of the subtitle, but this article helped push our bill over the finish line.

Unlock Higher Ed on the Hill. In 2019, UHE brought over fifty formerly incarcerated people from across the nation to the hill and had over one hundred meetings with lawmakers to advocate for ban the box and Pell Restoration. After a twenty-five-year battle, Pell was restored for incarcerated people in December 2020.

Discussing Ban the Box with Gov. Hogan,
after his veto of the bill. (c. June 2017)

Prison-to-Professionals (P2P)

Afunder once told me that "what P2P aspires for is too far out of reach for the people they serve in their mission. People with high recidivism risk shouldn't be aspiring for PhDs."

I was offended but responded calmly: (1) That's highly insulting to blanketly say a person in prison cannot or shouldn't aspire to a PhD. (2) P2P doesn't help people get PhDs. We help people pursue higher education. (3) Let us assume PhDs are far-fetched for people in prison. Isn't becoming Lil Wayne far-fetched? Isn't becoming LeBron James far-fetched? Isn't becoming Big Meech far-fetched? Yet we sell that dream to the Black community all the time. If we are going to sell something far-fetched, I'd rather it be advanced education. (4) We don't simply focus on higher education. We help people obtain "power" skills, useful in any profession. We help with case management to assist with navigating different services upon reentry. All that was missed while focusing on the PhD.

What I quickly discovered as I entered the world of reentry is that it is full of Jesus Christ saviors. Reentry and most services helping marginalized and vulnerable populations are full of big-hearted, well-intentioned, Jesus Christ-loving, cynical pessimists. They won't claim to be cynical or pessimistic or negative Nancies, but they are. They are often people with means and resources and a bright idea. Many of these bright ideas are backed with years of education, degrees, research, awards, and experiences. But rarely are these bright ideas backed with true, lived experiences. The people leading these efforts are not the people who lived the trauma, who sat in the cell, who were locked in a solitary cage for months, who witnessed the death of a friend, who survived the excursion of hopelessness.

Many of the people leading these efforts are white males and females often coming from high privilege, and they enter this field to heroically save the poor Black souls from despair. As with many things, it is helpful to be able to hold two truths at the same time. This is something that is challenging for many people to do. There are also many white people that don't fall into that category and are in this work not to be saviors, but to help change the world. I like to think that the white people on the P2P team are those in that second truth.

Because those closest to the problem were *not* the ones leading the solution, the solution had become a dilution and illusion of the savior. The savior with all his or her degrees created this delusion, this mirage of what the solution needed to be. Then the savior worded these solutions in fancy terminologies, such as "evidence-based practices," to further expand the divide between those closest to the problem and the resources, power, and money to create solutions. Further pillaging by the savior is readily and often promoted, as the savior regularly extorts data and knowledge from those closest to the problem without providing any or adequate compensation. The savior uses this data and knowledge to further validate their "evidence-based practices," thus using the knowledge of those closest to the problem to secure more resources and power for themselves to further validate themselves as the savior and creator of solutions. This is the world of reentry services.

I wanted no part in this world, as it was. So, I created my own lane. I created a new branch of reentry. With partners such as those from the Unlock Higher Ed Coalition, we embolden this new emerging movement of education justice, the mix of higher education and criminal justice reform. At first, it was very difficult to get funding for P2P. Nearly every funder we spoke with loved my inspirational story and liked the P2P idea, but could not figure out how it fit into their portfolio. The problem was that P2P was not higher education or criminal justice reform or workforce development. P2P was a near equal combination of all of these. But the biggest challenge we faced was what our name embodied; taking people from prison to a place of excellence and high achievement was too far-fetched and out of reach for people who've experienced prison. Sometimes when your dream is too big, it does not fit in the boxes people readily ascribe to them. That was okay with me. Dreams do not belong in boxes. Dreams belong in the sky, limitlessly bound.

As of 2021, Prison-to-Professionals had participants and team members in over thirty states and was continually growing, from a revenue of $8,000 with seven scholars in year one to $40,000 with thirty scholars in year two to $150,000 with 120-plus scholars in year three to over half a million dollars in year four with 200-plus scholars. We have grown five-fold in funding each of our first three years and anticipate continued years of growth. Proceeds from this book will be donated to P2P. You can visit our website to donate or get involved.

In 2019, P2P and partners received a $7.2 million, five-year government grant from the National Science Foundation.[18] When the traditional reentry funders would not buy into the P2P idea, we sought funders outside of the reentry space, such as the Robert Wood Johnson Foundation, National Science Foundation, and National Institutes of Health. P2P has received hundreds of thousands of dollars from these entities that had never funded reentry programs before. Dreams don't belong in boxes. Dreams live in the clouds.

✦ ✦ ✦

Featured in The Physiologist, *one of the leading journals in my field. (c. October 2020)*

Letter from President Obama. He expressed his gratitude
for the work I was doing to increase access to education.

Life Today

"If you stay ready, you ain't got to get ready,
youngsta." —Ole Skool, 2006

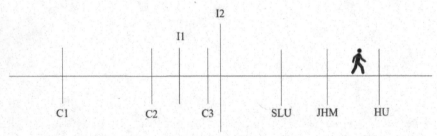

C = arrest that led to conviction; I = sentenced to incarceration; Numbers = number of that event
SLU = Saint Louis University; JHM = Johns Hopkins Medicine; HU = Howard University

I could not believe what had just happened. It was the early morning of December 30, 2014. Stephanie was at my tiny apartment in Baltimore. We were preparing to travel to NYC later that day to celebrate New Year's Eve in Times Square. We had been doing long-distance for six months. I could tell it was wearing on us. I wanted her in Baltimore with me. I wanted her with me for the rest of my life. I wanted to marry her. I was planning to propose to her at the turn of the new year at Times Square.

But I just encountered a huge problem. In my nervousness, I had just broken the key to the safe in the keyhole of the safe. I silently screamed, "Agghhhhhh!" The very expensive diamond engagement ring that I was to propose with was locked inside this safe, and I now no longer had a way to get inside said safe. It was about 5:00 in the morning. Stephanie was silently asleep just a few feet away from me.

The safe was in the closet of my bedroom. Back in my hustling days, I had many safes. I've had safes smaller than a shoebox to safes that looked like a dictionary to safes that were taller than a person. Back in my day, I could go to my safes blindfolded with a gun to my head and still be able to punch in the code, open the safe, and grab the dope or money in record speed. Back in my day, I would open and close safes almost every day. My safes were always hidden somewhere. Whether it be the hidden wall I built at the local's house at MOVAL after the campus police raid or the safe in Hazel's apartment in her closet before the Drug Task Force raid or my giant safe confiscated by the Feds. They were all in dark places. And many times, I was opening them under the pressure of a recent police raid or grabbing twenty-five pounds of dope out as I was rushing to make a $20,000 deal. I handled opening safes under extreme pressure and in the dark all the time. But this time was different. I was nervous.

This safe was one of my last remnants of my past life. This was one of my functional dope safes. It smelled like money and weed for a long time. While trying to keep quiet, I flipped the forty-pound safe over and attempted to shake the broken piece out. This proved to be too noisy and Stephanie began to wake up.

"Lovey? What are you doing? Why are you up so early? I thought we were sleeping in today," She muttered, still half-asleep with her eyes closed.

I jumped up and closed the closet door. "Oh, nothing, baby, go back to sleep. I actually remembered that I need to go into lab today for a little bit." I was still working at Hopkins.

In addition to going into lab, I shot over to a Jared jewelry store to inform my jewelers of my conundrum. I had come up with the idea that I would buy a second ring—a much less expensive ring—and inform Stephanie after the proposal that this was not the real ring. Then the jeweler threw a monkey wrench in my initial idea.

"You can't just buy some rinky-dink, bubblegum-machine ring," the jeweler mocked me as I selected a very inexpensive, simple ring, with no diamonds. "She's gonna say no to that thing. You want her to say yes, right?"

I could feel the sweat beading on my forehead. I had not quite thought of that. In reality, Stephanie would have said yes to a bubblegum-machine ring, but in my nervousness, I let this jeweler get in my head.

"What do you suggest?" I asked.

The jeweler showed me a ring twice the price of the already very expensive ring I had locked in my safe.

"Absolutely not. I'm not going to buy her a more expensive ring. What if she likes this one better than the one in my safe?"

"Then you give her that one," the jeweler nonchalantly advised, as if she were the one that was going to magically deposit $10,000 into my bank account.

I passed on that suggestion. I ended up buying a nice diamond ring that was half the price of the real ring locked in my safe. It was beautiful enough to say yes to—but not better than the other one—and if she did think it was better than the other one, then even better for my pockets since it was less costly.

I bought the second ring and darted back to the apartment to prepare for our fun NYC NYE trip. From that moment on, the ring never left my side. I wore sweatpants that had a very secure zipper pocket. The ring resided there for the next twenty-four-plus hours.

I was very much broke at the time. First-year postdoctoral scientists don't make big money. Despite NYC being an expensive city, we had an amazing time. I was an expert at "balling on a budget."

The day went exactly as planned. We had a great time visiting Times Square and walking around NYC during the day. For NYE, I got us VIP tickets to a rooftop club near Times Square overlooking the Empire State Building. We danced and partied the night away. At the turn of the new year, with the Empire State Building lit up in the background, I got down on one knee, professed my love to Stephanie, and popped the question. She said yes.

❖ ❖ ❖

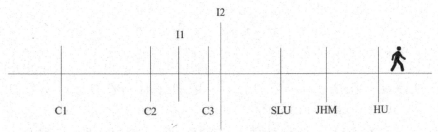

C = arrest that led to conviction; I = sentenced to incarceration; Numbers = number of that event
SLU = Saint Louis University; JHM = Johns Hopkins Medicine; HU = Howard University

Several major life events took place from 2015-2020 that are best explained thematically as opposed to purely chronologically. Let's jump to October 2018. Life was better than I could have ever possibly imagined. From sitting in a prison cell looking at seven years flat as a convicted drug trafficker and career criminal to being a professor at two world-renowned medical institutions performing cutting-edge diabetes research as an endocrinologist scientist, to starting and running a nonprofit aimed at helping people in the system pursue higher education, and to having a beautiful wife who was now pregnant with our first child. Life was good.

My nonprofit program Prison-to-Professionals (P2P) was doing well. In October 2018, I was in New Orleans for an induction ceremony for a grant called Culture of Health Leaders that P2P had just received from the Robert Wood Johnson Foundation. By that time, "Papa was a rolling stone." Ever since the initial public sharing of my story in February 2017, I was still on this roller coaster of speaking engagements. I was speaking roughly two to four times per week locally and nationally. It was grueling but exciting and necessary. It was for a greater good. I was fortunate to have my wife by my side. She leaned in more than I could have imagined. She traveled with me all over the world, from the West Coast to the Deep South to Puerto Rico and even China.

However, she could not make the trip to New Orleans, as she was thirty-nine weeks pregnant.

✦ ✦ ✦

I want to step back a second and mention that two years prior, in July 2016 (our first month of marriage), my wife was diagnosed with polycystic ovary syndrome (PCOS) by a Johns Hopkins reproductive endocrinologist. At that time, I was a Johns Hopkins endocrinologist studying PCOS. PCOS is the leading cause of female infertility with roughly 20 percent of women suffering from this condition. I did not believe that my wife had PCOS. She lacked one of the key features, obesity, and metabolic complications. My wife and I went down a one-year path of despair and lots of crying.

After months of failed attempts at inducing ovulation via assisted reproductive therapies (ART) at Johns Hopkins, we decided to go to Shady Grove Fertility. They helped us get pregnant on the very first attempt.

As many people close to us knew the year-and-a-half emotional roller coaster we had been going through, on February 14, 2019, Valentine's Day, we announced to the world that Stephanie was pregnant by posting a picture of us holding up a tiny onesie that said, "Made with Love and Science."

A few weeks later we found out the gender of our baby-to-be and released her name during a virtual gender reveal party with our family back in St. Louis. Our angel baby's name is Ashlynn Odette Hope Andrisse.

One point I often made in my talks was, "We must understand where we came from in order to understand where we are going." I would often give the history of my daughter's middle names. My mom's mom, Odette, died when my mom was only two years old. Thus, my daughter would give my mom the opportunity to meet and know Odette.

My daughter's second middle name, Hope, comes from the hope my wife and I held on to believing that God would one day deliver us a child. Stephanie's mom gave her tiny golden baby shoes as a tangible piece of hope to look at each day when we were battling through the months of infertility treatments. Stephanie hung the shoes up in our bathroom so that each morning she could see them. The very morning we were set to go into Shady Grove Fertility Center to do our first round of intrauterine insemination (IUI), she grabbed the tiny golden shoes, held them tightly, and kissed them. As she did this, she looked inside the shoes for the first time. The brand name of the shoes was Hope. She immediately began bawling. I walked in the bathroom and found her crying and held her. Finding Stephanie crying and me holding her without asking questions was almost an everyday thing in the years we were battling infertility. That very same day our beautiful daughter Ashlynn Odette Hope Andrisse was conceived into this world. Many people have rough estimates of their child's conception. We have a picture of the very moment it happened. Love and science.

❖ ❖ ❖

Back to New Orleans on October 16, 2018. The Robert Wood Johnson Foundation event was an exciting and energetic atmosphere. The event was four days long. On the morning of day two, October 16, at 4:00 a.m. CT (5:00 a.m. ET), my phone rang. I had already been up for about an hour getting some work done, my everyday work ethic.

"Hi, lovey," Stephanie's voice calmly said over the phone.

"Hi, baby, are you okay?" My voice was a little less calm.

"So, I think I'm in labor, but do not panic, everything is fine. I will not have this baby without you here," she stated. She explained how she had already called our good friend Sabrina and that Sabrina was about to drive her to Howard University Hospital.

The plan to get back home was already in place. In my mind, it felt like when Batman would say "To the Batmobile!" and secret bookshelves would turn and reveal hidden elevators and Batman would push a bunch of buttons and the Batmobile would magically appear with his Batman suit ready to go. It was almost as if I went into autopilot and I stayed in autopilot for the next forty-eight hours. I pressed some buttons and made some phone calls and, miraculously, from the Hilton Riverfront in downtown New Orleans, I was thirty thousand feet in the air within thirty minutes. I don't know how I got on the plane that quickly. It was as if I mysteriously conducted myself through TSA.

The plane ride was agonizing and anxiety-filled with moments of sporadic tears. I did not want to miss my angel being born. Thanks to modern technology, despite being tens of thousands of feet in the air, I was still connected to my wife. I purchased the eight-dollar in-flight Wi-Fi, and Stephanie and I were communicating live via Facebook Messenger.

Every five minutes or so, I would message her, "How're those contractions going?" She'd laugh and give me some silly reply, letting me know that everything was fine.

By the time I landed in BWI Airport, I was ready to shoot over to Howard University Hospital, but the hospital sent her home. I had never been happier to see my big-bellied, beautifully pregnant wife.

Later that evening, Stephanie's contractions increased, and her water broke. It was about 8:00 p.m. on October 16. We got all our birthing stuff together and drove back to Howard University Hospital.

At 11:11 p.m. on October 17, Ashlynn Odette Hope Andrisse came into this world. Stephanie was in labor from 5:00 a.m. on October 16 to 11:00 p.m. on October 17—nearly forty-eight hours. Despite the long labor, Mom and baby were both very happy and very healthy. The strength and resilience Stephanie showed during her unmedicated laboring reinforced my deep love for her.

Laying eyes on my angel for the first time was this soothing feeling. I felt the world was now in order. There was a weight released off my shoulders that I had not even known I was carrying. It would not be for a couple of days or weeks until I snapped out of this autopilot feeling that I truly realized the connection of her birth.

Ten years ago, to the exact day—October 17, 2008—I was in another out-of-body autopilot feeling. But I was not on a plane or in a hospital; I was sitting in a courtroom being told that I was a dangerous threat to society. I was being told that I had no hope for changing. I was being sentenced to ten years in prison as a career criminal. Ten years ago, to the exact day!

I suddenly realized that the soothing feeling Ashlynn brought was connected to the weight of the carceral system being fully and officially lifted from my shoulders. I had been physically free for several years now. But the birth of Ashlynn, my angel, into this world gave me emotional and psychological freedom from the carceral system.

Ashlynn's birth marked the full completion of my prison sentence, literally, figuratively, and spiritually. I felt it but I would not grasp it for probably another year. I no longer feared my story. I no longer feared the collateral consequences of my story. I was free.

❖ ❖ ❖

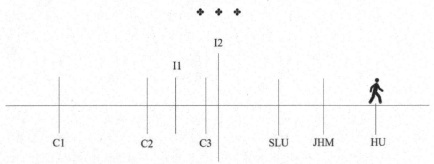

C = arrest that led to conviction; I = sentenced to incarceration; Numbers = number of that event
SLU = Saint Louis University; JHM = Johns Hopkins Medicine; HU = Howard University

Unemployment and Release from Hopkins: Spiritual and emotional freedom presented itself at a much-needed moment in my life. At the time of Ashlynn's birth, in October 2018, it had been roughly a year and a half since I had shared my story publicly in the *Washington Post*. A few weeks after that story, my boss, Sheng, released me, stating it was because of Donald Trump decreasing funding for science and medicine.

I chose not to focus my energy negatively. Sheng's and my relationship remains to this day as it had always been, a solid scientific relationship. I have always been a bottle-half-full person. I channeled my energy into finding a new job, as I would soon be an unemployed MBA and PhD holder with a Johns Hopkins postdoctoral certificate. All of that did not stop the discrimination of my criminal record. I remained unemployed for several months. I had managed to save up a very small rainy-day fund, but that was all gone relatively quickly. I started skipping payments, paying certain bills every two months instead of monthly and rotating which bills I did this with. I did not tell Stephanie the full extent of our financial struggles, but I did let her know that we were in a deep financial strain. Stephanie did not want to know detailed explanations of our finances. I may have been the executive director (ED) of P2P, but she was the executive director of our household. I was the chief financial officer (CFO) and the ED only wanted broad summaries from the CFO. That executive summary was, "We cannot do happy hours or brunches anymore, we can't plan any vacations, we have to cut back on groceries, we have to cut subscriptions, and we can't drive back to STL to see family anymore." The executive summary did not mention me skipping bills or that our mortgage was several months behind and nearing foreclosure. As the ED, Stephanie would ask, "Will we be okay?" and I would respond confidently, "Yes."

Some days I was truly confident; some days I was very down. The down days were usually tied to days where I had numerous bill collectors calling my phone on an hourly basis. It was not a good feeling. It left me feeling like less of man. Have you ever been out for dinner with your significant other or at a family gathering and your phone rings five to ten times in a row and you keep denying it because it's a bill collector? It's immensely embarrassing and looks like some side piece is calling or that you are hiding something. There's usually never a good place to interject, "I'm broke and nearing foreclosure."

From the very beginning of me pursuing my PhD studying diabetes, I had hopes of working for a drug company and being closer to the end product of medical research, developing new cutting-edge drugs and therapies. I applied to well over a hundred jobs in 2017, the year I was fired and unemployed.

At first, the same thing kept happening to me. On paper, I am amazing. My resume is phenomenal. PhD and MBA in four years, finishing at the top of my class in both. Postdoctoral scientist at the number-one endocrinology division at the number-one hospital in the nation. Leadership experience off the charts. I was president or captain of everything I have ever been a part of, from high school and college sports to high school and college student government.

My LinkedIn was so strong that I got headhunted by several companies. I would make it past the resume phase with ease. I am a great interviewer, so I'd make it past the initial interview phases relatively easily as well. I made it to the final interview phase of four big companies, and the same thing happened at all of them. I would knock the big interview day out of the park. But then the next day I would get the rejection email.

Each of these four companies spent big money to put me through eight-hour-long, multiple-team-member interviews. Becton Dickinson, the world's largest medical device company, flew me from San Francisco to New Jersey in one day's notice; the ticket was over $2,000 and then they had a private car drive me two hours to the location, another $1,000. I was certain I was going to get this job. Then I got the email the next day.

With the company that headhunted me, the Milken Institute, the recruiter stated that she was nearly 100 percent certain they were going to go with me. They wanted someone with an MBA/PhD with my exact experiences and expertise. I was informed that the job description was literally written *after* having found my LinkedIn page, and it was molded and modeled based on my credentials. Most interviewers did not meet with the president, but I did. I knocked this interview out of the park. We laughed. We joked. We politicked. We talked technical. If I was not going to get offered the job, I was surely going to get offered a date to catch up over coffee or a drink. The connection in the conversation was that strong. On top of all that, the company was founded by a formerly incarcerated person, Michael Milken,[19] a billionaire financier found guilty of racketing and fraud in 1989. But, just as in the other jobs, the very next day, I got the rejection email.

What was I doing wrong? Here lies my enigma. In every single one of these four eight-hour interviews, I was asked some variation of "So tell me the biggest mistake you've made, professionally or personally, and how you overcame it."

All the companies that I interviewed with were in states or were employers that had banned the box. I did not apply to many jobs that required me to answer the criminal conviction question. When I was asked the biggest challenge question, I told a story about a challenge I faced in work. Come to find out, because my story was now very public (in the *Washington Post*, NPR, ABC, and CBS), they were wanting me to tell my incarceration story. In my mind, if your state has banned the box, I am not legally obligated to tell you that. In the employer's perspective, me not sharing was viewed as me being dishonest. I still have the email from that headhunter apologizing that I did not get selected as she thought I would, stating it was because of my record—more precisely, because of me not sharing my story.

So, now I had to change my game plan. I had heard from four different employers that I *should* share my story. So, I began sharing my story up front. The catch-22 was that now that I was sharing my story up front, I did not receive a single offer for an interview the entire time I used this strategy.

Thus, I eventually moved into *strategy three*. I would not share up front, but I would share in the interview phase. I got to put this strategy into action relatively quickly after conceiving it.

❖ ❖ ❖

Thirty-Five Thousand Feet in the Sky: It was nearing the summer of 2017. I was pretty worn out from all the job rejections and my non-employment situation. However, I was headed to Chicago for one of my favorite scientific conferences, Experimental Biology (EB). EB is cohosted by the American Physiological Society. I had found my job at Hopkins through an ad that Sheng posted on APS. I had received my first grant award from APS as a doctoral student at SLU. APS was my beloved scientific family. I loved seeing all the APS staff and my science friends from across the country. APS was also paying me $2,000 to go to this meeting. I did not want to miss a single minute of the meeting. Thus, I was on a 5:00 a.m. flight on a Saturday morning. I was used to being up at 4:00 a.m. each morning, so I was naturally bubbly at that time.

As fate may have it, one of my APS mentors from over five years before sat in the seat right next to me on the plane. I was super excited to see him. I remembered him giving a speech at an EB event many years back about his journey to becoming a Black professor. He was incredibly inspiring for me. I eyed him down the entire time he was getting himself together as he was putting his luggage up and buckling his seatbelt. He never once made eye contact with me and immediately closed his eyes and put earbuds in.

I literally stayed awake, creepily watching him for the moment he'd open his eyes and make eye contact with me. The flight from BWI to Chicago Midway is only two and a quarter hours. We were one hour in when the opportunity presented itself. The flight attendant was coming around for the second time to get drinks. It was about 6:00 a.m. He opened his eyes and asked for coffee. Then he looked over my way.

"Heyyyy! What's up! How have you been?" I said super excitedly, like a little kid with a big Burger King smile on his face.

I was in the window seat. The middle seat was empty, and he was in the aisle seat. He looked over to the other side of the aisle without saying a word but giving the look of "Are you talking to me?"

Then he finally talked, mumbling out, "Do I know you?"

"Well, yes, well, kind of. I know you." I realized that I was tripping up on my words.

Experimental Biology is one of the biggest scientific conferences in the world. It has roughly fifteen thousand attendees from all over the globe. At these big conferences, there are scientists that give talks that often have five hundred to two thousand people in attendance. In science, this is equivalent to Jay-Z selling out the Garden. These people are science rock stars. I was sitting next to my science rock star. He didn't know me, but I knew him.

"I'm sorry. I'm Stan Andrisse. We met several years ago at EB. You were giving a talk," I managed to get out, in all my excitement. "We met when I was a second-year grad student. I'm now a postdoc at Johns Hopkins."

By this time, the attendant was back with his coffee and he was beginning to wake up. We went on talking for the remainder of the flight. A very in-depth, hour-and-fifteen-minute conversation where I did most of the talking. I told him how I was giving a big science talk and that he should come to my talk. I told him how my recent two papers were featured publications in the *Endocrine Society* journal, one of them winning the coveted cover spot. I told him how I founded and created a diversity group at Hopkins that was awarded a $5 million grant. I told him the details of my endocrinology research, essentially giving him my talk right there on the plane.

After an hour of talking about my endocrinology work, he looked at me and said, "You know, we're looking to hire an endocrinologist at Howard University College of Medicine in the physiology department." My eyes lit up. I had not even told him of my struggles with employment. I definitely did not mention that I had three felony convictions and was formerly incarcerated.

"Really?" I said.

"Yeah. Actually, I am the chair of the recruitment committee." He smiled at me. "We actually close the application today. I think you would be an excellent candidate. I know it might be hard to do today, but before we leave the conference in the next couple of days, please send me your CV, a research statement, and a teaching statement."

I was dumbfounded. I was at a loss for words. "O-Okay," I said, nodding my head in agreement.

"Even if it's not completely polished, just get something to me so we have you in the system. You've just given me the detailed, polished version right here on the plane." He smiled.

Wow. He was right. Without even knowing it, I just had a full-fledged one-hour interview thirty-five thousand feet up in the air at 6:00 in the morning. I could not have performed any better on an interview. I was beyond enthusiastic about my work. My passion was spilling over. I was clearly very energetic as I was delivering a dissertation at 6:00 in the morning. *It was the perfect interview, and I nailed it.*

One of the mottos that I live by, which I learned in prison from Ole Skool, the older gentleman I was incarcerated with, is, "*If you stay ready, you ain't got to get ready.*" Ole Skool told me this, referring to always having your boots strapped up because you never know what might pop off on the yard. My boots were always strapped up. I was always ready. As soon as we touched down, before I even left the airport, my CV, research statement, and teaching statement were in his inbox.

The EB meeting went extremely well. He and a few of his Howard colleagues came to two of my talks. Within one week, I had an HU interview email in my inbox. Going with strategy number three, I immediately sent the recruitment chair whom I spoke with on the plane my response to the criminal conviction statement, which of course I always had ready to go. In that email, I explained that my story was now very public and that I had no problem sharing it with the people I would talk with on my eight-hour interview.

The recruitment chair thanked me for sharing and congratulated me on overcoming those challenges—and then told me not to mention one word of this in the interview. The chair did not want this to bias any of his colleagues' views on my merit and accomplishments. I thought surely at Howard, the proclaimed mecca,[20] that could not be the case. But bias towards the criminal legal system exists in all aspects of American culture. Needless to say, I aced the interview as I always did, and the offer letter soon followed. Unfortunately for a person with criminal convictions, the offer letter does not quite equal getting the job. I had to pass the background check.

In academia, there are several stages of "yes" before that offer letter comes: (1) the department recruitment committee, then (2) the department chair, then (3) the dean of the college of medicine, then (4) the university's Appointments, Promotions, and Tenure Committee, and then (5) the provost and president. I went through all these stages without the recruitment chair mentioning my background to either these people or the committees. It was not until I was hired (when I signed the offer letter) that the recruitment chair informed the dean and provost of my situation. But, at this point, he had five legs to stand on. Five different committees had reviewed my application and said "Yes, we want this person as tenure-track faculty." This recruitment chair that I met just weeks ago (thirty-five thousand feet in the air) vouched for me, just as my mentor had done for me many years back at the start of my post-prison journey. *I was starting to observe a strong trend. As a person with criminal convictions, it is almost a requirement to have an inside person vouching for you to pull strings.*

After my offer letter, it took another two months to get things finalized before my official start date. It was a painful two months of still skipping bills and missing meals, but I knew reciprocity was coming soon. My salary was now twice as much as I had been receiving. On top of that, I had just recently been awarded the National Institutes of Health (NIH) Loan Repayment Program Award, which provided me an additional $35,000 per year to pay off my student loans. I was well into a six-figure salary. I hadn't been, as Jay-Z calls it, "a six-figga nigga" since back in my teenage/young adult years of hustling. I wasn't quite the six-figga nigga as I was back then. But I was doing quite well for myself. I had gone from prison cells to earning my PhD to being a Hopkins Med top nominee to the mecca of Black academic culture.

I am a Board member of the Formerly Incarcerated College Graduates Network (FICGN), that is connected to 1000s of formerly incarcerated college graduates and has the pulse for these types of things. To my knowledge and FICGN's knowledge, I am the only black male openly formerly incarcerated person who is a medical school professor.

Life today is good. I am a well-published endocrinologist scientist studying mechanisms of insulin resistance in animal and clinical models. I am a tenure-track professor at Howard University College of Medicine, which is the number-one producer of Black and brown PhD holders and medical doctors. I have a diverse research team of ten trainees that help me push forward in my cutting-edge research on insulin resistance. I founded and help run a nonprofit with twenty-six paid team members and over two hundred volunteers that are working to increase access to higher education for currently and formerly incarcerated people. But most of all, I have a loving wife, a beautiful baby girl, and a very supportive family that has been with me the entire time through this journey.

I am very fortunate. I hope to extend those blessings to as many people as I can through my nonprofit, through my academic work, and through the sharing of my life via this book. Wishing you all many blessings and good grace.

❖ ❖ ❖

Visiting China for a speaking engagement. Ruins of St. Paul, Macau. Upon returning, we started the fertility cycle that brought Ashlynn into the world. (c. November 2017)

Four months pregnant with Ashlynn. (c. 2018)

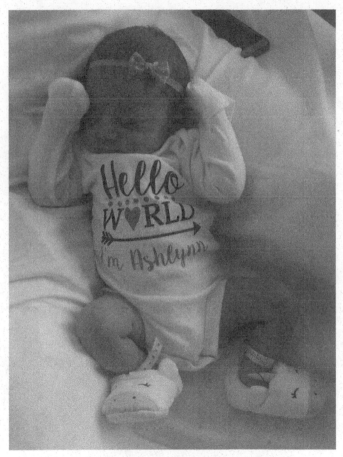

Hello World! My name is Ashlynn Odette Hope Andrisse. (October 17, 2018)

Holding my angel and closing the chapter of
my physical and psychological confinement
to the DOC. (October 17, 2018)

Message and Analysis

Education—Not Just Entry-Level Jobs—Is
Key for Those Returning from Prison

How should we reintegrate formerly incarcerated people back into society, outside the prison walls? Does education or labor present a better answer?

When you think of someone who is tagged as a dangerous criminal with multiple felony convictions and was formerly incarcerated, you may not immediately think "future CEO."[21] Researchers have found that you are more likely to think low-wage labor worker with minimal skills.[22] Is this by convention or intention?

Let's look back at the historical underpinnings of incarceration, and then reimagine the possibilities of a more educated population of formerly incarcerated persons (FIP) for the future. *We need a societal paradigm shift from the idea that FIP should focus on getting workforce development (or minimal educational attainment) for entry-level labor jobs.* We need to shift toward pushing and supporting FIP to move into higher degree attainment, STEM fields, and leadership roles.

Interestingly, 120 years ago—at the turn of the twentieth century—we were having a similar discussion. What are we to do with freed men that they have been released from slavery? Booker T. Washington won popularity with white people by saying freed Black folks should accept segregation and disfranchisement and instead work towards progress in labor and technical trades.[23] W. E. B. DuBois, the first Black PhD recipient from Harvard, took a different approach. He promoted higher education for previously enslaved persons to move toward equality with white people.

Ties Between Mass Incarceration and Slavery

Mass incarceration has been proclaimed the "new age slavery" by many scholars,[24] including Michelle Alexander[25] and Ta-Nehisi Coates[26] among others. The US imprisons far more people than any other nation. In 2017, the rate of Black incarcerated persons in the US was nearly six times as high as the rate for white imprisonment.[27] Yet after widening exponentially for several decades,[28] the gap in Black and white incarceration decreased by about 20 percent between 2007 and 2017 and has since plateaued. And leaders on both sides of the aisle are supporting measures to decrease Black incarceration even further.[29] The First Step Act[30] has potential to be the first major step towards drastically decreasing mass incarceration.[31] But what are we to do with all the formerly incarcerated folks, or "slaves of state," as they're referred to in the US Constitution,[32] once they regain their freedom?

Thus, the DuBois-versus-Washington, 125-year-old argument continues to be relevant in modern America—education or labor? On one hand, many advocates and reentry-focused, community-based organizations see workforce development as the path to successfully integrate FIP, taking the "labor perspective" of Washington.[33] Alternatively, myself and others in the #UnlockHigherEd movement promote higher education for the currently and formerly incarcerated as the #NextStep in decarcerating America, taking the "postsecondary education (PSE) perspective" of DuBois.

As with previously enslaved populations, there is a daunting disparity in postsecondary education for FIP compared to the public. The system has done well at getting incarcerated and FIP high school educated—75 percent of FIP attain their GED or high school diploma compared to 90 percent of the public—but is lagging in helping them obtain PSE. Less than 4 percent of FIP, compared to 32 percent of the public, have gone on to achieve PSE, an eight-and-a-half-fold difference. There are several prevailing theories as to why this is the case, most grounded in the stigma of incarceration.[34] Even in conversation with the funders and partners of my Prison-to-Professionals (P2P) program, it is a surprisingly tough sell[35] to convince folks that FIP need education along with, or even more importantly than, twelve-dollars-per-hour, entry-level work.

The Case for WFD

The argument for WFD[36] is that it can be obtained relatively quickly (certificates in less than one year), the salaries are livable, and the cost is relatively less than four-year college. The prevailing myth is that college is much too expensive[37] and as one of my P2P scholars once said, "college is only for rich white kids." Unfortunately, semi-rich or middle-class white and Black people have brought credence to this myth[38] by doing college all wrong. Busy middle-class parents don't have time to research colleges and costs. Thus, their academically mediocre child ends up going to the private "Harvard University" of their state, doesn't get any scholarships because they are mediocre at best, and as such pays full tuition for an art history degree. Moreover, the well-off middle-class parents wanting to be the truly wealthy Joneses don't have the money to help defray the high private-university cost. Then the media perpetuates the story of student debt[39] without telling the full story[40]—that these people did college wrong. Then, truly low-income people in poverty see "rich white people" struggling with student debt and think "this definitely isn't for me," perpetuating the generational inequity of higher education.

The Case for PSE

College can be affordable if done correctly. Going to a two-year public community college[41] then going to a four-year public university reduced debt by 82 percent. The annual tuition[42] at four-year public universities was $8,655 compared to $29,056 at four-year private universities, a three-and-a-third-fold higher cost.[43] The average annual amount paid at a four-year public is $2,490. Knowing where to shop around for scholarships and grants, like at CareerOneStop,[44] P2P on average finds its scholars $2,000 to $3,000 of *free* money. P2P regularly finds ways to get our scholars through two years of college with no money out of their pockets. Yes, vocational trades are obtained relatively quicker, but what is the rush? My partners in WFD will say, "People coming out of prison need jobs immediately." My response is, "But why? If a person's family or significant other has held down the household for five, six, seven-plus years since he/she has been gone, why can't they hold it down for two more years while the FIP gets an associate's degree?" Yes, sometimes the salaries are livable. But are people happy? Does the work bring them personal fulfilment? Do they have purpose and a sense of self-value and self-worth?

In a recent conversation, one of P2P's funding partners was ecstatically showing me the numbers of a labor force[45] social enterprise that was getting FIP construction jobs.

"Look at these numbers!" she proclaimed, showing me an ad with a Black guy wearing a hoodie, smiling, with a construction hat on. "Eighty-one percent employment compared to 30 percent! Incredible."

This is indeed notable. However, on the flipside, through P2P preliminary data, 95 percent of FIP state they are pursuing careers that are not their passion or top choice, and most program directors stated they only offered one major or career path in their programs. Thus, program directors are "forcing" FIP into careers they are not passionate about nor want to be in. But, as the people with resources and power, program directors and funders tell them they need to do this because "it's quick, it's easy, and it's what's best for you since you have a conviction."

Why aren't we letting FIP decide what's best for FIP? Oftentimes it's because the people with power and resources think they know what's best for FIP. Many people[46] think FIP aren't capable[47] of obtaining[48] middle-skill or high-skill jobs,[49] masking this true feeling with "Well, they are naturally good with their hands." Or "They did poorly in high school" or "College is not for everyone."[50] They are selling FIP short. At P2P, we let our scholars decide what's best. We utilize an asset-based methodology focusing on what's strong, not what's wrong. We help them tap into their strengths and make them stronger via pursuing their passions, then we help connect them to those passions via a variety of partnerships and connections to PSE. They do the work. We connect the dots.

Why aren't we pushing white kids to go into WFD,[51] certificate programs, and low-skill service jobs? Because society thinks white people are better[52] than that. Because of structural racism, low academically achieving white kids have the opportunity[53] to obtain middle-skill and high-skill jobs despite lower merit. Eighteen- to twenty-four-year-old white people are more than twice as likely to participate in PSE[54] than Black people. Blacks must earn a bachelor's degree[55] to make more than whites with only a HS diploma.

Why Education

PSE allows people to explore the world around them. The benefits of college[56] far outreach the most prominently known benefit, higher income. The benefits include increased community and civic engagement, increased voting, decreased unemployment, decreased poverty, increased health, increased medical insurance, increased home ownership, decreased smoking, decreased incarceration, increased school readiness for children, increased volunteerism, increased blood donations, increased public savings on social help programs, and the list goes on.

❖ ❖ ❖

Thoughts on Death, Dying, and Loss of Life

I've experienced a lot of death, dying, and loss of life, and my views on this have changed over the years. El Chapo,[57] a Mexican drug lord, was sentenced to die in prison. What gives us the right to sentence someone to death to protect our people and preserve our land and liberty? Manmade laws give us that right. We kill people who have heinously killed other people and who have egregiously disobeyed our laws. Why, then, is it so difficult for us to justify, accept, or understand why someone like El Chapo has killed before? He was following the laws of his land. Laws not too different than ours. Ones that are in place to protect this land and our people. Drug lords follow the same way of thinking and way of law—protect one's land and liberty. I, too, once followed that train of thinking.

Hear me out. I no longer believe in any of it. I don't believe that we as human beings, non-superhuman entities, non-deities, people that don't even understand life fully, have the right to take life away. Let's think deeply on death, dying, and loss of life. When is murder acceptable in our society? Quite frankly and literally—when it is ordered by a white man. Look throughout our history. Whether referring to war or in the streets, white men have been given the right to kill. George Zimmerman. Police killings. Mob bosses escaping conviction. Presidents of the United States of America. Kings and queens throughout European history. You might argue that kings and queens in African, Asian, and Middle Eastern history were given this right to kill as well. But let's think a little deeper on that. What is the prevailing thought on how people are getting killed in Middle Eastern countries? Murder. These dictators are murdering innocent people. As Americans, we don't care to learn much about why they are killing people. The picture painted for us is that it is wrong. When we (Americans) think of African countries and their killings, we think of savages and underdeveloped ways of thinking and living. Asian countries like China and North Korea are considered Communist and backwards. This leaves the authority of killing people to white men and their nations. I am simply speaking from looking at the facts of our nation's and world's history.

When a white man kills someone, it is generally seen as okay or justifiable. But when a Black man, person of color, or a non-white person kills someone, it is seen as murder and they must be harshly punished. Some might argue, "Well, there are plenty of white men in prison for murder." I would counter this with saying, "Let's take a look a mass shooting." Several white gunmen have been taken into custody peacefully after having heinously shot and killed multiple people in one setting. I, an unarmed drug dealer, was tased and beaten while taken into custody. These clearly white gunmen were given the benefit of the doubt, almost as if to say, maybe this shooting was justified. Let's treat them as innocent until proven guilty in a court of law.

❖ ❖ ❖

Thoughts on Perceptions of Sentencing Lengths and Prison Trauma

Some may ask—in fact, my wife may be the first—"Why did you include so much about your ex and your relationship?" I've come to learn through the experience of seeing it and feeling it that the pain of losing your significant other far exceeds any other separation pain, including separation from family, except from your children. In most cases, it is never talked about. It makes you look soft, weak, vulnerable, and thus targeted.

Another misnomer that I'd like to address is time of incarceration. Many non-formerly incarcerated people (and FIP) want to rate or score incarceration by length of time incarcerated. There are many faults, problems, and issues with this way of thinking. Within one week of my time in prison, I very tragically witnessed a close acquaintance of mine viciously and maliciously kill another man right in front of me. Within one week of time in prison, I was already having very serious, real, and gruesomely horrifying thoughts of killing myself. I had never experienced any of these things in my life. And yet these things alone have drastically reshaped my life, my thinking, and my physical and nonphysical psychology, as well as my emotional and mental well-being. Another very tragic example of how time does not equate trauma is the story of Kalief Browder,[58] the young man who took his life shortly after release and exoneration from a traumatic year of violence and abuse suffered in Rikers Island, a notorious New York City jail.

When asked how long I did, I'm reminded of how it was "only" one month into my sentence that I had very nearly killed myself. I'm reminded of how Kalief Browder or Sandra Bland were not as fortunate to be able to share the same words, "nearly killed." I've been told that

337

people aren't gauging or judging trauma; they just want to know the full truth. I've told these same editors and journalists that you can't get the full truth in the 1,800-word article you're writing about my life.

Additionally, would you ask a rape victim, "Did your rapist use lube when they raped you?" If they answered yes, imagine saying, "Oh, well, that's not really rape. I've had rough sex that probably hurt more." That statement is ridiculous and a journalist or any person would never say that, right? But asking years of incarceration is asking a similarly harmful question. It's asking a question to try and score how bad the incarceration was. I know. I have heard it so many times before. You are thinking, "That's not why I want to ask that." But your conscious is lying to your subconscious.

For someone, in particular a non-formerly incarcerated person, to put a score on incarceration time is emotionally damaging and retraumatizing. In this system of rating, for someone to understand my trauma, I must now explain it to you and relive it, all for this person's or society's perversion to "rate" my incarceration.

Thoughts on Sentencing

For this book, I interviewed and gathered recollections from many people in my life: lawyers, therapists, dealers, family, and friends. But the prosecuting attorney and judge declined on multiple occasions to respond to me. If the prosecuting attorney had her way, I'd still be locked up past the release date of this book. Two significant events happened regarding my sentencing. One, I was given ten years instead of the twenty to life that the prosecutor pushed for. Two, an unexplained blessing was bestowed upon me as my incarceration time changed from 70 percent to 30 percent in the blink of an eye. If these two things didn't happen, I would be in prison for fourteen years instead of the three years that I served (30 percent on my ten-year sentence). I'd still be in prison right now. Look at all the contributions I've made since my release. How many people got hit with that twenty or life instead of the ten? How many people got hit with the 70 percent instead of the 30 percent?

We partly know that answer. The data shows that it is a coin flip where 50 percent get their maximum and 50 percent get their minimum. However, a study by the U.S Sentencing Commission showed that Black men got their max sentence for the same crime (life in my case) 19.1 percent more frequently than their white male counterparts.[59] When I tell people that the two white guys in my DEA drug bust never stepped foot in prison but the three black guys all got caged in prison, audiences immediately jump to, "Well, it must be because you had priors or got caught with more drugs or some other reasonable difference." Many don't want to believe systemic racism exists. The above study showed that the racial disparity in sentencing could not be accounted for by past criminal history.

❖ ❖ ❖

We Must Understand Where We Came from to Understand Where We Are Going.

New Generation, Same Problem, In a Different Format.

Each generation has had legislation that has emboldened racial inequities. Our forefathers grounded this nation through the blood of the Revolutionary War and built it upon breaking the backs of black slaves. And from that, consecrated the Constitution for which we are founded. In that was a firm understanding that slavery[60] would be the driving industrial force[61] and that whiteness was a blessing and bestowed power and privilege of citizenship.[62] The next generation was the Civil War Era, where abolitionists were pinned against confederate beliefs. The abolishing of slavery was replaced with reconstruction laws that resulted in Jim Crow and segregation. This ensued for two generations. Riddled with lynching and enforced by the Ku Klux Klan and government policies. The next generation and its biggest policy was the new deal. The creation of the FHA and things like redlining brought generational wealth to whites and generational poverty to Blacks. And again, this era was still riddled with lynching.[63] The Civil Rights Era brought about changes like affirmative action which sought to close the wealth gap that redlining, segregation, and Jim Crow politics had been creating for over 200 years now.[64] Our generation, the sons and daughters and grandchildren of civil rights, face yet another descendant of our forefathers' vision—another descendant of the ever-evolving racial inequalities: mass incarceration.

The problem has changed from **Slavery to Reconstruction to Jim Crow to Mass incarceration**.[65] Here are some points to that argument. Blacks born in the middle class in the 1960s withdrew to poverty at three times that of whites.[66] Blacks making one-hundred-thousand dollars live with whites making thirty-thousand dollars.[67] Daniel Patrick Moynihan in the 1970s stated the Negro experience is like a diseased patient, caught up in a web of pathology.[68] He suggested social aid, but President Nixon suggested mass incarceration of primarily Black people. From 1970 to present, incarceration rose by seven-fold. Blacks without a conviction have more difficulty getting a job than whites with a conviction.[69] Whites entangled in the system are actually caught in a web that was *not* intended for them. The creators of the system essentially say, "Tough luck. At least you're still white."

Mass Incarceration.[70] One in three black men will be incarcerated in their lifetime. Black males and females go to prison at a rate six times more than whites. Since the launch of the war on drugs with things like mandatory minimums and giving prosecutors the right to sentence people as career criminals, incarceration has gone up nearly 800 percent. Furthermore, mass incarceration is a race issue. Non-poor people of color make up nearly more than the poor and non-poor white prison populations combined. **It's not just poor Black people going to prison—it's all Black people.**

School-to-Prison Pipeline.[71] Let's talk briefly about the school-to-prison pipeline and zero tolerance policies. From 2017 to 2018, students in foster care from pre-K to second grade were three times more likely to receive in-school suspension. This data is from a Texas study, but similar numbers exist across the nation. Blacks made up 13 percent of the student population but 33 percent of out-of-school suspensions and 25 percent of in-school suspensions. Black girls were suspended six times more frequently than white girls. Use of zero tolerance punishments and criminalization policies are being used **on two- and three-year-old Black babies**. If I find out that the day care teacher is criminalizing my two-year-old daughter, there are going be some real problems. That's crazy. We are criminalizing babies. In high school, I lived in, in- and out-of-school suspension. I was one suspension away from expulsion. I escaped expulsion because I was the high school's track star. I was considered a criminal in school before prison.

How did we get here? We must understand where we came from to understand where we are going. Let's dive deeper into the history. Between 1525 and 1866, 12.5 million people were kidnapped from Africa in the transatlantic slave trade.[72] Only 10.7 million survived the two-month journey. How American society remembers and teaches the horrors of slavery is crucial. Many textbooks offer a sanitized view of this history.[73] We supposedly rebuke slavery, yet we knowingly elect politicians that choose to enshrine this savagery. In the decade prior, American taxpayers contributed $40 million to maintain Confederate monuments.[74]

Systemic Inequality[75] has led to racial, economic, and educational disparities that are deeply entrenched in *all* U.S. institutions, including universities. Here are a few of these discriminatory policies: Poll taxes that disenfranchised Black voters; marginalization of Black soldiers; Black innovators barred from filing patents; white medical professionals' exploitation of Black women's bodies; the Lovings' decade-long fight for interracial marriage; the Jim Crow Era and segregation of American cities and schools—to name a few. I of course could go on much longer.

Beyond enslavement, exploitation, and inequality, Blacks have long been the targets of racially-charged physical violence. The Equal Justice Initiative stated that more than 4,400 lynchings[76] took place in the U.S. between the end of Reconstruction and WWII. The Senate *only* passed legislation declaring lynching a federal crime in 2018.[77] Between 1918 and 2018, more than 200 anti-lynching bills failed. Because the politicians we elected didn't think that Black lives mattered. Incidents of Black bodies lying (or hanging) dead in the streets is not new to this country.

❖ ❖ ❖

Analysis of "Poverty Porn" and How the Media Propagates a Negative Narrative

"Poverty porn, also known as development porn, famine porn, or stereotype porn, has been defined as 'any type of media, be it written, photographed or filmed, which exploits the poor's condition in order to generate the necessary sympathy for selling newspapers or increasing charitable donations or support for a given cause.'"

The media has an infatuation with lengthy sentences. A 2017 Huffington Post article[78] detailed the fourteen reasons America is obsessed with prison and lengthy sentences, titled, "The 14 Most F#$%ed Up Things about America's Obsession with Putting People Behind Bars."

A 2019 Politico article[79] argues that shorter sentences will end prison crowding and even reduce crime. One of the main issues, as I see it, is that the media[80] perpetuates the use of long sentences. Think about how many crime drama TV shows there are: here is a list of the top two hundred by IMDb.[81] Then there are the crime reality TV shows: here is a list of the top one hundred by Ranker.[82]

Wikipedia[83] has an A-to-Z list of over a thousand in the past fifty years. Why are we so addicted to crime TV?[84] It is not by mistake; it is by intention. Look at the years when most of these popular dramas and reality shows began, in the late 1980s through the early 2000s. This was the height of the war on drugs, and it was the exponential phase of mass incarceration.

A 2020 *Hill* article[85] argued that TV crime shows present a warped view of our criminal justice system. Crime series on television are changing the way Americans see reality. For politics, big-money interests, and structural racism to continue thriving, they need to lie to the masses.

They need to scare society. They need to keep them intrigued with the foul portrayal of crime and criminals. This is accomplished very discreetly and covertly through media.

In order to turn this tide of negative portrayals, we need more uplifting portrayals of prison life, such as PBS's 2019 miniseries *College Behind Bars*, which details the triumphs of people in New York prisons as they complete college on the inside through Bard's Prison Initiative. We need more accurate portrayals of the system such as Bryan Stevenson's 2019 book-to-film *Just Mercy*, which details the blatantly racist practices of the Southern criminal system to unjustly prosecute and execute Black bodies. Here is a list of ten prison movies,[86] most of which propagate a negative portrayal of prison.

Blackness and Criminality

I mentioned my Blackness and its affiliation with criminality in Chapter 3.1 (my first hundred-pound deal with my Mexican friends), Chapter 3.4 (pulling a gun on Jake in front of his wife, and child), and in Chapter 5.1 (the prosecutor seeing hope in whiteness but hopelessness in Blackness). I mentioned my criminality in Chapter 7.1 (treatments attempt at breaking criminality), Chapter 7.4 (my fears while attending my players' basketball game after being fired, and my fears at Dion's funeral), Chapter 8.1 (institutionalization and my feelings towards my graduate student friends), and Chapter 8.2 (dating and women repeatedly rejecting me). My Blackness has been viewed by society and me as intimately tied to criminality. Imagine a world where Blackness was tied to excellence. A world where if I walk into a job interview, my Blackness says that I'm highly educated and well accomplished, with endless potential. We need to change the narrative.

Transferable Skills

In my nonprofit's Prison-to-Professionals program, one of the activities we do is called "Criminal Skills." This is one of several epiphany moments for most of our currently and formerly incarcerated participants, whom we call scholars. We ask them to dive back into the days of their deepest criminality and to inform the group on the "criminal skills" they were using then. Every single time, after twenty plus cohorts, a room full of twenty to forty men and women completely fill up an entire white board with skills. The anticipation and excitement is building as the classroom erupts into participants sharing intricate details of dedication, leadership, project management, people relations, customer management, fearlessness, and much more. We have two to three team members frantically writing down skills on the white board. The epiphany moment comes as the white board is completely full and we then scratch out the word criminal skills and replace it with "transferable skills." You can literally see the light bulbs clicking as we explain this concept to the scholars.

As with my case, the system (my prosecutor) tells us that we are worthless, that our skills are criminal and no good and that we need to get rid of those criminal skills. They don't tell us that these are the same skills that white men and people of privilege and power have sitting at long fancy walnut boardroom tables with plush seats closing million and billion dollar deals. They don't tell us that these are the same skills that white students and people with access and opportunity have sitting in classrooms at places like Johns Hopkins and Harvard University solving Calculus II equations and acing graduate admissions exams.

Take me for example. I had been using a multitude of leadership skills since I was fourteen years old. I was running a business that pulled in a million dollars (street value) of revenue at nineteen years old. I was closely managing several director-level positions (Fab Five 1.0 and 2.0), coaching team members, providing one-on-one feedback, handing out promotions for good performance, and delivering sanctions for subpar behaviors. I held regular strategic planning meetings, set monthly and yearly financial projections for sales and revenue, and developed a supply chain management and logistics plan. I was tireless with the hustle, often working long days on the road with little sleep. I was dedicated to sticking to the script and achieving the goals set out in our strategic plans. In prison, I honed in on patience, built upon my resilience and intuition, and continued showing leadership, fearlessness, compassion, and love for others. All of these skills, now re-purposed, are exactly why I completed my MBA and PhD in record time and at the top of my class.

Over four hundred currently and formerly incarcerated people from across the nation apply to P2P each year with roughly one hundred starting and completing the program. Nearly 100 percent of scholars who completed our program matriculated into college and maintained a 3.75 GPA and recidivated at less than 2 percent. We employ dozens of formerly incarcerated people which make up 85 percent of our team. We have P2P scholars or team members in over thirty states. In 2020, we opened the first P2P House in Baltimore which is transitional housing for people returning from prison that operates like a college dorm. Over 80 percent of the people we work with are people with crimes considered to be violent and dangerous. We help them see themselves as scholars instead of the violent criminals that society has labeled them.

Analysis of Empathy Towards Crime

The movie *Just Mercy* brings me to another point: the media's and society's deep empathy for innocence project stories[87] where people erroneously, blatantly, and unjustly got lengthy sentences. The Innocence Project, the Innocence Network, and Equal Justice Initiative are just a few organizations geared at exonerating the innocent. I don't think anyone would argue that there is no one more deserving of being released from prison than someone who truly should not be there in the first place because they are innocent. Bryan Stevenson's Equal Justice Initiative specifically works to exonerate people on death row who are innocent or wrongly convicted. He often quotes a statistic that "for every nine people executed, one person on death row has been exonerated." Stevenson argues, "The question we need to ask about the death penalty in America is not whether someone deserves to die for a crime. The question is whether we deserve to kill."

I had the pleasure of meeting Bryan Stevenson in 2018, as I was a Johns Hopkins faculty member sitting near him on the stage at the 2018 Hopkins graduation ceremony for which he delivered the keynote. I walked with him as we were entering the Royal Farms Arena's center stage. I gave him my thirty-second elevator pitch of being a formerly incarcerated Johns Hopkins faculty member. He was amazed. Holding back my childish, starstruck feelings, I calmly handed him my business card. Bryan Stevenson is a rock star to me. His work gives me chills and often brings me to tears, as the film *Just Mercy* did.

However, the success of Brian Stevenson and all the great work he has done are part of this conundrum. Please understand that *he* or *his* work is not the problem. The popularity of *innocence stories* is part of the problem. Think of the work that Kim Kardashian West[88] did with Donald Trump in 2018–2019 to help free Alice Johnson and others from prison. Think of the compassion people felt for this unjustly convicted mother. How could the system do that to a mother? In this space of "innocence stories mixed with crime drama and reality TV," there's little room left for the other stories. The "bad people"-turned-good stories. The Stan Andrisse stories.

This brings me to another point: the media's empathy for drug crimes. Crime and people who commit crimes are seen as black and white. There are good people and there are bad people. This is why there is so much empathy for innocence projects. These are good people. In the era of the opioid crisis, drug crimes have moved into this territory. People with low-level drug crimes are good people with a health problem. These "good people" need medical attention, not incarceration. Thus, media and society very easily show empathy for people with drug crimes. For instance, I have mentioned several times now that I do two to four speaking engagements per week. Depending on my audience, I detail my crimes and convictions very differently to get my message across more effectively. In audiences with less proximity to crime and conviction, I share much less detail about my drug convictions. In audiences with very close proximity to crime and conviction, like when I speak in prisons, I share the whole pie and talk about me carrying guns and moving hundreds of pounds of dope. For the audiences where I share less about my crimes, it is assumed that I was harshly sentenced to ten years for a rather minor drug possession charge. This assumption is something that I intentionally play on. I know that the audience will have more empathy for me and thus accept my message more readily if they don't know that I was more like a drug lord as opposed to a nickel-and-dimer or drug user. This is why I chose to be so open in this book in detailing some of the aspects of my life and drug dealing that I have never shared before.

The media and society have a lack of understanding of drug crimes. Many tend to think all people with drug crimes were petty dealers and got hammered by the system. This is why there is a strong push to release people with drug convictions from prison. I am in agreeance with this push. However, this in particular does not leave room for empathizing with the person who truly behaved as a "dangerous person." This focuses the narrative again on there being good people and bad people, and that bad people will always be bad people. This does not leave the ability or room to truly believe in change. This empathizes with people who were never really "bad people" or did anything majorly wrong. But what about people who did do serious wrong but are different people now? Aren't they deserving of empathy? Aren't they deserving of a second chance? Don't we want to believe in the human capacity to change?

So many things in my life I have done terribly wrong. I was seeking to solve adult challenges and inequities with adolescent knowledge and philosophies. It's easy to find mercy for someone who was wrongfully convicted or someone who was charged with a minor crime or something less serious or heinous, but can we find it within ourselves to have mercy for those who are truly guilty of serious crimes? I don't think we are there yet. That is what I hope to do. That is what I hope to have you see. That change is possible. That *it is never too late to do good.*

I battled with including some of the things that I've added, but I felt that I had to tell the whole truth. I felt that this had to lay it all out. I felt that people needed to understand that what someone did is not who they are.

When you have empathy stories like the drug dealer who had to sell drugs to feed his two-year-old daughter and pay her medical bills because she had cancer, your heart feels for this person and his sick daughter. But does your heart allow your mind to simultaneously know that this drug dealer had to pistol-whip another man in front of that man's wife and kids? Do you still hold empathy for that drug dealer?

Through interacting with hundreds of people with convictions, engaging thousands of people through my many speaking appearances, and conversing with dozens of thought leaders and key stakeholders, the answer most often is no. Society no longer holds empathy for a person once any sort of violence is attached to the crime.

I have received empathy from thousands if not hundreds of thousands of people that have read articles about me or have heard me speak. None of these articles or my speaking engagements dove deep into the violence of my past life.

My hope is that since hundreds of thousands have already extended me their empathy, they will continue to extend that empathy knowing the violence I engaged in. I hope they can hold the two, empathy and my violent past, with the guiding principle that *it is never too late to do good*. Humans by nature of design are not static characters. We are dynamic. We change over time. That is the beauty of our human being.

Does Incarceration Work?

The Prison Policy Initiative[89] broke down the incarceration pie and debunked the biggest five myths of the system with suggestions. The first myth: releasing "nonviolent drug offenders" would end mass incarceration. The second myth: private prisons are the corrupt heart of mass incarceration. The third myth: prisons are "factories behind fences" that exist to provide companies with a huge slave labor force. The fourth myth: people in prison for violent or sexual crimes are too dangerous to be released. The fifth myth: expanding community supervision is the best way to reduce incarceration.

The Equal Justice Initiative[90] offered a short and to-the-point response that "no, incarceration does not work." They offered the "age-out theory," where crime is drastically reduced among people over the age of twenty-five. Research shows that crime starts to peak in the mid- to late-teenage years and begins to decline when individuals are in their mid-twenties. After that, crime drops sharply as adults reach their thirties and forties.

The Vera Institute's *The Prison Paradox*[91] summarizes research about the relationship between incarceration rates and crime rates, finding that, since 2000, the increased use of jails and prisons accounted for nearly 0 percent of the overall reduction in crime. Instead, between 75 and 100 percent of the drop in crime rates since the 1990s is explained by other factors, including the aging population, increased wages, increased employment, increased graduation rates, increased consumer confidence, and changes in policing strategies.

The Sentencing Project[92] offered great facts sheets and infographics, saying:

> Incarceration has some impact on crime, but the impact is one of diminishing returns. Crime rates have declined substantially since the early 1990s, but studies suggest that rising imprisonment has not played a major role in this trend. The National Research Council concluded that while prison growth was a factor in reducing crime, "the magnitude of the crime reduction remains highly uncertain and the evidence suggests it was unlikely to have been large." Several factors explain why this impact was relatively modest. First, incarceration is particularly ineffective at reducing certain kinds of crimes; in particular, youth crimes, many of which are committed in groups, and drug crimes. When people get locked up for these offenses, they are easily replaced on the streets by others seeking an income or struggling with addiction.

The Sentencing Project offered these suggestions: "(1) Eliminating mandatory minimum sentences and cutting back on excessively lengthy sentences. (2) Shifting resources to community-based prevention and treatment for substance abuse. (3) Investing in interventions that promote strong youth development and respond to delinquency in age-appropriate ways. (4) Examining and addressing the policies and practices, conscious or not, that contribute to racial inequity at every stage of the legal system. (5) Removing barriers that make it harder for individuals with criminal records to turn their lives around."

What Would I Tell the Teenage Me?

Be patient with yourself and the world. Give yourself time to grow and learn more about people, society, and ineptitudes on human behavior. I felt the cards were unfairly stacked against certain people. Tupac and rap (and Key amongst others) taught me that. But they didn't exactly teach me how or why. Selling drugs was a way to quickly even the odds and promote financial empowerment.

Am I a Rare Exception?

To write my story as an exceptional one inherently says, "Them other niggaz is just niggaz," and that's why they still are where they are. The story must be phrased as, "The *system* is why there are not more Stan Andrisses." It is not that Stan Andrisse is a rare exception.

I refer you to Ibram Kendi, *How to Be an Antiracist*. In chapter eleven, "Black," he tells a story of how the Black editor-in-chief of the FAMU (a well-known HBCU) newsletter scolded him in his senior year. Kendi wrote a controversial article about white people after the 2000 election recount debacle in Florida. His editor opened the conversation by telling Kendi an anecdote about how he was recently pulled over by the cops and that the cops treated him like he was one of "them niggaz." Kendi then went on to explain how Chris Rock made that phrase "them niggaz" popular by making a slew of skits about "them niggaz."

Kendi stated that successful Black people are often likely to want to find ways to separate themselves from "them niggaz." Indirectly and subconsciously, if you envision me as exceptional, then you are calling the other people I was locked up with "them niggaz."

I am not a rare exception. There are many exceptional people in prison, but they lack access and opportunities. Talent is distributed evenly, but access and opportunity are not. And I'm going to do everything in my power to change that.

Society can benefit from understanding that *it is never too late to do good.*

REFERENCES

Chapter 1

[1] Andrew Schiller, "NeighborhoodScout's Murder Capitals of America – 2021," *Blog*, NeighborhoodScout, January 2, 2021, https://www.neighborhoodscout. com/top-lists/highest-murder-rate-cities/.

[2] "Justice Department Finds a Pattern of Civil Rights Violations by the Ferguson Police Department," USDOJ, March 2015, https://www.justice.gov/opa/ pr/justice-department-announces-findings-two-civil-rights-investigations-ferguson-missouri.

[3] "The World Bank In Haiti," The World Bank, https://www.worldbank.org/en/ country/haiti/overview#1.

[4] Smucker, Glenn R. "The Middle Class," *A Country Study: Haiti* (Richard A. Haggerty, editor), Library of Congress Federal Research Division (December 1989).

[5] "Haiti profile – Timeline." BBC News, February 2019, https://www.bbc.com/ news/world-latin-america-19548814.

[6] "Haiti - Poverty and wealth," Encyclopedia of Nations, https://www.nation-sencyclopedia.com/economies/Americas/Haiti-POVERTY-AND-WEALTH. html.

Chapter 2

[1] Robert C. Bartlett, "Masters of Greek Thought: Plato, Socrates, and Aristotle," (online course, The Great Courses), https://www.thegreatcourses.com/courses/ masters-of-greek-thought-plato-socrates-and-aristotle.html.

[2] Victor Luckerson, "Black Wall Street: The African American Haven That Burned and Then Rose from the Ashes," The Ringer, June 28, 2018, https:// www.theringer.com/2018/6/28/17511818/black-wall-street-oklahoma-greenwood-destruction-tulsa.

Chapter 3

1 Nelson George, *Hip Hop America* (New York: Penguin Books, 2005), Kindle.

2 Ben Westhoff, "The City Next to Ferguson Is Even More Depressing," Vice, June 2, 2015, https://www.vice.com/en_us/article/bnpzda/the-spectacular-decline-of-the-historic-town-next-to-ferguson-missouri-602.

Chapter 4

1 David Mikkelson, "'Dry Now' Billboards," Snopes, last updated July 4, 2011, https://www.snopes.com/fact-check/the-weed-whacker/.

2 Sean Sands et. al. "How Long Can You Be Held Without Charges?" Find Law, 2020, https://www.findlaw.com/criminal/criminal-rights/how-long-may-police-hold-suspects-before-charges-must-be-filed.html.

3 The State of Bail Reform, "The System" 4, The Marshall Project, updated October 30, 2020, https://www.themarshallproject.org/2020/10/30/the-state-of-bail-reform.

4 "Manhattan Project Spotlight: Deak Parsons," Atomic Heritage Foundation, September 2016, https://www.atomicheritage.org/article/manhattan-project-spotlight-deak-parsons.

5 Si Cantwell. "A 'self-made man' armed Hiroshima bomb," Star News Online, March 2008, https://www.starnewsonline.com/article/NC/20080326/News/605084747/WM.

6 John Gramlich, "Only 2% of Federal Criminal Defendants Go to Trial, and Most Who Do Are Found Guilty," Pew Research Center, June 11, 2019, https://www.pewresearch.org/fact-tank/2019/06/11/only-2-of-federal-criminal-defendants-go-to-trial-and-most-who-do-are-found-guilty/.

7 "06LF-CV00862 - STANLEY ANDRISSE V WILLIAM PAGE BELLAMY ET AL," Missouri Courts, 16 Oct. 2006, https://www.courts.mo.gov/casenet/cases/header.do?inputVO.caseNumber=06LF-CV00862&inputVO.courtId=SMPDB0001_CT15&inputVO.isTicket=false.

8 Wikipedia, s.v. "Lindenwood Lions Football," last edited January 30, 2021, 03:28 (UTC), https://en.wikipedia.org/wiki/Lindenwood_Lions_football.

9   "04CV127227-STATE OF MISSOURI V STAN ANDRISSE ET AL," Missouri Courts, 7 June 2004, https://www.courts.mo.gov/casenet/cases/header.do?inputVO.caseNumber=04CV127227&inputVO.courtId=CT11&inputVO.isTicket=false.

10   Colin Wilson, "666: The Day of the Devil," *Daily Mail*, last updated June 6, 2006, https://www.dailymail.co.uk/news/article-389081/666-day-Devil.html.

11   "Centralia[']s Biggest Drug Bust," KOMU 8, August 30, 2006, https://www.komu.com/news/centralias-biggest-drug-bust/article_e609c82a-6ef0-5d9e-a543-06278dadae75.html.

12   DEA Public Affairs, "30 People Indicted for Involvement in St. Louis Drug Trafficking Network," news release no. 202-307-7977, January 19, 2006, https://www.dea.gov/sites/default/files/divisions/stl/2006/pr011906p.html.

13   "22 Indicted after 18-Month Federal Drug Conspiracy Probe," News on 6, August 29, 2007, https://www.newson6.com/story/5e367bfa2f69d76f6208ec3d/22-indicted-after-18month-federal-drug-conspiracy-probe.

Chapter 5

1   Prior and Persistent Drug Offenders, Definitions, Sentencing, Revisor of Missouri § 579.170 (2017), https://revisor.mo.gov/main/OneSection.aspx?section=579.170.

2   "0811-CR01450-01 - ST V STAN ANDRISSE," Missouri Courts, 3 Sept. 2008, https://www.courts.mo.gov/casenet/cases/header.do?inputVO.caseNumber=0811-CR01450-01&inputVO.courtId=CT11&inputVO.isTicket=false.

3   Anthony E. Bottoms, "Interpersonal Violence and Social Order in Prisons," *Crime and Justice* 26 (1999): 205–281, http://www.jstor.org/stable/1147687.

4   Wendy Sawyer, "New Government Report Points to Continuing Mental Health Crisis in Prisons and Jails," Prison Policy Initiative, June 22, 2017, https://www.prisonpolicy.org/blog/2017/06/22/mental_health/.

5   *Procedures Governing the Granting of Paroles and Conditional Releases*, Board of Probation and Parole, State of Missouri Department of Corrections, January 1, 2017, https://doc.mo.gov/sites/doc/files/2018-01/Blue-Book.pdf.

6   "Habeas Corpus," last edited June 2017, Legal Information Institute, Cornell Law School, https://www.law.cornell.edu/wex/habeas_corpus.

Chapter 6

1   *Reimagining Prison Web Report*, Vera Institute of Justice, October 2018, https://www.vera.org/reimagining-prison-web-report.

2   "109. RICO Charges," US Department of Justice Archives, updated January 22, 2020, https://www.justice.gov/archives/jm/criminal-resource-manual-109-rico-charges.

3   Ryan Delaney, "St. Louis School Desegregation Program Begins Its Long Wind Down," St. Louis Public Radio, November 1, 2018, https://news.stlpublicradio.org/education/2018-11-01/st-louis-school-desegregation-program-begins-its-long-wind-down.

4   JD Bremner, "Traumatic Stress: Effects on the Brain," *Dialogues in Clinical Neuroscience* 8, no. 4. (2006): 445–461, https://www.ncbi.nlm.nih.gov/pmc/articles/PMC3181836/.

5   *The Importance of the Company You Keep: The Effectiveness of Social Support Interventions for Prisoners*, American Enterprise Institute, October 10, 2018, https://www.aei.org/research-products/report/the-importance-of-the-company-you-keep-the-effectiveness-of-social-support-interventions-for-prisoners/.

6   Marc Mauer, "Long-Term Sentences: Time to Reconsider the Scale of Punishment," The Sentencing Project, November 5, 2018, https://www.sentencingproject.org/publications/long-term-sentences-time-reconsider-scale-punishment/.

7   Hollie McKay, "Pedophiles in Prison: The Hell That Would Have Awaited Epstein If He'd Stayed Behind Bars," Fox News, August 21, 2019, https://www.foxnews.com/us/jeffrey-epstein-pedophiles-prison-hell.

8   "High School Reading Books," Goodreads, https://www.goodreads.com/shelf/show/high-school-reading.

Chapter 7

1   Virginia Gewin, "Moving from Prison to a PhD," *Nature*, October 31, 2019, https://www.nature.com/articles/d41586-019-03370-1.

2   Peter Wagner and Bernadette Rabuy, "Mass Incarceration: The Whole Pie 2016," Prison Policy Initiative, March 14, 2016, https://www.prisonpolicy.org/reports/pie2016.html.

3   Lauren-Brooke Eisen et al., "How Many Americans Are Unnecessarily Incarcerated?" Brennan Center for Justice, December 9, 2016, https://www.brennancenter.org/our-work/research-reports/how-many-americans-are-unnecessarily-incarcerated.

4   Michelle Ye Hee Lee, "Does the United States Really Have 5 Percent of the World's Population and One Quarter of the World's Prisoners?" *Washington Post*, April 30, 2015, https://www.washingtonpost.com/news/fact-checker/wp/2015/04/30/does-the-united-states-really-have-five-percent-of-worlds-population-and-one-quarter-of-the-worlds-prisoners/.

5   Michelle Ye Hee Lee, "Yes, U.S. Locks People Up at a Higher Rate Than Any Other Country," *Washington Post*, July 7, 2015, https://www.washingtonpost.com/news/fact-checker/wp/2015/07/07/yes-u-s-locks-people-up-at-a-higher-rate-than-any-other-country/.

6   Gergő Baranyi et al., "Prevalence of Posttraumatic Stress Disorder in Prisoners," *Epidemiologic Reviews* 40, no. 1 (2018): 134–145, https://www.ncbi.nlm.nih.gov/pmc/articles/PMC5982805/.

7   Angela Davis, "Masked Racism: Reflections on the Prison Industrial Complex," History Is a Weapon, https://www.historyisaweapon.com/defcon1/davisprison.html.

8   Melinda D. Anderson, "How Mass Incarceration Pushes Black Children Further Behind in School," *Atlantic*, January 16, 2017, https://www.theatlantic.com/education/archive/2017/01/how-mass-incarceration-pushes-black-children-further-behind-in-school/513161/.

9   Lucius Couloute and Daniel Kopf, "Out of Prison & Out of Work: Unemployment among Formerly Incarcerated People," Prison Policy Initiative, July 2018, https://www.prisonpolicy.org/reports/outofwork.html.

10 "Sleep Paralysis," WebMD, last reviewed October 17, 2020, https://www.webmd.com/sleep-disorders/sleep-paralysis#1.

11 Valerie Schremp Hahn, "Man Found Fatally Shot inside Vehicle in St. Louis Is Identified," *St. Louis Post-Dispatch*, March 6, 2014, https://www.

stltoday.com/news/local/crime-and-courts/man-found-fatally-shot-inside-vehicle-in-st-louis-is/article_088a52bb-19a0-5860-b059-fc45d19a0fe6.html.

12   Denise Hollinshed, "One Killed, Three Wounded in Two St. Louis Shootings," *St. Louis Post-Dispatch*, November 16, 2013, https://www.stltoday.com/news/local/crime-and-courts/one-killed-three-wounded-in-two-st-louis-shootings/article_f47c16ba-2713-5504-8e91-361655b93f93.html.

13   "Voting Rights," The Sentencing Project, http://www.sentencingproject.org/issues/felony-disenfranchisement/.

14   "State-by-State Data," The Sentencing Project, http://www.sentencingproject.org/the-facts/#detail?state1Option=U.S.%20Total&state2Option=Missouri.

15   *Felony Disenfranchisement* (Washington, DC: The Sentencing Project, updated April 2014), http://www.sentencingproject.org/wp-content/uploads/2015/12/Felony-Disenfranchisement-Laws-in-the-US.pdf.

16   Ari Berman, "How the 2000 Election in Florida Led to a New Wave of Voter Disenfranchisement," *Nation*, July 28, 2015, https://www.thenation.com/article/how-the-2000-election-in-florida-led-to-a-new-wave-of-voter-disenfranchisement/.

17   Andrisse, Stan. "From Prison Cells to Ph.D.: Felony Disenfranchisement and My Voting Rights." Biomedical Odyssey: Life at the Johns Hopkins School of Medicine. 31 Jul. 2017, https://biomedicalodyssey.blogs.hopkinsmedicine.org/2017/07/from-prison-cell-to-ph-d-felony-disenfranchisement-and-my-voting-rights/.

Chapter 8

1   National Research Council, *The Growth of Incarceration in the United States: Exploring Causes and Consequences* (Washington, DC: The National Academies Press, 2014), https://www.nap.edu/read/18613/chapter/8.

2   Ellen Kjelsberg et al., "Attitudes towards Prisoners, as Reported by Prison Inmates, Prison Employees and College Students," *BMC Public Health* 7, no. 71 (May 4, 2007): https://www.ncbi.nlm.nih.gov/pmc/articles/PMC1891097/.

3   "The Origins of Jim Crow," Jim Crow Museum, Ferris State University, https://www.ferris.edu/jimcrow/origins.htm.

4   Craig Haney, "The Psychological Impact of Incarceration: Implications for Post-prison Adjustment," Office of the Assistant Secretary for Planning and Evaluation, Department of Health and Human Services, December 2001, https://aspe.hhs.gov/basic-report/psychological-impact-incarceration-implications-post-prison-adjustment.

5   Richard McCorkle, "Personal Precautions to Violence in Prison," *Criminal Justice and Behavior* 19 (1992): 161.

6   A. J. Taylor, "Social Isolation and Imprisonment," *Psychiatry* 24 (1961): 373.

7   "2014 Best Graduate Schools Preview: Top 10 Medical Schools," US News and World Report, March 11, 2013, https://www.usnews.com/education/best-graduate-schools/top-medical-schools/articles/2013/03/11/2014-best-graduate-schools-preview-top-10-medical-schools.

8   Rana Campbell and Yariela Kerr-Donovan, "Employers Must Understand Their Role in Post-incarceration Success," Vera Institute of Justice, November 19, 2014, https://www.vera.org/blog/unlocking-potential/employers-must-understand-their-role-in-post-incarceration-success.

9   "Transforming the Culture for Basic Scientists," Office of Diversity, Inclusion and Health Equity, Johns Hopkins Medicine, January 25, 2017, https://www.hopkinsmedicine.org/diversity/annual-reports/2016-annual-report/transforming-the-culture-for-basic-scientists.

10 "Cohorts 2016-2019," Faculty Affairs, Office of the Provost, Johns Hopkins University, https://facultyaffairs.jhu.edu/provosts-office-faculty-initiatives-3/faculty-diversity-initiative/postdoctoral-fellowship-program/postdoctoral-fellowship-program-cohorts/.

11 "Postdoc Diversity and Inclusion," Office of the Provost, Johns Hopkins University, https://provost.jhu.edu/education/postdoctoral-affairs/the-postdoc-community/postdoc-diversity-and-inclusion/.

12 Nivet MA, Minorities in academic medicine: review of the literature, J Vasc Surg, 2010;51(4 Suppl):53S-58S.

13 Kendi, Ibram X., *How to Be an Antiracist*, New York: One World, 2019.

14 Alexander, M. (2010). *The new Jim Crow: Mass incarceration in the age of colorblindness*. The New Press.

15 DiAngelo, Robin J., *White Fragility: Why It's so Hard for White People to Talk About Racism*, Boston: Beacon Press, 2018.

Chapter 9

1   Ovetta Wiggins, "Taking a Lawbreaking Past Out of College Applications," *Washington Post*, February 2017, https://www.washingtonpost.com/local/md-politics/taking-a-lawbreaking-past-out-of-college-applicati ons/2017/02/27/c98efe3e-f311-11e6-a9b0-ecee7ce475fc_story.html.

2   Kelly Swoope, "From Prison to PhD: One man's second chance," ABC2 WMAR Baltimore, May 2017, https://www.wmar2news.com/news/region/baltimore-city/from-prison-to-phd-one-mans-second-chance.

3   "Benefits of Higher Education – In Prison and After Prison" https://static1.squarespace.com/static/53af218ee4b00644e6dad9f8/t/5611b736e4b0b-3f00aabb888/1444001590685/Benefits-of-Higher-Ed.pdf.

4   "Criminal Justice Facts," The Sentencing Project, http://www.sentencingproj-ect.org/criminal-justice-facts/.

5   Andrisse, Stan. "Spreading Hope to Those Deemed Hopeless." Biomedical Odyssey: Life at the Johns Hopkins School of Medicine. 22 Jun. 2017, https://biomedicalodyssey.blogs.hopkinsmedicine.org/2017/06/spreading-hope-to-those-deemed-hopeless/.

6   "On Time: May 14, 2017," CBS Baltimore, May 14, 2017, http://baltimore.cbslocal.com/2017/05/14/on-time-may-14-2017/.

7   "Collateral Consequences," The Sentencing Project, http://www.sentencing-project.org/issues/collateral-consequences/.

8   Andrisse, Stan. "From Prison Cells to PhD: Words Matter." Biomedical Odyssey: Life at the Johns Hopkins School of Medicine. 29 Aug. 2017, https://biomedicalodyssey.blogs.hopkinsmedicine.org/2017/08/from-prison-cells-to-phd-words-matter/.

9   Maryland Fair Access to Education Act of 2017, SB 543, Maryland General Assembly, 2017 Session (MD 2017), http://mgaleg.maryland.gov/2017RS/fnotes/bil_0003/sb0543.pdf.

10 America Now, "Obama Calls to 'Ban the Box,'" YouTube video, 02:04, November 3, 2015, https://www.youtube.com/watch?v=Ec2o8qiMeGA.

11 *Beyond the Box: Increasing Access to Higher Education for Justice-Involved Individuals* (Washington, DC: US Department of Education, 2016), https://www2.ed.gov/documents/beyond-the-box/guidance.pdf.

12 *The Use of Criminal History Records in College Admissions Reconsidered* (New York: Center for Community Alternatives), http://www.communityalternatives.org/pdf/Reconsidered-criminal-hist-recs-in-college-admissions.pdf.

13 "NRRC Facts & Trends," National Reentry Resource Center, https://csgjusticecenter.org/nrrc/facts-and-trends/.

14 "Boxed Out Criminal History Screening and College Application Attrition" Center For Community Alternatives, March 2015, :http://www.communityalternatives.org/wp-content/uploads/2019/11/boxed-out.pdf.

15 "Home," Unlock Higher Ed, https://www.unlockhighered.org/.

16 From Prison Cells to PhD Inc, "From Prison Cells to PhD - Stan Andrisse," YouTube video, 04:51, November 24, 2017, https://www.youtube.com/watch?v=HQ68ihYOnjk.

17 Andrisse, Stan. "Ban the Box on College Applications." Biomedical Odyssey: Life at the Johns Hopkins School of Medicine. 2 Oct. 2017, https://biomedicalodyssey.blogs.hopkinsmedicine.org/2017/10/ban-the-box-on-college-applications/.

18 "Princeton Prison Teaching Initiative Awarded NSF Grant to Promote STEM Careers," Prison Teaching Initiative, Princeton University, September 23, 2019, https://www.princeton.edu/news/2019/09/23/princeton-prison-teaching-initiative-awarded-nsf-grant-promote-stem-careers.

19 William D. Cohan, "Michael Milken Invented the Modern Junk Bond, Went to Prison, and Then Became One of the Most Respected People on Wall Street," Business Insider, May 2, 2017, https://www.businessinsider.com/michael-milken-life-story-2017-5.

20 Ta-Nehisi Coates, "The Journey to Mecca," *The Atlantic*, April 2013, https://www.theatlantic.com/politics/archive/2013/04/the-journey-to-mecca/274980/.

21 Couloute and Kopf, "Out of Prison."

22 *Highlights from the U.S. PIAAC Survey of Incarcerated Adults: Their Skills, Work Experience, Education, and Training* (Washington, DC: US Department of Education, 2014), https://nces.ed.gov/pubs2016/2016040.pdf.

23 "The Debate between W.E.B. Du Bois and Booker T. Washington," FRONTLINE, https://www.pbs.org/wgbh/pages/frontline/shows/race/etc/road.html.

24 Aristotle Jones, "The Evolution: Slavery to Mass Incarceration," updated October 6, 2016, HuffPost, https://www.huffpost.com/entry/the-evolution-slavery-to-mass-incarceration_b_57f66820e4b087a29a54880f.

25 "Plantation to Prison," *New York Times*, https://www.nytimes.com/paidpost/netflix-13th/plantation-to-prison.html.

26 Ta-Nehisi Coates, "The Black Family in the Age of Mass Incarceration," *Atlantic*, October 2015, https://www.theatlantic.com/magazine/archive/2015/10/the-black-family-in-the-age-of-mass-incarceration/403246/.

27 John Gramlich, "The Gap between the Number of Blacks and Whites in Prison Is Shrinking," Pew Research Center, April 30, 2019, https://www.pewresearch.org/fact-tank/2019/04/30/shrinking-gap-between-number-of-blacks-and-whites-in-prison/.

28 James Cullen, "The History of Mass Incarceration," Brennan Center for Justice, July 20, 2018, https://www.brennancenter.org/blog/history-mass-incarceration.

29 Michael Waldman et al., "Ending Mass Incarceration: Ideas from Today's Leaders," Brennan Center for Justice, May 16, 2019, https://www.brennan-center.org/publication/ending-mass-incarceration-ideas-todays-leaders.

30 James Mooney, "Four Steps for Getting Republicans On Board with Criminal Justice Reform," *Slate*, March 1, 2019, https://slate.com/news-and-politics/2019/03/republicans-criminal-justice-reform-first-step.html.

31 Ed Chung, Betsy Pearl, and Lea Hunter, "The 1994 Crime Bill Continues to Undercut Justice Reform—Here's How to Stop It," Center for American Progress, March 26, 2019, https://www.americanprogress.org/issues/criminal-justice/reports/2019/03/26/467486/1994-crime-bill-continues-undercut-justice-reform-heres-stop/.

32 "Prison Labor and the Thirteenth Amendment," Equal Justice Initiative, February 1, 2016, https://eji.org/history-racial-injustice-prison-labor.

33 "Transition and Offender Workforce Development," National Institute of Corrections, US Department of Justice, https://nicic.gov/transition-and-offender-workforce-development.

34 James Forman Jr., "A Prison Sentence Ends. But the Stigma Doesn't," *New York Times*, September 15, 2017, https://www.nytimes.com/2017/09/15/opinion/a-jail-sentence-ends-but-the-stigma-doesnt.html.

35 "Colleges & Degrees for Felons," Affordable Colleges Online, February 12, 2021, https://www.affordablecollegesonline.org/college-resource-center/college-after-prison/.

36 Rose Leadem, "Trade School vs. College: Which Is Right for You? (Infographic)," *Entrepreneur*, July 8, 2018, https://www.entrepreneur.com/article/316320.

37 Morgan Polikoff, Jerome A Lucido, and Julie Renee Posselt, "Why Meritocracy Is a Myth in College Admissions," *Chicago Reporter*, August 16, 2019, https://www.chicagoreporter.com/why-meritocracy-is-a-myth-in-college-admissions/.

38 Sara Lindberg, "The Worst Myth: College Is for Rich Kids," CollegeXpress, last updated March 20, 2019, https://www.collegexpress.com/articles-and-advice/financial-aid/blog/worst-myth-college-rich-kids/.

39 Harmeet Kaur, "They're Lawyers, Scientists and Health Care Professionals. They're Also Still Struggling to Pay Off Their Student Loans," CNN, June 2, 2019, https://www.cnn.com/2019/06/01/us/student-loan-debt-stories-trnd/index.html.

40 Kelley Holland, "The High Economic and Social Costs of Student Loan Debt," CNBC, updated June 15, 2015, https://www.cnbc.com/2015/06/15/the-high-economic-and-social-costs-of-student-loan-debt.html.

41 Leadem, "Trade School vs. College."

42 "How Much Do In-State Students Pay in Tuition and Fees to Attend Four-Year Public Universities?" Association of Public and Land-Grant Universities, https://www.aplu.org/projects-and-initiatives/college-costs-tuition-and-financial-aid/publicvalues/college-costs.html.

43 *Fact Sheet: College Costs* (Washington, DC: Association of Public and Land-Grant Universities), https://www.aplu.org/library/fact-sheet-college-costs/File.

44 "Scholarship Finder," CareerOneStop, https://www.careeronestop.org/Toolkit/Training/find-scholarships.aspx.

45 "Pro Employment," Project Return, https://www.projectreturninc.org/pro-employment/.

46 Couloute and Kopf, "Out of Prison."

47 Elena Holodny, "'It Still Haunts Me': What It's like to Get a Job after Prison in America," Business Insider, July 30, 2017, https://www.businessinsider.com/finding-job-after-prison-2017-7.

48 Spencer Shanholtz, "It's Time to Think about Middle-Skill Jobs and Education," *Stat Chat* (blog), University of Virginia Weldon Cooper Center for Public Service, July 18, 2019, http://statchatva.org/2019/07/18/middle-skill-jobs-and-education/.

49 Harry J. Holzer and Robert I. Lerman, *America's Forgotten Middle-Skill Jobs* (Skills2Compete, November 2007), https://www.urban.org/sites/default/files/publication/31566/411633-America-s-Forgotten-Middle-Skill-Jobs.PDF.

50 Yasmine Mian, "College Is Not for Everyone," *State Press*, April 20, 2017, https://www.statepress.com/article/2017/04/spopinion-asu-college-isnt-necessary-for-everyone-opinion.

51 Meg St-Esprit, "The Stigma of Choosing Trade School over College," *Atlantic*, March 9, 2019, https://www.theatlantic.com/education/archive/2019/03/choosing-trade-school-over-college/584275/.

52 Robin DiAngelo, "White Fragility," *International Journal of Critical Pedagogy* 3, no. 3 (2011): 54–70, https://libjournal.uncg.edu/ijcp/article/viewFile/249/116.

53 Dylan Matthews, "The Massive New Study on Race and Economic Mobility in America, Explained," Vox, March 21, 2018, https://www.vox.com/policy-and-politics/2018/3/21/17139300/economic-mobility-study-race-black-white-women-men-incarceration-income-chetty-hendren-jones-porter.

54 "Degrees/Certificates Conferred by Postsecondary Institutions, by Control of Institution and Level of Degree/Certificate: 1970-71 through 2014-15," Digest of Education Statistics, National Center for Education Statistics, Institute of Education Sciences, US Department of Education, https://nces.ed.gov/programs/digest/d16/tables/dt16_318.40.asp.

55 "Trends in Higher Education," CollegeBoard, https://trends.collegeboard.org/sites/default/files/education-pays-2004-full-report.pdf.

56 Ibid.

57 Alan Feuer, "'El Chapo' Guzmán Sentenced to Life in Prison, Ending Notorious Criminal Career," *New York Times*, July 17, 2019, https://www.nytimes.com/2019/07/17/nyregion/el-chapo-sentencing.html.

58 Jennifer Gonnerman, "Kalief Browder, 1993–2015," *New Yorker*, June 7, 2015, https://www.newyorker.com/news/news-desk/kalief-browder-1993-2015.

59 Erica Y. King, "Black men get longer prison sentences than white men for the same crime: Study," ABC News, November 17, 2017, https://

abcnews.go.com/Politics/black-men-sentenced-time-white-men-crime-study/story?id=51203491.

60 Henry Louis Gates, Jr. "Why Was Cotton 'King'?" PBS, https://www.pbs.org/wnet/african-americans-many-rivers-to-cross/history/why-was-cotton-king/.

61 Dina Gerdeman. "The Clear Connection Between Slavery And American Capitalism," Forbes, May 3, 2017 https://www.forbes.com/sites/hbsworking-knowledge/2017/05/03/the-clear-connection-between-slavery-and-american-capitalism/?sh=348fe45c7bd3.

62 "Race – The Power of Illusion: The House we live in," PBS, 2003, https://www.pbs.org/race/000_About/002_04-about-03.htm.

63 "The Truth About Jim Crow," The American Civil Rights Union, 2014, http://theacru.org/wp-content/uploads/The-Truth-About-Jim-Crow.pdf.

64 Ta-Nehisi Coates. "The case for reparations," *The Atlantic*, June 2014, https://www.theatlantic.com/magazine/archive/2014/06/the-case-for-reparations/361631/.

65 Graff G. Redesigning Racial Caste in America via Mass Incarceration. J Psychohist. 2015 Fall;43(2):120-33. PMID: 26462404.

66 Angela Hanks, Danyelle Solomon, and Christian E. Weller. "Systemic Inequality," Center For American Progress, February 21, 2018 https://www.americanprogress.org/issues/race/reports/2018/02/21/447051/systematic-inequality/.

67 Patrick Sharkey. "Neighborhoods and the Black white mobility gap," Pew Trusts, July 2009, https://www.pewtrusts.org/-/media/legacy/uploadedfiles/wwwpewtrustsorg/reports/economic_mobility/pewsharkeyv12pdf.pdf.

68 "The Moynihan Report: The negro family, the case for national action," Black Post, 1965, https://www.blackpast.org/african-american-history/moynihan-report-1965/#chapter4.

69 Devah Pager, Bruce Western, and Naomi Sugie. "Sequencing Disadvantage: Barriers to employment facing young black men and white men with criminal records." Annals, May 2009 https://scholar.harvard.edu/files/pager/files/annals_sequencingdisadvantage.pdf.

70 "Criminal Justice Facts," The Sentencing Project, 2020, https://www.sentencingproject.org/criminal-justice-facts/.

71 Alycia Castillo, Jemima Abalogu, and Lindsey Linder. "Reversing the pipeline to prison in Texas," Texas Criminal Justice Coalition, 2020, https://www.texascjc.org/system/files/publications/Reversing%20the%20Pipeline%20Report%202020.pdf.

72 Allison Keyes. "Few Artifacts of the Transatlantic Slave Trade Still Exist. These Iron Blocks Help Tell That Gut-Wrenching Story," Smithsonian, 2016, .

73 Jason Daley. "Study Reveals Deep Shortcomings With How Schools Teach America's History of Slavery," Smithsonian, February 2018, https://www.smithsonianmag.com/smart-news/slavery-taught-shortcomings-history-180968061/.

74 Cynthia Greenlee. "A Senator Speaks Out Against Confederate Monuments… in 1910," Smithsonian, October 2017, https://www.smithsonianmag.com/history/senator-speaks-out-against-confederate-monuments-1910-180965299/.

75 Meilan Solly. "158 resources to understand racism in America," Smithsonian, June 2020, https://www.smithsonianmag.com/history/158-resources-understanding-systemic-racism-america-180975029/.

76 "Lynching in America: Confronting the Legacy of Racial Terror," Equal Justice Initiative, 2017, https://eji.org/reports/lynching-in-america/.

77 Brigit Katz. "Legislation Declaring Lynching a Federal Crime Hits New Roadblock," Smithsonian, December 2018, https://www.smithsonianmag.com/smart-news/after-200-failed-attempts-us-has-made-lynching-federal-crime-180971092/.

78 Amanda Scherker, "The 14 Most F#$%ed Up Things about America's Obsession with Putting People Behind Bars," HuffPost, updated December 6, 2017, https://www.huffpost.com/entry/us-prison-size_n_5398998.

79 Ben Miller and Daniel S. Harawa, "Why America Needs to Break Its Addiction to Long Prison Sentences," Politico, September 3, 2019, https://www.politico.com/magazine/story/2019/09/03/why-america-needs-to-break-its-addiction-to-long-prison-sentences-227999.

80 Sara Sun Beale, "The News Media's Influence on Criminal Justice Policy: How Market-Driven News Promotes Punitiveness," *William & Mary Law Review* 48, no. 2 (November 2006), https://scholarship.law.wm.edu/cgi/viewcontent.cgi?article=1103&context=wmlr.

81 "TV Series, Crime (Sorted by IMDb Rating Descending)," IMDb, https://www.imdb.com/search/title/?genres=crime&title_type=tv_series&sort=uscr_rating,dcsc.

82 "The Best True Crime TV Shows," Ranker, updated February 10, 2021, https://www.ranker.com/list/true-crime-tv-shows-and-series/reference.

83 Wikipedia, s.v. "List of Police Television Dramas," last edited February 15, 2021, 16:39 (UTC), https://en.wikipedia.org/wiki/List_of_police_television_dramas.

84 Kathryn VanArendonk, "Why Is TV So Addicted to Crime?" Vulture, January 25, 2019, https://www.vulture.com/2019/01/why-is-tv-addicted-to-crime-shows.html.

85 Anagha Srikanth, "TV Crime Shows Present a Warped View of Our Criminal Justice System: Report," The Hill, January 24, 2020, https://the-hill.com/changing-america/respect/diversity-inclusion/479773-tv-crime-shows-present-a-warped-view-of-our.

86 CommuniTV, "Top 10 Prison Movies," YouTube video, 10:48, November 25, 2019, https://www.youtube.com/watch?v=WgYnp1-qRrg.

87 Alicia Maule, "Meet the Men and Women of the 2017 Innocence Network Conference," Innocence Project, March 27, 2017, https://www.innocenceproj-ect.org/2017-innocence-network-conference/.

88 Joanne Rosa, "Kim Kardashian West Reacts to Trump Backlash on 'The View,'" ABC News, September 13, 2019, https://abcnews.go.com/Entertainment/kim-kardashian-west-backlash-working-trump-choose-alice/story?id=65571704.

89 Wendy Sawyer and Peter Wagner, "Mass Incarceration: The Whole Pie 2020," Prison Policy Initiative, March 24, 2020, https://www.prisonpolicy.org/reports/pie2020.html.

90 "Study Finds Increased Incarceration Has Marginal-to-Zero Impact on Crime," Equal Justice Initiative, August 7, 2017, https://eji.org/news/study-finds-increased-incarceration-does-not-reduce-crime/.

91 "The Prison Paradox," Vera Institute of Justice, July 2017, https://www.vera.org/publications/for-the-record-prison-paradox-incarceration-not-safer.

92 "Criminal Justice Facts."

ACKNOWLEDGMENTS

Quotes from the Real People

The recollections of my life presented here are primarily my own. However, I couldn't tell my story without telling pieces of their stories. Thus, in putting together these recollections, I reached out to and had conversations with many of the people included in this book. In many cases, at the request of the person or from my discretion, I changed their names for privacy and for creative flow. It should be noted that several people declined or did not respond. Some of them happened to be people that I hurt the most. Thus, the personal responses from the real people whom I hurt the most are mostly missing from below. To guide these conversations, I created a survey that was both a consent to include or de-identify and asked several questions. Below are some of the real responses from those who consented to be identified and those who asked to be de-identified.

1. How do you know Stan?

Dr. Bayla Myer: I was Stan's treating psychologist.

Cortney Harley: I've known Stan since he was 14. We met at a basketball camp and he later attended the same high school as I.

Jeff P. Lerno: Met him in college.

Austin: From a friend.

Richard Shaw: Friend.

Sydney N. Rodgers: Dated him in college for like a week.

Liz: Stan was from North County [NC] which is where I grew up. I started to really get to know Stan when he started dating one of my best friends who later became his fiancé but the engagement was called off due to his prison sentence.

Taron K. Harrison: We stayed in the same neighborhood together.

Julie: Stan and I went to the same high school but were never in school together with the age gap between us. How I officially met and became friends with Stan was from him and my sister dating.

Renee Billups: Through my husband and college.

Michael S. Arbogast Jr.: Met in mid-teens through friends so just from living in [the] same area.

Sheng Wu, PhD: He was my postdoctoral fellow.

Barrie Bode, PhD: Stan was a graduate [fellow] in my research laboratory at Saint Louis University.

Michael Nenninger: He's a good friend.

2. What was/were your relationship(s) or interaction(s) with Stan? In the past and presently?

Dr. Myer: I was Stan's clinical psychologist when he was charged with felony drug crimes.

Cortney: Friend: PAST: Stan & I became close, as I dated a girl he was good friends with at the time in 2001. Once my relationship with that girl ended in 2003, Stan and I stayed friends. Through the years, we shared many memories from partying with friends to me driving hours to visit him in prison several times a year. We corresponded through letters. I assisted with completing his Saint Louis University application while he was incarcerated. PRESENT: Stan remains probably my closest friend. I was a groomsman in his June 2016 wedding. He will be the same in my 2018 wedding. I consider him family. Colleague: We eventually attended grad school together at Lindenwood University & earned our MBAs.

Jeff: I met Stan in college. While smoking weed together he informed me how much he was paying for a pound of weed. I told him I could get it for a lot cheaper in KC.

Austin: Drug dealing, buyer from him. Became friends from the initial business relationship and had other business ventures together outside of the drugs.

Rich: Friend.

Sydney: Friend.

Taron: My best friend—we pretty much shared a lot from hustling to knowledge to getting money to making our own drugs.

Liz: Well, I've had a lot of them... Friend—I've always been friends with Stan. God, now for about twenty years. When we were in HS, we did a lot of partying together. We smoked A LOT of weed, we tried other drugs such as ecstasy. We used to drive around and get high or go to "the river" and drink and smoke and hope the cops didn't come. I never really bought weed off of Stan. We were in a group where the girls got to smoke for free most of the time, haha. I think once I bought a triple stacked [S] uperman off of him but that was it. Stan has always been there for me—he and Jennifer saved my life one time when I tried to kill myself. He helped me through a tough breakup by working out with me like three days a week. He even got close with my daughter, when she was little. Stan really was one of my best friends in HS but after his imprisonment we really took a lean on each other to help both of us through hard times. It's a REAL friendship that I will always value.

Julie: Stan and I have been friends for many years, grateful to still have him in my life even with all the miles in between us.

Renee: College friend

Mike: We were friends, but I was the main supplier of pot and other drugs for our area of St Louis, so we were connected in that way too. I had the plug and I supplied to all my people [that] I could trust. Stan was one of them. We made a lot of money together, but I went to jail and prison eventually and lost contact for a number of years. I ran across his profile or he ran across mine and we reconnected like that about a year or two ago. Where we grew up, there was never any positive, there was just positive reinforcement for negative actions. We didn't know any other way—not an excuse, but an explanation.

Sheng: In the past, he worked in my lab as a postdoctoral fellow to conduct research.

Barrie: Academic/personal advisor; I counseled and supported Stan through his journey from court to conviction, to incarceration and subsequent re-matriculation into a PhD program.

Mickey: A very good friend of mine for almost 25 years. We were roommates [at Missouri Valley College] for a few minutes. I did buy small amounts from time to time.

3. What was your perception of Stan? Past and present?

Dr. Myer: Very high intellectual and academic potential both past and present.

Cortney: Past: I felt he was living 2 lives. The Stan I always saw & interacted with never sold drugs around me. He never put me in a position where I could get in trouble for those types of actions. But then there was the Stan I would "hear" about [through] others. This was the drug dealing Stan. Present: My perception of him currently is a man who experienced going through the "system." He took notes along the way and wants to make a positive change for others currently experiencing what he experienced in the past. Specifically, what is wrong with the system, how people similar to Stan get into the system, and how to not only educate those people but to also ensure they have opportunities to make those positive changes & not be held back by our current judicial system.

Jeff: My perception has never changed. I was proud of him then and I'm proud of him now. Everybody makes mistakes. It could have been me.

Austin: PAST—College student selling drugs who also created music. I never knew if he had a direction he was wanting to head towards, however we did not get into that conversation. PRESENT—Someone taking full advantage of a second chance, trying to make something of himself and prove that you can alter your life with hard work and good thoughts. Standing up for others who want to make the same change. Successful.

Rich: Genius.

Sydney: I loved him! Lol he was very attractive—still is—and he's smart and funny [and] very fun to be around.

Taron: He [has] always been my brother to me still til this day, from when we first met til now.

Liz: Past—being older and looking back[,] I think Stan was trying to "fit in" in a sense. He wasn't a "gang banger." He was intelligent and came from a [good] family upbringing. Stan went to a predominately white [C]atholic high school but lived in a predominately black neighborhood. I think at times it was hard to juggle who he really wanted to be. Stan was flashy—wore big chains, flashy clothes, had a nice car with rims.… But had the grades, was an athlete, and very likable. Present—I would say I am shocked but I am not. The positive changes Stan is making in lives of those who were previously incarcerated or who are a "minority" or his students…his wife, Stephanie's life, his daughter's life…it's just remarkable. But when you are in prison and you keep in touch with professors from college (SLU) what [should] we have expected. He had a plan and he is delivering his plan to many. I am proud of who Stan was and who Stan is. I am a white female who has done her fair share of breaking the law or doing drugs but I never got in trouble. I was not selling drugs though :).

Julie: My past and future perception of Stan would be the same, he was always like a big brother/role model to me. He has always been super smart and driven, so proud of who he has become.

Renee: Stan has always been respectful and genuine.

Mike: He's always been a friend. You just have a different relationship with people you grew up with.

Sheng: In the past, I realized that he had a talent to become a politician since he had a lot of passion in attending politically related activities. He also spent a lot of time and effort helping other minority groups.

Barrie: I have always perceived Stan as a hard-working and driven individual with high intelligence and motivation to achieve. He is also humble and very polite. In the past he made some very bad decisions - likely driven by the thrill-seeking of youth and lure of money. People have the ability to mature and learn from their mistakes; Stan certainly did so.

Mickey: A good guy.

4. What were others' perceptions of Stan? Past and present?

Dr. Myer: I cannot speak for anyone else in his life.

Cortney: PAST: Depends on who you ask. Friends & Family would say Stan was a loyal, good human being, who wasn't perfect (but who is?) but would do anything he could to help you. Outsiders, or those who didn't know him as well, would say he's a troublemaker. He's sneaky. He's a drug dealer and drug dealers are not good people. PRESENT: Again, depends who you ask. I think outsiders may say he is seeking attention by his social media posts. It's like he's bragging or bigger and better than everyone because he's in Washington DC meeting with lawmakers & government leaders trying to enact change in the judicial system & college application system. Me personally, I disagree with those assertions. Others will say that they totally admire the guts he has to put his story out there to the world. It gives inspiration to people who may need that today.

Jeff: I could not tell you. I do not know anyone he knows.

Austin: PAST—Drug dealer rapper up to no good. PRESENT—Successful [and] wanting to make something of his life.

Rich: Gangster.

Sydney: Fun[,] intelligent[,] sexy.

Taron: He was a full sneaky hustler[,] big time hustler.

Liz: For me this is hard to say.... I know my parents really like him, thought he was very polite and respectful but made poor decisions. I think some thought he was great—sold you drugs, played football with you, and [you] enjoyed his presence. Others probably seen him as a "thug."

Julie: I would say back in the day, Stan was looked up to in many ways. I would say the same thing would be true to today as well.

Renee: Stan has always just been a good person.

Mike: He was always looked at as a good dude.

Sheng: He also knew how to advertise himself when he was helping other minorities so that his voice and opinions could be heard. His work related presentations were easy to follow with clear purposes.

Barrie: Many of his fellow students really liked and respected him. During his troubled period many faculty members considering his re-admission to the PhD program were understandably skeptical given his history. Those perceptions changed as he re-entered and excelled in the PhD program. He is now admired for his resilience, resolve and achievement post-incarceration. His story is inspirational and uplifting for those I share it with, who did not know him.

Mickey: I really can't vouch for others' perceptions.

5. Explain your most memorable memory or memories of or with Stan.

Dr. Myer: My information is privileged between doctor and patient.

Cortney: There are really too many to count. The time I busted him stealing his brother's car at the age of 14. The time he helped me remodel [...] both of my bathrooms of my condo. The countless number of vacations, parties & celebrations (March Madness, Birthdays, Super Bowls) during our 20s & 30s. Watching him graduate from Saint Louis University with his PhD. Being a groomsman in his wedding.

Jeff: First time I ever saw Stan was late at night outside my room. He was blacked out arguing with some huge overweight RA. I don't remember what it was about. I doubt he does either. I remember this 5'8" Haitian scream[ing] and talk[ing] shit so much at this 6'3 RA until he screamed "I am going to skull fuck you" to Stan. Stan without missing a beat screamed "[W]ell do it then mother fucker." I knew we were going to be friends after that night. I introduced myself the next morning and told Stan what happened. We both laughed really hard.

Austin: Grand Prix and bricks :) Rapper. Nice guy.

Rich: A lot of years of memories.

Sydney: Lol well there's so many[;] probably just seeing his face always brought a smile to my face we had a lot of really good times.

Taron: When I went to go visit St. Louis and I realize[d] how Stan was so far up [in the game]. We both took a trip came to Atlanta and then came to Florida[.] [We was basically living it up[.] [We] went to a club and [there] was [a] shooting and I got grazed by a bullet[.] [At that time in life,] we were having so much fun when he went back home he caught that case.

Liz: My list can GO ON! I have stories for years—some good, some bad, happy, and sad. It is truly hard to pick just one but one of the memories that will stick with me is when I went to visit him in prison with Jennifer and Cortney. I have never been near a prison let alone been in one. It was hard to see him "locked up" in his prison suit. We had a great time visiting and playing cards and catching up but I walked out the door a free woman and Stan was still serving his time. After we left Bowling Green, the 3 of us went to Classics (bar in NC) and really we just were so down. It was one of the most unordinary feelings I think I have ever experienced—visiting my best friend in jail who was more intelligent than anyone we hung out with. All and all, I love Stan and I think he is an awesome friend, father, husband, mentor, professor, etc. He is making an impact in this world and I couldn't be any prouder. He is a leader.

Julie: So many memories and great times really, it's hard to pick! We were big into Wings day Wednesday every week a while ago, that was always something I looked forward to. Stan has taught me so much and I appreciate his outlook on life, he will always be like family to me.

Renee: I have a few stories with Stan—mainly parties and college dorm days.

Mike: I'll have to think on that. I have a few that will blow your mind.

Sheng: 1. When he joined my lab, our lab had a hepatocyte androgen receptor knockout mouse model. At that moment, we only knew that knocked out AR mice had different metabolic responses compared to wild type mice, but we did not know the mechanism behind it. He led this project very well and collected a lot of meaningful data under a reasonable time. 2. He was very persistent in helping young minority kids since he organized a class for a Baltimore city elementary school every year to enhance their interest in science. He understands that education is a very important part in improving life quality.

Barrie: I remember very good, personal conversations with Stan - describing growing up in North County in St. Louis (we are both from the Ferguson area), where we talked football, life, and science. Stan always struck me with how he was quick to grasp and implement complex information (as in the design of scientific experiments), and was very good at the bench. He clearly was family-oriented, and I could tell that he was a good person. I really enjoyed the time I was able to spend with him - and knew that supporting him through his bad periods was not only defensible - it was the right thing to do. So proud of him.

Mickey: There's too many items to list from when we crashed his [Grand Prix] racing my wife to a road trip to [Miami] Florida. He's always been there for me.

Author photo by Tchad Dublin

Dr. Stanley Andrisse is an endocrinologist scientist and assistant professor at Howard University College of Medicine researching type 2 diabetes and insulin resistance. Dr. Andrisse holds a visiting professorship at Georgetown University Medical Center and held an adjunct professorship at Johns Hopkins Medicine after completing his postdoctoral training. Dr. Andrisse completed his PhD at Saint Louis University and his MBA and bachelor's degree at Lindenwood University, where he played three years of Division II collegiate football.

Dr. Andrisse's service commitments include: Executive Director and Founder of From Prison Cells to PhD, board member on the Formerly Incarcerated College Graduates Network (FICGN), past president of the Johns Hopkins Postdoctoral Association, founder of the Diversity Postdoctoral Alliance, member on several local and national committees aimed at community outreach, youth mentor, motivational speaker, and community activist.